MTEL Early Childhood
02 Teacher Certification Exam

By: Sharon Wynne, M.S
Southern Connecticut State University

"And, while there's no reason yet to panic, I think it's only prudent that we make preparations to panic."

XAMonline, INC.
Boston

To obtain permission(s) to use the material from this work for any purpose including workshops or seminars, please submit a written request to:

XAMonline, Inc.
21 Orient Ave.
Melrose, MA 02176
Toll Free 1-800-509-4128
Email: info@xamonline.com
Web www.xamonline.com
Fax: 1-781-662-9268

Library of Congress Cataloging-in-Publication Data

Wynne, Sharon A.
    Early Childhood 02: Teacher Certification / Sharon A. Wynne. -2nd ed.
    ISBN 978-1-58197-676-2
    1. Early Childhood 02.   2. Study Guides.   3. MTEL
    4. Teachers' Certification & Licensure.   5. Careers

Disclaimer:
The opinions expressed in this publication are the sole works of XAMonline and were created independently from the National Education Association, Educational Testing Service, or any State Department of Education, National Evaluation Systems or other testing affiliates.

Between the time of publication and printing, state specific standards as well as testing formats and website information may change that is not included in part or in whole within this product. Sample test questions are developed by XAMonline and reflect similar content as on real tests; however, they are not former tests. XAMonline assembles content that aligns with state standards but makes no claims nor guarantees teacher candidates a passing score. Numerical scores are determined by testing companies such as NES or ETS and then are compared with individual state standards. A passing score varies from state to state.

Printed in the United States of America

MTEL: Early Childhood 02
ISBN: 978-1-58197-676-2

Project Manager:	Sharon Wynne, MS
Project Coordinator:	Victoria Anderson, MS
Content Coordinators/Authors:	Fran Stanford, MS Victoria Anderson, MS Christina Godard, BS Kimberly Putney, BS Vickie Pittard, MS Deborah Suber. BS Kelley Eldredge, MS
Sample test:	Shelley Wake, MS Deborah Harbin, MS Christina Godard, BS Kim Putney, BS Carol Moore, BS Vickie Pittard, MS
Editors: Managing Proof reader Copy editor Sample test Production	Dr. Harte Weiner, PhD James Stark, MS James Stark, MS Shelley Wake, MS David Aronson
Graphic Artist	Jenna Hamilton

Table of Contents

SUBAREA II.   KNOWLEDGE OF CHILDREN'S LITERATURE AND THE WRITING PROCESS

COMPETENCY 3.0   UNDERSTAND CHILDREN'S LITERATURE, INCLUDING GENRES, LITERARY ELEMENTS, AND LITERARY TECHNIQUES

SUBAREA IV.   INTEGRATION OF KNOWLEDGE AND UNDERSTANDING

COMPETENCY 8.0   PREPARE AN ORGANIZED, DEVELOPED ANALYSIS THAT RELATES CHILD DEVELOPMENT TO TWO OR MORE OF THE FOLLOWING: LANGUAGE ARTS, MATHEMATICS, HISTORY AND SOCIAL SCIENCE, AND SCIENCE

Great Study and Testing Tips!

What to study in order to prepare for the subject assessments is the focus of this study guide but equally important is *how* you study.

You can increase your chances of truly mastering the information by taking some simple, but effective, steps.

Study Tips:

1. Some foods aid the learning process. Foods such as milk, nuts, seeds, rice, and oats help your study efforts by releasing natural memory enhancers called CCKs (*cholecystokinin*) composed of *tryptophan*, *choline*, and *phenylalanine*. All of these chemicals enhance the neurotransmitters associated with memory. Before studying, try a light, protein-rich meal of eggs, turkey, and fish. All of these foods release the memory-enhancing chemicals. The better the connections, the more you comprehend.

Likewise, before you take a test, stick to a light snack of energy boosting and relaxing foods. A glass of milk, a piece of fruit, or some peanuts all release various memory-boosting chemicals and help you to relax and focus on the subject at hand.

2. Learn to take great notes. A by-product of our modern culture is that we have grown accustomed to getting our information in short doses (i.e. TV news sound bites or *USA Today*-style newspaper articles.)

Consequently, we've subconsciously trained ourselves to assimilate information better in neat little packages. If your notes are scrawled all over the paper, it fragments the flow of the information. Strive for clarity. Newspapers use a standard format to achieve clarity. Your notes can be much clearer through use of proper formatting. A very effective format is called the *"Cornell Method."*

> Take a sheet of loose-leaf lined notebook paper and draw a line all the way down the paper about 1-2" from the left-hand edge.

> Draw another line across the width of the paper about 1-2" up from the bottom. Repeat this process on the reverse side of the page.

Look at the highly effective result. You have ample room for notes, a left-hand margin for special emphasis items or inserting supplementary data from the textbook, a large area at the bottom for a brief summary, and a little rectangular space for just about anything you want.

3. <u>Get the concept then the details</u>. Too often we focus on the details and don't gather an understanding of the concept. However, if you simply memorize only dates, places, or names, you may well miss the whole point of the subject.

A key way to understand things is to put them in your own words. If you are working from a textbook, automatically summarize each paragraph in your mind. If you are outlining text, don't simply copy the author's words.

Rephrase them in your own words. You remember your own thoughts and words much better than someone else's, and subconsciously tend to associate the important details to the core concepts.

4. <u>Ask Why?</u> Pull apart written material paragraph by paragraph and don't forget the captions under the illustrations.

Example: If the heading is "Stream Erosion," flip it around to read, "Why do streams erode?" Then answer the questions.

If you train your mind to think in a series of questions and answers, not only will you learn more, but it also helps to lessen the test anxiety because you are used to answering questions.

5. <u>Read for reinforcement and future needs</u>. Even if you only have ten minutes, put your notes or a book in your hand. Your mind is similar to a computer; you have to input data in order to have it processed. *By reading, you are creating the neural connections for future retrieval.* The more times you read something, the more you reinforce the learning of ideas.

Even if you don't fully understand something on the first pass, *your mind stores much of the material for later recall.*

6. <u>Relax to learn so go into exile</u>. Our bodies respond to an inner clock called biorhythms. Burning the midnight oil works well for some people, but not everyone.

If possible, set aside a particular place to study that is free of distractions. Shut off the television, cell phone, and pager and exile your friends and family during your study period.

If you really are bothered by silence, try background music. Light classical music at a low volume has been shown to aid in concentration over other types. Music that evokes pleasant emotions without lyrics is highly suggested. Try just about anything by Mozart. It relaxes you.

7. <u>Use arrows not highlighters</u>. At best, it's difficult to read a page full of yellow, pink, blue, and green streaks. Try staring at a neon sign for a while and you'll soon see that the horde of colors obscure the message.

A quick note, a brief dash of color, an underline, and an arrow pointing to a particular passage is much clearer than a horde of highlighted words.

8. <u>Budget your study time</u>. Although you shouldn't ignore any of the material, *allocate your available study time in the same ratio that topics may appear on the test.*

Testing Tips:

1. Get smart, play dumb. Don't read anything into the question. Don't make an assumption that the test writer is looking for something else than what is asked. Stick to the question as written and don't read extra things into it.

2. Read the question and all the choices _twice_ before answering the question. You may miss something by not carefully reading, and then re-reading, both the question and the answers.

If you really don't have a clue as to the right answer, leave it blank on the first time through. Go on to the other questions, as they may provide a clue as to how to answer the skipped questions.

If later on, you still can't answer the skipped ones . . . _Guess._ The only penalty for guessing is that you _might_ get it wrong. Only one thing is certain; if you don't put anything down, you will get it wrong!

3. Turn the question into a statement. Look at the way the questions are worded. The syntax of the question usually provides a clue. Does it seem more familiar as a statement rather than as a question? Does it sound strange?

By turning a question into a statement, you may be able to spot if an answer sounds right, and it may also trigger memories of material you have read.

4. Look for hidden clues. It's actually very difficult to compose multiple-foil (choice) questions without giving away part of the answer in the options presented.

In most multiple-choice questions you can often readily eliminate one or two of the potential answers. This leaves you with only two real possibilities, and automatically your odds go to fifty-fifty for very little work.

5. Trust your instincts. For every fact that you have read, you subconsciously retain something of that knowledge. On questions that you aren't really certain about, go with your basic instincts. **Your first impression on how to answer a question is usually correct.**

6. Mark your answers directly on the test booklet. Don't bother trying to fill in the optical scan sheet on the first pass through the test. _Just be very careful not to miss-mark your answers when you eventually transcribe them to the scan sheet._

7. Watch the clock! You have a set amount of time to answer the questions. Don't get bogged down trying to answer a single question at the expense of 10 questions you can more readily answer.

THIS PAGE BLANK

SUBAREA I.   KNOWLEDGE OF CHILD DEVELOPMENT

Competency 001   **Understand child development from prenatal through the early elementary years**

Skill 1.1   **Major theories of child development and learning (e.g., Piaget, Erikson, Kohlberg, Bronfenbrenner, Vygotsky, brain research)**

Some of the most prominent learning theories in education today include brain-based learning and the Multiple Intelligence Theory. Supported by recent brain research, brain-based learning suggests that knowledge about the way the brain retains information enables educators to design the most effective learning environments. As a result, researchers have developed twelve principles that relate knowledge about the brain to teaching practices. These twelve principles are:

- The brain is a complex adaptive system
- The brain is social
- The search for meaning is innate
- We use patterns to learn more effectively
- Emotions are crucial to developing patterns
- Each brain perceives and creates parts and whole simultaneously
- Learning involves focused and peripheral attention
- Learning involves conscious and unconscious processes
- We have at least two ways of organizing memory
- Learning is developmental
- Complex learning is enhanced by challenged (and inhibited by threat)
- Every brain is unique

(Caine & Caine, 1994, Mind/Brain Learning Principles)

Educators can use these principles to help design methods and environments in their classrooms to maximize student learning.

The Multiple Intelligence Theory, developed by Howard Gardner, suggests that students learn in (at least) seven different ways. These include visually/spatially, musically, verbally, logically/mathematically, interpersonally, intrapersonally, and bodily/kinesthetically.

Jean Piaget

Jean Piaget, a European scientist who died in the late 20th Century, developed many theories about the way humans learn. Most famously, he developed a theory about the stages of the development of human minds. It's very simple. The first stage is the "sensory-motor" stage that lasts until a child is in the toddler years. In this stage, children begin to understand their senses.

The next stage, called the "pre-operational" stage, is where children begin to understand symbols. For example, as they learn language, they begin to realize that words are symbols of thoughts, actions, items, and other elements in the world. This stage lasts into early elementary school.

The third stage is referred to as the "concrete operations" stage. This lasts until late elementary school. In this stage, children go one step beyond learning what a symbol is. They learn how to manipulate symbols, objects, and other elements. A common example of this stage is the displacement of water. In this stage, they can reason that a wide and short cup of water poured into a tall and thin cup of water can actually have the same amount of water.

The next stage is called the "formal operations" stage. It usually starts in adolescence or early teen years and it continues on into adulthood. This stage is what allows critical thinking, hypothesis, systematic organization of knowledge, etc.

Generally, when we say that children move from a stage of concrete thinking to logical and abstract thinking, we mean that they are moving from the "pre-operational" and "concrete" stage TO the "formal operations" stage. But as anyone who spends time with children knows, there are many bumps in the way to a person's ability to be a strong critical thinker. And remember, just because a child has moved into a particular stage does not mean that they will be able to complete function at the specified level. For example, adolescents may be able to think critically, but they need plenty of instruction and assistance to do so at an adequate level. This does not necessarily mean that critical thinking skills should be taught out of context; rather, through all lessons, teachers should work to instill components that help develop the thinking of children.

Benjamin Bloom

In 1956, Benjamin Bloom, an educational psychologist developed a detailed classification of critical thinking and learning skills/objectives into tiered levels. These hierarchal levels ordered thinking skills from the simplest (or lower-ordered) thinking skills to the highest (or higher-ordered) thinking skills. The goal of Bloom's taxonomy was to motivate teachers to teach at all levels of critical thinking and not just at the most common level – the lower-ordered thinking skills such as memorize, restate, define.

The six levels of Bloom's taxonomy and the skills each entails, from simplest to most complex, are as follows:

1. **Knowledge:** This level is the most basic level of learning where students learn terminology and specific facts; tasks at this level ask students to define, label, recall, memorize, and list
2. **Understanding/Comprehension:** This level of learning requires students grasp the meaning of a concept; tasks at this level ask students to classify, explain, identify, locate, and review
3. **Application:** This level of learning requires students to take previous learning and utilize it in a new way; tasks at this level ask students to demonstrate, illustrate, distinguish, solve, write, choose, and dramatize
4. **Analysis:** This level of learning involves the breakdown of material to its component parts and requires students to utilize those parts; tasks at this level ask students to calculate, categorize, compare, contrast, criticize, distinguish, examine, and experiment
5. **Synthesis:** This level of learning requires students to take the analyzed parts from the previous level and converge them into creative new wholes; tasks at this level ask students to collect, compose, design, manage, plan, organize, and formulate
6. **Evaluation:** This is the highest level of learning on the taxonomy, and according to research, is the level that is least often achieved. This level of learning requires students to judge the value of material based on experience, prior knowledge, opinions, and/or the resulting product; tasks at this level ask students to assess, appraise, predict, rate, support, evaluate, judge, and argue

Lawrence Kohlberg

Lawrence Kohlberg outlined what is now known as "Kohlberg's stages of moral development" in 1958. Kohlberg's six stages are grouped into three levels: pre-conventional, conventional, and post-conventional. Each level consists of two stages according to Kohlberg.

- Pre-conventional (Egocentric: up to age 9)
    - Punishment/obedience: morality is based on established rules. Children in this stage see that following the rules and/or avoiding negative consequences defines moral behavior
    - Instrumental purpose: In this stage, whatever satisfies the child's needs is considered moral by that child
- Conventional (Socio-centric: age 9 to adolescence)
    - Interpersonal: Children begin to understand that good behavior is expected, and achieving those expectations is moral
    - Social system: Adolescents at this stage understand that there is a need for them to fulfill obligations and expectations, and that this fulfillment constitutes moral behavior
- Post-conventional (adulthood)
    - Social contract: We understand that various cultures, as well as individuals, have different definitions of morality, and good moral behavior is seen as living up to the moral standards of that person's social norm
    - Universal Ethical Principles: At this stage, reasoning is based on ethical fairness, and individuals are able to judge themselves and others based on their own sense of morality

For additional reference
http://allpsych.com/psychology101/moral_development.html
http://www.utmem.edu/~vmurrell/dissertation/Kohlberg.htm

Erikson

Eric Erikson articulated a theory that humans go through eights stages of development as they go from infancy to adulthood. These stages are:

- Infancy to 12 months

During this phase the young child develops the ideas of trust and mistrust. This is evident when the child can't lose sight of the mother or cries when strangers get too close. One has to slowly approach a baby of this age in order to let the child learn whether or not the person is to be trusted.

- Young Childhood - Ages 1 to 3

During this stage, the child develops feelings of shame and doubt along with learning about autonomy. The child wants to be independent and if denied, this could translate into temper tantrums as he tests the adults in charge. Play of all kinds is very important as the child learns the language and self-control.

- Early Childhood – Ages 3 – 5

Here the child learns how to initiate tasks and carry them out. However, the child also learns the quality of guilt in this stage when tasks are not completed. He/She learns how to dream about goals associated with adult life. During this stage the child will begin playing with other children and become aware of the differences between the sexes. There is also some moral development taking place as well.

- Middle Childhood – Ages 6 – 10

The child begins to take pride in work and has a sense of achievement. Friendships develop during this stage as well as learning skills. The child also learns how to act as part of a team.

- Adolescence – Ages 11 – 18

Ego is very important in this stage as the young teen starts to wonder how he/she appears to others. Emotional maturity is very important here as well as physical maturity. Relationships also start to develop with groups and between the sexes.

- Early Adulthood – Ages 18 – 34

This is the stage when people start to develop a sense of isolation and intimacy. Close relationships are formed with others. This is the childbearing stage when stable relationships and work are the focus of attention.

- Middle Adulthood – Ages 35 – 60

A commitment to family and career is the focus of this stage.

- Late Adulthood – Ages 60 – Death

This stage is characterized by ego integrity versus despair. The despair comes into play as one faces the inevitable possibility of death. Many seniors tackle life at this stage as they would if they were younger, remaining active and living a healthy lifestyle, thus maintaining their ego integrity, which makes it easier for them to face death.

Bronfenbrenner

Urie Bronfenbrenner is regarded as a leader in the field of child psychology and development. In his Ecological Systems Theory, he outlined four types of nested systems. These are:

- Microsystem – family or classroom
- Mesosystem – interaction of two microsystems
- Exosystem – influence of external influences on development
- Macrosystem – the whole socio-cultural context

He later added a fifth system, which he called the Chronosystem, referring to the natural evolution of development.

His approach to human development shows that the development from infancy to adulthood is a natural progression. It helped to break down barriers between disciplines and show a connection between all of them.

Vygotsky

According to Vygotsky, higher mental functions develop through all the interactions a child has with adults and other children. It is only through these interactions that a child learns his/her language, culture and family background. All of these are essential for normal childhood development. Through the interactions, a child internalizes the concepts of life, family and school.

Vygotsky also did a lot of work on the psychology of play and its importance in child development. He concluded that through play, a child develops the abstract meaning needed to differentiate between objects in the world.

Another of his contributions to the field of early childhood learning was his metacognition theory about speech. He said there is a direct connection between speech and thought, calling thoughts inner speech. Though develops through social interactions and when children think out loud they are externalizes their inner speech.

Constructivist Learning

The most current learning theory of constructivist learning allows students to construct learning opportunities. For constructivist teachers, the belief is that students create their own reality of knowledge and how to process and observe the world around them. Students are constantly constructing new ideas, which serve as frameworks for learning and teaching. Researchers have shown that the constructivist model is comprised of the four components:

1. Learner creates knowledge
2. Learner constructs and makes meaningful new knowledge to existing knowledge
3. Learner shapes and constructs knowledge by life experiences and social interactions
4. In constructivist learning communities, the student, teacher and classmates establish knowledge cooperatively on a daily basis.

Constructivist learning for students is dynamic and ongoing. For constructivist teachers, the classroom becomes a place where students are encouraged to interact with the instructional process by asking questions and posing new ideas to old theories. The use of cooperative learning that encourages students to work in supportive learning environments using their own ideas to stimulate questions and propose outcomes is a major aspect of a constructivist classroom.

Other Theories

The metacognition learning theory deals with "the study of how to help the learner gain understanding about how knowledge is constructed and about the conscious tools for constructing that knowledge" (Joyce and Weil 1996). The cognitive approach to learning involves the teacher's understanding that teaching the student to process his/her own learning and mastery of skill provides the greatest learning and retention opportunities in the classroom. Students are taught to develop concepts and teach themselves skills in problem solving and critical thinking. The student becomes an active participant in the learning process and the teacher facilitates that conceptual and cognitive learning process.

Social and behavioral theories look at the social interactions of students in the classroom that instruct or impact learning opportunities in the classroom. The psychological approaches behind both theories are subject to individual variables that are learned and applied either proactively or negatively in the classroom.

No single approach will work for every classroom, and a good practice is to incorporate a range of learning styles in a classroom. Still, under the guidance of any theory, good educators will differentiate their instructional practices to meet the needs of their students' abilities and interests using various instructional practices.

Skill 1.2   Development within the cultural context of the family

Like students, every family is different. There are many different ways families exist today, and it is important for teachers to consider a student's background when their education is concerned.

Examples of Issues/Situations
- Students from multicultural backgrounds: Curriculum objectives and instructional strategies may be inappropriate and unsuccessful when presented in a single format which relies on the student's understanding and acceptance of the values and common attributes of a specific culture which is not his or her own.

- Parental/family influences: Attitude, resources and encouragement available in the home environment may be attributes for success or failure. Families with higher incomes are able to provide increased opportunities for students. Students from lower income families will need to depend on the resources available from the school system and the community. This should be orchestrated by the classroom teacher in cooperation with school administrators and educational advocates in the community.

Family members with higher levels of education often serve as models for students, and have high expectations for academic success. And families with specific aspirations for children (often, regardless of their own educational background) encourage students to achieve academic success, and are most often active participants in the process.

A family in crisis (caused by economic difficulties, divorce, substance abuse, physical abuse, etc.) creates a negative environment which may profoundly impact all aspects of a student's life, and particularly his or her ability to function academically. The situation may require professional intervention. It is often the classroom teacher who will recognize a family in crisis situation and instigate an intervention by reporting on this to school or civil authorities.

Regardless of the positive or negative impacts on the students' education from outside sources, it is the teacher's responsibility to ensure that all students in the classroom have an equal opportunity for academic success. This begins with the teacher's statement of high expectations for every student, and develops through planning, delivery and evaluation of instruction which provides for inclusion and ensures that all students have equal access to the resources necessary for successful acquisition of the academic skills being taught and measured in the classroom.

SEE also Skill 2.8

Skill 1.3 Factors that may facilitate or impede a child's development in various domains

In an era of academic accountability, all teachers must remember that they are still teaching children, who are whole individuals. While teachers are not substitutes for parents, they certainly do have a responsibility to look out for the well-being of their students. In early elementary school, children are particularly affected by emotional stress within the family, and they are particularly susceptible to emotional harm when they are not cared for in an appropriate manner at home.

While it would be too easy to say that teachers should look out for children who show signs of emotional abuse or emotional neglect, whenever a teacher does notice something unusual in a child's behavior, it is a good idea to look into it. A note of caution, however. teachers should remember that a student's privacy is extremely important.

Furthermore, teachers should remember that all schools, districts, and states have very specific procedures and laws about the reporting of concerns. Yet, it goes without saying that teachers who see problems should seek an effective intervention.

When children are emotionally neglected or have recently endured family distress, their school work can suffer. First, the level of attention toward school will be greatly reduced. While children may actually think about these things, they may also show signs of jealousy of other children, or they may feel a sense of anger toward other children, the teacher, or their parents. Aggression is a very common behavior of emotionally-neglected children.

When a child has had little verbal interaction, the symptoms can be rather similar to the symptoms of abuse or neglect. The child might have a "deer in the headlights" look and maintain a very socially awkward set of behaviors. In general, such a child will have a drastically reduced ability to express him or herself in words, and often, aggression can be a better tool for the child to get his or her thoughts across.

Although cognitive ability is not lost due to such circumstances (abuse, neglect, emotional upset, lack of verbal interaction), the child will most likely not be able to provide as much intellectual energy as the child would if none of these things were present. But, also, note that the classroom can be seen as a "safe" place by a child, so it is imperative that teachers be attentive to the needs and emotions of their students.

Skill 1.4   How children use play to develop understanding and acquire knowledge

Too often, recess and play is considered peripheral or unimportant to a child's development. It's sometimes seen as a way to allow kids to just get physical energy out or a "tradition" of childhood. The truth is, though, that play is very important to human development. First, an obvious point, in this country, even though we are very industrious, we believe strongly that all individuals deserve time to relax and enjoy the "fruits of our labors."

But even more importantly, for the full development of children (who will soon be active citizens of our democracy, parents, spouses, friends, colleagues, and neighbors), play is an activity that helps teach basic values such as sharing and cooperation. It also teaches that taking care of oneself (as opposed to constantly working) is good for human beings and further creates a more enjoyable society.

The stages of play development do indeed move from solitary (particularly in infancy stages) to cooperative (in early childhood), but even in early childhood, children should be able to play on their own and entertain themselves from time to time. Children who do not know what to do with themselves when they are bored should be encouraged to think about particular activities that might be of interest.

But it is also extremely important that children play with peers. While the emerging stages of cooperative play may be awkward (as children will at first not want to share toys, for example), with some guidance and experience, children will learn how to be good peers and friends.

Play—both cooperative and solitary—helps to develop very important attributes in children. For example, children learn and develop personal interests and practice particular skills. The play that children engage in may even develop future professional interests.

Finally, playing with objects helps the child to develop motor skills. The objects that children play with should be varied and age appropriate. For example, playing with a doll can actually help to develop hand-eye coordination. Sports, for both boys and girls, can be equally valuable. Parents and teachers, though, need to remember that sports at young ages should only be for the purpose of development of interests and motor skills—not competition. Many children will learn that they do not enjoy sports, and parents and teachers should be respectful of these decisions.

In general, play is an appropriate place of children to learn many things about themselves, their world, and their interests. Children should be encouraged to participate in different types of play, and they should be watched over as they encounter new types of play.

Skill 1.5   Interrelationships between cognitive development and other developmental domains

Child development does not occur in a vacuum. Each element of development impacts other elements of development. For example, as cognitive development progresses, social development often follows. The reason for this is that all areas of development are fairly inter-related. People laugh about how adolescents often develop slower in the physical domain than they do in the social or cognitive domain (e.g., they may think like teenagers, but they still look like children), however, the truth is that even in such cases, physical development is under progress—just not as evident on the surface.

And as children develop physically, they develop the dexterity to demonstrate cognitive development, such as writing something on a piece of paper (in this case, this is cognitive development that only can be demonstrated by physical development). Or, as they develop emotionally, they learn to be more sensitive to others and therefore enhance social development.

What does this mean for teachers? The concept of latent development is particularly important. While teachers may not see some aspects of development present in their students, other areas of development may give clues as to a child's current or near-future capabilities. For example, as students' linguistic development increases, observable ability may not be present (i.e., a student may know a word but cannot quite use it yet). As the student develops emotionally and socially, the ability to use more advanced words and sentence structures develops because the student will have a greater need to express him or herself.

In general, by understanding that developmental domains are not exclusive, teachers can identify current needs of students better, and they can plan for future instructional activities meant to assist students as they develop into adults.

Competency 002   Understand child development and learning in students with disabling conditions or exceptionalities

Skill 2.1   Types of disabilities, developmental delays, and exceptionalities

In the early childhood classroom, the teacher has to be cognizant of the various types of disabilities, developmental delays and exceptionalities that the students can exhibit. They need to be aware of what is appropriate for each individual and to approach the classroom situation with a respect for the students' capabilities. They will need to vary the length of lessons and activities to support each child's individual development.

The qualities of an effective teacher in understanding and creating learning conditions for students with disabilities and exceptionalities include:
- Selects activities based on specific learning objectives from the mandated curriculum
- Selects activities that optimize student learning including the use of manipulatives and group learning situations
- Introduces activities and concepts in an instructional sequential order
- Use a child-centered approach to address the needs and abilities of all students
- Help students identify their own learning needs and structure learning experiences to meet these needs
- Pay attention to the emotional needs of the children and be aware of this when planning lessons
- Be watchful of the children and take advantage of opportunities to teach children how to control or modify behavior
- Use safe interventions in the classroom for children with emotional disabilities
- Establish an environment that promotes appropriate behavior by all students

How can a teacher know when a child needs help with his/her behavior? The child will indicate by what they do that they need and want help. Breaking rules established by parents, teachers, and other authorities and destroying property can signify that a student is losing control especially when these behaviors occur frequently. Other signs that a child needs help may include frequent bouts of crying, a quarrelsome attitude, and constant complaints about school, friends, or life in general. Anytime a child's disposition, attitude, or habits change significantly, teachers and parents need to seriously consider the existence of emotional difficulties.

Emotional disturbances in childhood are not uncommon and take a variety of forms. Usually these problems show up in the form of uncharacteristic behaviors. Most of the time, children respond favorably to brief treatment programs of psychotherapy. At other times, disturbances may need more intensive therapy and are harder to resolve. All stressful behaviors need to be addressed, and any type of chronic antisocial behavior needs to be examined as a possible symptom of deep-seated emotional upset.

Serious Illness/Disabilities

Students with severe illnesses and disabilities are accommodated in the regular classroom. In some instances, this may mean that the child needs a medical aid for the administration of medicines. In most cases, though, a child with a severe illness or disability will qualify for a teacher assistant who will work in the regular classroom. Physical accommodations may need to be done in the school or the classroom to make it possible for children with disabilities to come to school. This includes such things as installing wheelchair ramps or elevators, making the doors larger or having special chairs for the children to use.

Eligibility for special education services is based on a student having one of the above disabilities (or a combination thereof) and demonstration of educational need through professional evaluation.

Seldom does a student with a disability fall into only one of the characteristics listed in IDEA 2004. For example, a student with a hearing impairment may also have a specific learning disability, or a student on the autism spectrum may also demonstrate a language impairment. In fact, language impairment is inherent in autism. Sometimes the eligibility is defined as multiple disabilities (with one listed as a primary eligibility on the IEP and the others listed as secondary). Sometimes there are overlapping needs that are not necessarily listed as a secondary disability.

Teachers of special education students should be aware of the similarities between areas of disabilities, as well as the differences.

Students with disabilities (in all areas) may demonstrate difficulty in social skills. For a student with a hearing impairment, social skills may be difficult because of not hearing social language. However, the emotionally disturbed student may have difficulty because of a special type of psychological disturbance. An autistic student, as a third example, would be unaware of the social cues given with voice, facial expression, and body language. Each of these students would need social skill instruction but in a different way.

Students with disabilities (in all areas) may demonstrate difficulty in academic skills. A student with mental retardation will need special instruction across all areas of academics while a student with a learning disability may need assistance in only one or two subject areas.

Students with disabilities may demonstrate difficulty with independence or self-help skills. A student with a visual impairment may need specific mobility training while a student with a specific learning disability may need a checklist to help in managing materials and assignments.

Special education teachers should be aware that although students across disabilities may demonstrate difficulty in similar ways, the causes may be very different. For example, some disabilities are due to specific sensory impairments (hearing or vision), some due to cognitive ability (mental retardation), and some due to neurological impairment (autism or some learning disabilities). The reason for the difficulty should be a consideration when planning the program of special education intervention.

Additionally, special education teachers should be aware that each area of disability has a range of involvement. Some students may have minimal disability and require no services. Others may need only a few accommodations and have a 504 plan. Some may need an IEP that outlines a specific special education program which might be implemented in an inclusion/resource program, self-contained program, or in a residential setting.

A student with ADD may be able to participate in the regular education program with a 504 plan that outlines a checklist system to keep the student organized and additional communication between school and home. Other students with ADD may need instruction in a smaller group with fewer distractions and would be better served in a resource room.

Special educators should be knowledgeable of the cause and severity of the disability and its manifestations in the specific student when planning an appropriate special education program. Because of the unique needs of the child, such programs are documented in the child's IEP – Individualized Education Program.

Neurotic Disorders

Emotional disorders can seriously hamper a child's normal development. When a child is experiencing trauma or emotional stress of some kind, this causes the child to become nervous and afraid of the simplest things. Thus the child will shy away from some experiences that could be very educational and necessary for social, emotional and moral development.

Sometimes emotional disorders escalate so quickly and become so severe that the child's well-being is threatened. Teachers and parents must recognize the signs of severe emotional stress that may be detrimental to the child. Various forms of emotional disorders, including neurosis, are potentially dangerous. Neuroses are the second most common group of psychiatric disturbances of childhood, and symptoms include extreme anxiety related to over dependence, social isolation, sleep problems, unwarranted nausea, abdominal pain, diarrhea, and headaches.

Some children exhibit irrational fears of particular objects or situations; others become consumed with obsessions, thoughts, or ideas. Depression is one of the most serious neuroses. The child is sad, cries, shows little or no interest in people or activities, has eating and sleeping problems, and sometimes talks about wanting to be dead. Teachers must listen to what the child is saying and take these verbal expressions very seriously. Perhaps what happened at Columbine, Colorado; Jonesboro, Arkansas; and Lake Worth, Florida could have been prevented if adults had recognized the signs.

For more information on neurotic disorders in childhood:

http://www.depression-guide.com/child-psychiatry/childhood-disorder.htm

---

Psychotic Disorders

Psychosis, which is characterized by a loss of contact with reality, is an even more serious emotional disorder. Psychosis is rare in childhood, but when it does occur, it is often difficult to diagnose. One fairly constant sign is the child's failure to make normal emotional contact with other people. The most common psychosis of childhood is schizophrenia, which is a deliberate escape from reality and a withdrawal from relationships with others. When this syndrome occurs in childhood, children continue to have some contact with people; however, a curtain exists between them and the rest of the world. Schizophrenia is more common in boys than in girls. A habitually flat or agitated facial expression is one of the major signs of this disorder. Children suffering from schizophrenia are occasionally mute, but at times they talk incessantly and use bizarre words in ways that make no sense. Their incoherent speech often contributes to their frustration and compounds their fears and preoccupations and is the most significant sign of this very serious disturbance.

Read more about psychotic disorders:

http://www.webmd.com/schizophrenia/guid e/mental-health-psychotic-disorders

---

Early Infantile Autism

Unlike genetic disorders, research has not supported hereditary links to having this disorder. Early infantile autism may occur as early as the fourth month of life. Suddenly the infant lies apathetic and oblivious in the crib. In other cases, the baby seems perfectly normal throughout infancy, and the symptoms appear without warning at about eighteen months of age. Because of the nature of the symptoms, autistic children are often misdiagnosed as mentally retarded, deaf-mute, or organically brain-damaged. Boys are twice as likely to be autistic as girls.

According to many psychologists who treat autistic children, these children seem to have built a wall between themselves and everyone else, including their families and even their parents. They do not make eye contact with others and do not appear to hear those who speak to them. They cannot empathize with others and cannot appreciate humor.

Autistic children usually have language disturbances. One third of them never develop speech at all but may grunt or whine. Others may repeat the same word or phrase over and over or parrot what someone else has said. They often lack inner language as well and cannot play by themselves above a primitive, sensory-motor level.

Frequently, autistic children appear to fill the void left by the absence of interpersonal relationships with a preoccupation with things. They become compulsive about the arrangements of objects and often engage in simple, repetitive physical activities with objects for long periods of time. If these activities are interrupted, they may react with fear or rage. Others remain motionless for hours sometimes moving only their eyes or hands.

On intelligence tests, autistic children score from severely subnormal to high average. Some, while functioning poorly in general, exhibit astonishing ability in isolated skill areas. They may be able to memorize volumes of material, sing beautifully, or perform complicated mathematical problems.

The cause of early infantile autism is unknown. Years ago some psychiatrists speculated that these children did not develop normally because of a lack of parental warmth. Since the incidence of autism in families is usually limited to one child, experts now think this cause is unlikely. Other theories include metabolic or chromosomal defects as causes; however, no evidence substantiates these theories.

The prognosis for autistic children is discouraging. Only about five percent of autistic children become socially well adjusted in adulthood. Another twenty percent make fair social adjustments. The remaining seventy-five percent are socially incapacitated and must be supervised for the duration of their lives. Treatment may include outpatient psychotherapy, drugs, or long-term treatment in a residential center, but neither the form of treatment nor the lack of treatment seems to make a difference in the long run.

Find out more about autism:

http://en.wikipedia.org/wiki/Early_infantile
_autism

Behaviors Indicating Drug/Alcohol Abuse

Students are using drugs and alcohol at surprisingly young ages today. Cases exist of ten year old alcoholics. Young people start using drugs and alcohol for one of four reasons:

1) out of curiosity

2) to party

3) from peer pressure

4) to avoid dealing with problems

It is first necessary to clarify abuse vs. dependency. Abuse is a lesser degree of involvement with substances; usually implying the person is not physically addicted. They may have just as many soft signs of involvement, but lack true addiction. Dependency indicates a true physical addiction, characterized by several hard signs, some of which are less likely to be seen in a school setting. The person may experience withdrawal symptoms when deprived of the substance. The person may experience blackouts. They may use more and more of the substance to get the same effect (tolerance). And they will exhibit irresponsible, illogical, and dangerous use of the substance. Soft signs, declines in functioning, are seen clearly in social, occupational, mental and emotional, and spiritual life. These last symptoms are most likely to be observed by an educator. Because determining addiction is not a concern for the educator, we will use the term abuse in this paper. The difference clinically may be academic for this age group, as addiction occurs at a high rate, and rapidly after first use in young people, sometimes after only a few tries. Legally, any use of an illicit substance for a minor, including alcohol, is automatically considered abuse.

In the school setting, hard signs of dependency are to be considered very serious. Any student who exhibits hard signs associated with substance ingestion must be treated by medical staff at a medical facility immediately. Seizures due to withdrawal are fatal 17% of the time and overdoses due to mixed substances or overuse of a single substance are rapidly fatal, including overdoses with alcohol alone.

Never, under any circumstances, attempt to treat, protect, tolerate, or negotiate with a student who is showing signs of a physical crisis. They are to be removed from the school center by EMS or police as soon as possible, and given constant one to one supervision away from the regular classroom before being taken to the hospital. Police must be called as this student is a danger to self or others in their condition. If it is questionable whether one should do the summoning, find out what the protocol is for each step.

The use of any substance by young people constitutes irresponsible, illogical and dangerous use, if for no other reason than substances of abuse, including alcohol, are all illegal. In the eyes of medical science, there exists a zero level of tolerance because of the inherent physical risk ingesting street drugs, the possibility of brain damage, the loss of educational levels, and lost social development, diminishing a student's ability and chances in life. Psychologically, the use of drugs and alcohol prohibits the youth from struggling with non-chemical coping skills to solve problems. Typically, sophisticated anger modulation techniques usually learned in late adolescence are missed, leaving the person limited in handling that most important of emotions. Substance abuse is also dangerous, considering the terrible number of automobile crash deaths, teen pregnancies attained while intoxicated, overdose on contaminated substances, and the induction of mental disorders from exposure to harsh substances, such as activation of a latent schizophrenia by use of hallucinogens.

There are three soft signs, less rapacious and life threatening, yet each a debilitating nightmare. They are the three psychosocial declines. The young substance abuser will exhibit losses in functional levels socially and academically previously attained. The adage, "Pot makes a smart kid average and an average kid dumb," is right on the mark. There exist not a few families where pot smoking is a known habit of the parents. The children may start their habit by stealing from the parents. Parental use is hampering national efforts to clean up America, making it almost impossible to convince the child that drugs and alcohol are not good for them,

Typically, a student on drugs and/or alcohol will show:

- lack of muscle coordination
- wobbly, ataxic gait
- reddened, puffy eyes (reddened sclera)
- averted gaze
- dilated pupils
- dry eyes
- dry mouth (anticholinergia)
- sneezing or sniffing excessively
- gazing off into space nervousness
- fine trembling
- failure to respond to verbal prompts
- passive-aggressive behavior
- sudden sickness in class
- vomiting and chills
- slurred speech
- aggression
- sleep
- odd, sudden personality changes

- withdrawal
- an appearance of responding to internal stimuli
- the smell of alcohol or the smell of marijuana (pungent, sharp odor, similar to burning cane)
- the appearance of powder around the nasal opening, on the clothes or hands

Students in early childhood classrooms would not have the same experience with drugs and alcohol as older students. They do, however, need to have instruction as to the danger of taking prescription drugs. They see the medicine cabinet at home full of pills and medicine and need to know that these things, while legal, are very dangerous and that they should not take them. Teachers need to make this part of Health class so that students know they only take medicine when needed.

Skill 2.2   Effects of disabling conditions on cognitive, physical, language, social, and emotional development and functioning

In today's push toward academic achievement and standards, it is easy to forget the importance of the development of a child's emotional and physical growth and health. New teachers may be tempted to just teach more or harder for fear that if they don't, their students will not learn. Yet, the new (and veteran) teacher must remember that child development plays a huge part in the academic development of individuals.

While all children develop at different rates, and every child will have unique attributes, we can generally say that teachers have some responsibility to note concerns regarding the emotional or physical states of their students. Indeed, this is a legal responsibility of teachers, particularly where abuse is noted. Yet, other concerns may be justifiable for discussion with counselors or administrators, as well.

Let's start with the legal issues of abuse. While the symptoms of abuse are usually thought to be physical (and therefore visible), mental and emotional abuse is also possible. The best action is to immediately contact a superior at the school if abuse is suspected. The impact of abuse of a child's development in other domains is often extensive. Abused children can be socially withdrawn, and typically, as one might suspect, their minds will not always be on their schoolwork. Significant emotional damage does occur, as well, and teachers may notice very awkward social behavior around other children, as well as adults.

Other issues of physical health might include the prenatal exposure to drugs, alcohol, or nicotine. In all cases, moderate to severe brain damage is possible; however, more subtle impairment can also occur (trouble with breathing, attention deficit disorder, etc.). Because drugs, alcohol, and nicotine can impair brain development, children exposed to such things in the womb may need significant extra classroom support. Some of these children will also need to be referred to the Special Education teacher in order to be tested for learning disabilities.

Day-to-day issues, such as lack of sufficient sleep or nutrition, can harm children in a more temporal fashion. While a child who has had sleep disruptions or insufficient nutrition can bounce back easily when these things are attended to, it is often the case that children living in environments where sleep and proper nutrition are not available will continue through childhood to struggle for these things. Through federal and local funds, many schools are able to provide free or reduced-price breakfasts and lunches for children, however, consider that if this is a necessity, such children may not get a decent dinner, and during weekends and holidays, may struggle even more.

Symptoms of a lack of nutrition and sleep most notably include a lack of concentration, particularly in the classroom. Furthermore, children who lack sufficient sleep or nutrition may become agitated more easily than other children.

In summary, it is always a good idea for teachers to pay attention to the abnormalities in behavior of children, or even sudden drop-offs in achievement or attention, and notify superiors at the school with concerns.

In an era of academic accountability, all teachers must remember that they are still teaching children, who are whole individuals. While teachers are not substitutes for parents, they certainly do have a responsibility to look out for the well-being of their students. In early elementary school, children are particularly effected by emotional upsets in family structure, and they are particularly susceptible to emotional harm when they are not cared for in an appropriate manner at home.

When children are emotionally neglected or have recently endured family upsets, what sorts of things would this impact in a child? Well, first, the level of attention toward school will be greatly reduced. While children may actually think about these things, they may also show signs of jealousy of other children, or they may feel a sense of anger toward other children, the teacher, or their parents. Aggression is a very common behavior of emotionally-neglected children.

When a child has had little verbal interaction, the symptoms can be rather similar to the symptoms of abuse or neglect. The child might have a "deer in the headlights" look and maintain a very socially awkward set of behaviors. In general, such a child will have a drastically reduced ability to express him or herself in words, and often, aggression can be a better tool for the child to get his or her thoughts across.

Although cognitive ability is not lost due to such circumstances (abuse, neglect, emotional upset, lack of verbal interaction), the child will most likely not be able to provide as much intellectual energy as the child would if none of these things were present. But, also, note that the classroom can be seen as a "safe" place by a child, so it is imperative that teachers be attentive to the needs and emotions of their students.

Teachers need to be aware of any traumatic events in a student's life. What may seem trivial to an adult can be very emotionally upsetting for a child. Talk is a great therapy for emotional events and children need time to talk about their problems. This does take time for the teacher, who does have many things to do, but it is essential to provide the time a child needs to talk. However, if a teacher knows something about any emotional event in a child's life, the child should not be forced to talk about it. This should occur naturally.

Skill 2.3   Significance of disabling conditions and exceptionalities for aspects of development and learning

Speech or language delays in children can be cause for concern or intervention. Understanding the development of language in young children can provide information on delays or differences. The efficiency of language for children develops in a pragmatic manner from the caregivers and social environment that they are exposed to during this crucial time of language acquisition. The focus during this period of development should not be on perceived problems such as a child's ability to pronounce certain vowels or consonants (for example a child's pronunciation of /r/ that sounds like /w/ making the word "right" sound like "white.")

Parents and teachers must understand the difference between developmental speech, word development and language delays/differences that may present potential oral language acquisition. The ability to differentiate between the natural ability of children's language patterns and the delayed development of those patterns should be the educated focus for the adult caregivers that provide environmental stimulus and language experience for children.

The mimic pattern of children developing patterns of language is learned from the vocal experiences of word and sentence usage that they hear on a daily basis. The constant exposure to language provides a virtual Webster's Dictionary of repetitive terms and word meanings that children will acquire and use as their word usage increases exponentially through the developmental years.

- Speech intelligibility guidelines provide a tracking of a child's oral speech development. General researchers have shown that the following guidelines are recognizable age/language acquisition: Children at 2 years old should have speech patterns that are about 70% intelligible.
- Children at 3 years old should have an increased 10% speech pattern that is about 80% intelligible.
- Children at 4 years old should have a 20% speech pattern that is about 90% intelligible.
- Children at 5 years old should have a speech pattern that is 100% intelligible.
- Children >5 years old will develop speech patterns that continue at 100% intelligibility with increased vocabulary databases.

Given the speech intelligibility guidelines, parents, adult caregivers and teachers are able to track what is normal development versus language developmental delays or differences. If a child is not developing intelligible and recognizable speech patterns at age appropriate development levels, intervention and additional in depth evaluations will provide the proper tools to address and correct language delays that could have long range impacts on a child's final development of speech pattern intelligibility of language.

Teachers and parents who have concerns about a child's language development should be proactive in addressing language delays. Contacting speech pathologists, auditory specialists to test for hearing disorders, pediatricians to test for motor functioning delays, and utilizing other assessment resources for evaluation are effective steps for those concerned about a child's language delays or differences. Early intervention is the key to addressing children's language delays or differences.

Skill 2.4 Identification and evaluation of students with exceptional learning needs, including academically advanced or artistically talented students

Identify the Characteristics of Emotionally Disturbed Children

Children with emotional disturbances or behavioral disorders are not always easy to identify. It is, of course, easy to identify the acting-out child who is constantly fighting, who cannot stay on task for more than a few minutes, or who shouts obscenities when angry. It is not always easy to identify the child who internalizes his or her problems, on the other hand, or may appear to be the "model" student, but suffers from depression, shyness, or fears. Unless the problem becomes severe enough to impact school performance, the internalizing child may go for long periods without being identified or served.

Studies of children with behavioral and emotional disorders indicate that children with these disorders share some general characteristics:

Lower academic performance: While it is true that some emotionally disturbed children have above average IQ scores, the majority are behind their peers in measures of intelligence and school achievement. Most score in the "slow learner" or "mildly mentally retarded" range on IQ tests, averaging about 90. Many have learning problems that exacerbate their acting out or "giving-up" behavior. As the child enters secondary school, the gap with non-disabled peers widens until the child may be as many as 2 to 4 years behind in reading and/or math skills by high school. Children with severe degrees of impairment may be difficult to evaluate.

Social skills deficits: Students with deficits may be uncooperative, selfish in dealing with others, unaware of what to do in social situations, or ignorant of the consequences of their actions. This may be a combination of lack of prior training, lack of opportunities to interact, and dysfunctional value systems and beliefs learned from their family.

Classroom behaviors: Often, emotionally disturbed children display classroom behavior that is highly disruptive to the classroom setting. Emotionally disturbed children are often out of their seat or running around the room, hitting, fighting, or disturbing their classmates, stealing or destroying property, defiant and noncompliant, and/or verbally disruptive. They do not follow directions and often do not complete assignments.

Aggressive behaviors: Aggressive children often fight or instigate their peers to strike back at them. Aggressiveness may also take the form of vandalism or destruction of property. Aggressive children also engage in verbal abuse.

Delinquency: As emotionally disturbed, acting-out children enter adolescence, they may become involved in socialized aggression (i.e., gang membership) and delinquency. Delinquency is a legal term, rather than medical, and describes truancy and actions that would be criminal if they were committed by adults. Not every delinquent is classified as emotionally disturbed, but children with behavioral and emotional disorders are especially at risk for becoming delinquent because of their problems at school (the primary place for socializing with peers), deficits in social skills that may make them unpopular at school, and/or dysfunctional homes.

Withdrawn behaviors: Children who manifest withdrawn behaviors may consistently act in an immature fashion or prefer to play with younger children. They may daydream or complain of being sick in order to "escape". They may also cry often, cling to the teacher, and ignore those who attempt to interact, or suffer from fears or depression.

Schizophrenia and psychotic behaviors: Children may have bizarre delusions, hallucinations, incoherent thoughts, and disconnected thinking. Schizophrenia typically manifests itself between the ages of 15 and 45, and the younger the onset, the more severe the disorder. These behaviors usually require intensive treatment beyond the scope of the regular classroom setting.

Gender: Many more boys than girls are identified as having emotional and behavioral problems, especially hyperactivity and attention deficit disorder, autism, childhood psychosis, and problems with under control (aggression, socialized aggression). Girls, on the other hand, have more problems with over control (i.e., withdrawal and phobias). Boys are much more prevalent than girls in problems with mental retardation and language and learning disabilities.

Age characteristics: When they enter adolescence, girls tend to experience affective or emotional disorders such as anorexia, depression, bulimia, and anxiety at twice the rate of boys, which mirrors the adult prevalence pattern.

Family characteristics: Having a child with an emotional or behavioral disorder does not automatically mean that the family is dysfunctional. However, there are family factors that create or contribute to the development of behavior disorders and emotional disturbance.
- Abuse and neglect
- Lack of appropriate supervision
- Lax, punitive, and/or lack of discipline
- High rates of negative types of interaction among family members
- Lack of parental concern and interest
- Negative adult role models
- Lack of proper health care and/or nutrition
- Disruption in the family

Children with Mild Learning, Intellectual, and Behavioral Disabilities

Some characteristics of students with mild learning and behavioral disabilities are as follows:

- Lack of interest in schoolwork
- Prefer concrete rather than abstract lessons
- Possess weak listening skills
- Low achievement; limited verbal and/or writing skills
- Respond better to active rather than passive learning tasks
- Have areas of talent or ability often overlooked by teachers
- Prefer to receive special help in regular classroom
- Higher dropout rate than regular education students
- Achieve in accordance with teacher expectations
- Require modification in classroom instruction and are easily distracted

Identify characteristic of students who have a learning disability:

- hyperactivity: a rate of motor activity higher than normal
- perceptual difficulties: visual, auditory, and perceptual problems
- perceptual-motor impairments: poor integration of visual and motor systems, often affecting fine motor coordination
- disorders of memory and thinking: memory deficits, trouble with problem-solving, concept formation and association, poor awareness of own metacognitive skills (learning strategies)
- impulsiveness: act before considering consequences, poor impulse control, often followed by remorselessness
- academic problems in reading, math, writing or spelling; significant discrepancies in ability levels

Identify characteristics of individuals with mental retardation or intellectual disabilities:

- IQ of 70 or below
- limited cognitive ability; delayed academic achievement, particularly in language-related subjects
- deficits in memory which often relate to poor initial perception or inability to apply stored information to relevant situations
- impaired formulation of learning strategies
- difficulty in attending to relevant aspects of stimuli; slowness in reaction time or in employing alternate strategies

Identify characteristics of individuals with autism:

This exceptionality appears very early in childhood. Six common features of autism are:

- **Apparent sensory deficit** –The child may appear not to see or hear or react to a stimulus, then react in an extreme fashion to a seemingly insignificant stimulus.
- **Severe affect isolation**—The child does not respond to the usual signs of affection such as smiles and hugs.
- **Self-stimulation** – Stereotyped behavior takes the form of repeated or ritualistic actions that make no sense to others, such as hand flapping, rocking, staring at objects, or humming the same sounds for hours at a time.
- **Tantrums and self-injurious behavior (SIB)** – Autistic children may bite themselves, pull their hair, bang their heads, or hit themselves. They can throw severe tantrums and direct aggression and destructive behavior toward others.
- **Echolalia** (also known as "parrot talk")—The autistic child may repeat what is played on television, for example, or respond to others by repeating what was said to him. Alternatively, he may simply not speak at all.
- **Severe deficits in behavior and self-care skills**—Autistic children may behave like children much younger than themselves.

Advanced Students

Students with disabilities are not the only ones who require adjusted instruction in a classroom. Often advanced/gifted students or students with exceptional talents are left unaddressed because the teacher assumes the student does not require additional instruction because they are so bright and handle assignments well. Not to say that the teacher purposely does this, but with the high demands teaching, it is often the case that teachers are so overtaxed that these students just are not as high on the instructional priority list. IAs a result, these students are not encouraged to achieve to their fullest potential. Instead, these students often become bored with school as their coursework fails to challenge them. This can lead to the common problem of underachievement among talented learners.

Gifted students are typically most identifiable by the three following characteristics:

- They master concepts and assignments much more quickly than others, and therefore, are left with open time
- They inquire about assignments, ideas and concepts at a higher level than other classmates; they may even seek further direction on assignments
- They maintain interests in unique topics or in areas that are of interest to older students

Depending on the student, free time can be spent in many ways including: being bored, being mischievous or reading or doing some other task. The effective teacher will ensure that these students have additional tasks to complete that perhaps compliment a current assignment. For example, suppose an advanced second-grade student completed his or her reading assignment. To modify this child's instruction, a teacher may propose one or more of the following directions (according to the student's interest):

- Research the author
- Connect the theme of this book to other books the child has read and complete a Venn diagram comparing and contrasting the books
- Design a poster that illustrates the book's theme
- Complete a computer presentation about the story
- Transform the story into a play
- Compose a musical piece that reflects the mood of a scene in the book
- Create a game based on the book for others to play
- Write a story following the same theme of the book
- Write another ending to the book
- Create a brochure that promotes the book

It is important to recognize advanced learners in more than just the traditional areas. Typically, students who excel in reading, writing and math are more easily recognized because of standardized testing results, as well as the fact that this is where most of early childhood education falls. However, students may show significant achievement in all areas including music, drama, art, social skills, science and other areas.

Students tend to be more motivated when they find a task meaningful and they know they have the skills to be successful. This is ever truer with advanced students as their assignments tend to need to be even more meaningful to propose a challenging task. When any form of giftedness is observed, teachers should also concern themselves with ensuring that such children get the attention they need and deserve so that they can continue to learn and grow.

Skill 2.5 **Criteria and procedures for selecting, creating, and modifying materials and equipment to provide differentiated instruction that addresses and accommodates individual students' strengths and challenges**

Differentiated Instruction

The effective teacher will seek to connect all students to the subject matter through multiple techniques, with the goal that each student, through their own abilities, will relate to one or more techniques and excel in the learning process. Differentiated instruction encompasses several areas:

- Content: What is the teacher going to teach? Or, perhaps better put, what does the teacher want the students to learn? Differentiating content means that students will have access to content that piques their interest about a topic, with a complexity that provides an appropriate challenge to their intellectual development.
- Process: A classroom management technique where instructional organization and delivery is maximized for the diverse student group. These techniques should include dynamic, flexible grouping activities, where instruction and learning occurs both as whole-class, teacher-led activities, as well as peer learning and teaching (while teacher observes and coaches) within small groups or pairs.
- Product: The expectations and requirements placed on students to demonstrate their knowledge or understanding. The type of product expected from each student should reflect each student's own capabilities.

Creating a Differentiated Classroom

The first month of school gives the teacher time to get to know the students and their strengths and needs. This month is also a planning month in which the teacher can determine the groupings for the various subjects and the various strategies and concepts that students need to learn within these groups. It is impossible to meet the needs of children in the classroom individually, so teachers differentiate their instruction to meet the needs of students in a group. Teachers don't have to differentiate all of the time, either – only when they see a need.

There are guiding principles the teacher can use to help create a differentiated classroom that meets the needs of special education students, the regular mainstream students and those that are academically advanced.

- Begin instruction keeping individual differences in mind and modify the lesson based on individual needs
- Adjust the pace and the content in response to student needs, such as learning difficulties, learning styles and problem areas.
- Employ a range of instructional strategies, such as learning stations, compacting the curriculum, cluster groups, etc.
- Assess individual achievement through assessment for learning, rather than assessment of learning. Through assessment, teachers can see where the students have achieved the objectives and where they may still need help. In this way, assessment drives instruction.
- Allow the students to participate in their own learning and give them choices in the activities they complete
- Modify assignments, up or down, according to student needs.
- Maintain flexibility in how the students move from one concept to another.
- Vary the areas where students work in the classroom. For example, some students work best when sitting on the floor, while others might like to work in the hallway.

Special Education Students

IDEA 2004 defines *a child with a disability. . . as having mental retardation, a hearing impairment (including deafness), a speech or language impairment, a visual impairment (including blindness), a serious emotional disturbance (referred to in this part as emotional disturbance), an orthopedic impairment, autism, traumatic brain injury, an other health impairment, a specific learning disability, deaf-blindness, or multiple disabilities, and who, by reason thereof, needs special education and related services.*

Eligibility for special education services is based on a student having one of the above disabilities (or a combination thereof) and demonstration of educational need through professional evaluation.

Seldom does a student with a disability fall into only one of the characteristics listed in IDEA 2004. For example, a student with a hearing impairment may also have a specific learning disability, or a student on the autism spectrum may also demonstrate a language impairment. In fact, language impairment is inherent in autism. Sometimes the eligibility is defined as multiple disabilities (with one listed as a primary eligibility on the IEP and the others listed as secondary). Sometimes there are overlapping needs that are not necessarily listed as a secondary disability.

Teachers of special education students should be aware of the similarities between areas of disabilities, as well as the differences.

Students with disabilities (in all areas) may demonstrate difficulty in social skills. For a student with a hearing impairment, social skills may be difficult because of not hearing social language. However, the emotionally disturbed student may have difficulty because of a special type of psychological disturbance. An autistic student, as a third example, would be unaware of the social cues given with voice, facial expression, and body language. Each of these students would need social skill instruction but in a different way.

Students with disabilities (in all areas) may demonstrate difficulty in academic skills. A student with mental retardation will need special instruction across all areas of academics while a student with a learning disability may need assistance in only one or two subject areas.

Students with disabilities may demonstrate difficulty with independence or self-help skills. A student with a visual impairment may need specific mobility training while a student with a specific learning disability may need a checklist to help in managing materials and assignments.

Special education teachers should be aware that although students across disabilities may demonstrate difficulty in similar ways, the causes may be very different. For example, some disabilities are due to specific sensory impairments (hearing or vision), some due to cognitive ability (mental retardation), and some due to neurological impairment (autism or some learning disabilities). The reason for the difficulty should be a consideration when planning the program of special education intervention.

Additionally, special education teachers should be aware that each area of disability has a range of involvement. Some students may have minimal disability and require no services. Others may need only a few accommodations and have a 504 plan. Some may need an IEP that outlines a specific special education program which might be implemented in an inclusion/resource program, self-contained program, or in a residential setting.

A student with ADD may be able to participate in the regular education program with a 504 plan that outlines a checklist system to keep the student organized and additional communication between school and home. Other students with ADD may need instruction in a smaller group with fewer distractions and would be better served in a resource room.

Special educators should be knowledgeable of the cause and severity of the disability and its manifestations in the specific student when planning an appropriate special education program. Because of the unique needs of the child, such programs are documented in the child's IEP – Individualized Education Program.

SEE also Skill 2.7

Skill 2.6 Legal requirements and responsibilities for providing education to students with special needs

One of the first things that a teacher learns is how to obtain resources and help for his/her students. All schools have guidelines for receiving this assistance especially since the implementation of the Americans with Disabilities Act. The first step in securing help is for the teacher to approach the school's administration or exceptional education department for direction in attaining special services or resources for qualifying students. Many schools have a committee designated for addressing these needs such as a Child Study Team or Core Team. These teams are made up of both regular and exceptional education teachers, school psychologists, guidance counselors, and administrators. The particular student's classroom teacher usually has to complete some initial paper work and will need to do some behavioral observations.

The teacher will take this information to the appropriate committee for discussion and consideration. The committee will recommend the next step to be taken. Often subsequent steps include a complete psychological evaluation along with certain physical examinations such as vision and hearing screening and a complete medical examination by a doctor. The referral of students for this process is usually relatively simple for the classroom teacher and requires little more than some initial paper work and discussion. The services and resources the student receives as a result of the process typically prove to be invaluable to the student with behavioral disorders.

At times, the teacher must go beyond the school system to meet the needs of some students. An awareness of special services and resources and how to obtain them is essential to all teachers and their students. When the school system is unable to address the needs of a student, the teacher often must take the initiative and contact agencies within the community. Frequently there is no special policy for finding resources. It is simply up to the individual teacher to be creative and resourceful and to find whatever help the student needs. Meeting the needs of all students is certainly a team effort that is most often spearheaded by the classroom teacher.

There is a saying, "If you're going to be an alcoholic or drug addict in America, you will be." Cynical but true, this comment implies exposure to alcohol and drugs is 100%. We now have a wide-spread second generation of drug abusers in families. And alcohol is the oldest drug of abuse known to humankind, with many families affected for three and four or more known generations. It's hard to tell youth to eschew drugs when Mom and Dad, who grew up in the early illicit drug era, have a little toot or smoke and a few drinks on the weekends, or more often. Educators, therefore, are not only likely to, but often do face students who are high on something in school. Of course, they are not only a hazard to their own safety and those of others, but their ability to be productive learners is greatly diminished, if not non-existent. They show up instead of skip, because it's not always easy or practical for them to spend the day away from home, but not in school. Unless they can stay inside they are at risk of being picked up for truancy. Some enjoy being high in school, getting a sense of satisfaction by putting something over on the system. Some just don't take drug use seriously enough to think usage at school might be inappropriate.

Family Involvement

Under the IDEA, parent/guardian involvement in the development of the student's Individualized Education Program (IEP) is required and absolutely essential for the advocacy of the disabled student's educational needs. IEPs must be tailored to meet the student's needs, and no one knows those needs better than the parent/guardian and other significant family members. Optimal conditions for a disabled student's education exist when teachers, school administrators, special education professionals and parents/guardians work together to design and execute the IEP.

Due Process

Under the IDEA, Congress provides safeguards for students against schools' actions, including the right to sue in court, and encourages states to develop hearing and mediation systems to resolve disputes. No student or their parents/guardians can be denied due process because of disability.

Inclusion, Mainstreaming, and Least Restrictive Environment

Inclusion, mainstreaming and least restrictive environment are interrelated policies under the IDEA, with varying degrees of statutory imperatives.
- Inclusion is the right of students with disabilities to be placed in the regular classroom.
- Least restrictive environment is the mandate that children be educated to the maximum extent appropriate with their non-disabled peers.

Mainstreaming is a policy where disabled students can be placed in the regular classroom, as long as such placement does not interfere with the student's educational plan

Abuse Situations

A suspected case gone unreported may destroy a child's life, and their subsequent life as a functional adult. It is the duty of any citizen who suspects abuse and neglect to make a report, and it is especially important and required for State licensed and certified persons to make a report. All reports can be kept confidential if required, but it is best to disclose your identity in case more information is required of you. This is a personal matter that has no impact on qualifications for license or certification. Failure to make a report when abuse or neglect is suspected is punishable by revocation of certification and license, a fine, and criminal charges.

It is the right of any accused individual to have counsel and make a defense, as in any matter of law. The procedure for reporting makes clear the rights of the accused, who stands before the court innocent until proven guilty, with the right to representation, redress and appeal, as in all matters of United States law. The State is cautious about receiving spurious reports, but investigates any that seem real. Some breaches of standards of decency are not reportable offenses, such as possession of pornography that is not hidden from children. But go ahead and make the report and let the counselor make the decision. Your conscience is clear, and you have followed all procedures that keep you from liability. Your obligation to report is immediate when you suspect abuse.

There is no time given as an acceptable or safe period of time to wait before reporting, so hesitation to report may be a cause for action against you. Do not wait once your suspicion is firm. All you need to have is a reasonable suspicion, not actual proof, which is the job for the investigators.

Many safe and helpful interventions are available to the classroom teacher when dealing with a student who is suffering serious emotional disturbances. First, and foremost, the teacher must maintain open communication with the parents and other professionals who are involved with the student whenever overt behavior characteristics are exhibited. Students with behavior disorders need constant behavior modification, which may involve two-way communication between the home and school on a daily basis.

The teacher must establish an environment that promotes appropriate behavior for all students as well as respect for one another. The students may need to be informed of any special needs that their classmates may have so they can give due consideration. The teacher should also initiate a behavior modification program for any student that might show emotional or behavioral disorders. Such behavior modification plans can be effective means of preventing deviant behavior. If deviant behavior does occur, the teacher should have arranged for a safe and secure time-out place where the student can go for a respite and an opportunity to regain self-control.

Often when a behavior disorder is more severe, the student must be involved in a more concentrated program aimed at alleviating deviant behavior such as psychotherapy. In such instances, the school psychologist, guidance counselor, or behavior specialist is directly involved with the student and provides counseling and therapy on a regular basis. Frequently they are also involved with the student's family.

As a last resort, many families are turning to drug therapy. Once viewed as a radical step, administering drugs to children to balance their emotions or control their behavior has become a widely used form of therapy. Of course, only a medical doctor can prescribe such drugs. Great care must be exercised when giving pills to children in order to change their behavior, especially since so many medicines have undesirable side effects. It is important to know that these drugs relieve only the symptoms of behavior and do not get at the underlying causes. Parents and teachers need to be educated as to the side effects of these medications.

Skill 2.7 Purposes and procedures for developing and implementing Individualized Education Plans (IEPs), 504s, and Individualized Family Service Plans (IFSPs)

Teachers develop plans to help students who need extra support, whether it is with their academics, behavior or with social and emotional problems. These plans are knows Individualized Educational Plans (IEPs). IEPs are plans designed to assist students in ways other than what the teacher in the regular classroom can provide. It can be a plan developed by the classroom teacher, though, but which modifications made to the instruction or assessment. Some IEP's focus on enrichment, but for the most part they focus on areas of need.

In order for a student to have an IEP, there must be testing done to determine the areas in which the student needs help. In some cases, psychological testing needs to be in place. There is a team involved in the IEP process, which include the parents, classroom teacher, the administration and if the student will be receiving help and instruction from other staff members, these people will also be part of the team.

An IEP will list the strategies needed to help the student succeed. They must be measurable goals and a time frame needs to be set during which the student will work on these goals. Sample strategies that could be included in an IEP are:
- Providing extra time to finish tasks
- Having the aid of a reader or scribe for Language Arts or other subjects that require reading and writing
- The use of manipulatives
- Getting extra assistance from an educational assistant, reading specialist or speech therapist

Students may also need resources that are not provided by the school and there are community resource personnel who provide this extra support.

The IEP is monitored during the year to ensure that students are meeting the goals. On occasion, the goals may have to be modified up or down throughout the year according to the student's needs.

For students diagnosed with a physical or emotional disability, the plan of action is called a 504. It is not an IEP, but it is similar in some respects in that it lists accommodations that are to be made for the student within the regular classroom setting. There are four steps in the process for putting a student on a 504. First the student has to be referred by the teacher, parent, physician or some other school personnel. A meeting is held and a plan is put in place. Like the IEP, regular monitoring is necessary and adjustments may need to be made throughout the year.

Some of the accommodations that might be included in a 504 include:
- The location of the child's seat in the classroom
- Diabetic children may be allowed to have food in the classroom
- Administering medication to the child in the school office
- Adjustment of student assignments or extra time allotted.

An IFSP is an Individual Family Service Plan and is a legal document. This plan is put in place for young children who have disabilities, such as deafness or other special needs. The focus of the plan is to help the family and the child by providing services, such as family based programs and the services of professionals to deal with the child's disability.

The IFSP is a way of providing early intervention under IDEA (Individuals with Disabilities Education Act). It is not only designed to enhance the child's education but it is also designed to help the family facilitate the child's development.

SEE also Skill 2.5

Skill 2.8   Role and influence of family in development and learning

Teachers today will deal with an increasingly diverse group of cultures in their classrooms. And while this is an exciting prospect for most teachers, it creates new challenges in dealing with a variety of family expectations for school and teachers.

First, teachers must show respect to all parents and families. They need to set the tone that suggests that their mission is to develop students into the best people they can be. And then they need to realize that various cultures have different views of how children should be educated.

Second, teachers will have better success when they talk personally about their children. Even though teachers may have many students, when they share personal things about each child, parents will feel more confident that their child will be "in the right hands."

Third, it is very important that teachers act like they are partners in the children's education and development. Parents know their children best, and it is important to get feedback, information, and advice from them.

Finally, teachers will need to be patient with difficult families, realizing that certain methods of criticism (including verbal attacks, etc.) are unacceptable. Such circumstances would require the teacher to get assistance from an administrator. This situation, however, is very unusual, and most teachers will find that when they really attempt to be friendly and personal with parents, the parents will reciprocate and assist in the educational program.

One way of interacting with families includes the parent-teacher conference.

Parent Conferences

The parent-teacher conference is generally for one of three purposes. First, the teacher may wish to share information with the parents concerning the performance and behavior of the child. Second, the teacher may be interested in obtaining information from the parents about the child. Such information may help answer questions or concerns that the teacher has. A third purpose may be to request parent support or involvement in specific activities or requirements. In many situations, more than one of the purposes may be involved.

Planning the Conference

When a conference is scheduled, whether at the request of the teacher or parent, the teacher should allow sufficient time to prepare thoroughly. Collect all relevant information, samples of student work, records of behavior, and other items needed to help the parent understand the circumstances. It is also a good idea to compile a list of questions or concerns you wish to address. Arrange the time and location of the conference to provide privacy and to avoid interruptions.

Conducting the Conference

Begin the conference by putting the parents as ease. Take the time to establish a comfortable mood, but do not waste time with unnecessary small talk. Begin your discussion with positive comments about the student. Identify strengths and desirable attributes, but do not exaggerate.

As you address issues or areas of concern, be sure to focus on observable behaviors and concrete results or information. Do not make judgmental statements about parent or child. Share specific work samples, anecdotal records of behavior, etc., which demonstrate clearly the concerns you have. Be a good listener and hear the parent's comments and explanations. Such background information can be invaluable in understanding the needs and motivations of the child.

Finally, end the conference with an agreed plan of action between parents and teacher (and, when appropriate, the child). Bring the conference to a close politely but firmly and thank the parents for their involvement.

After the Conference

A day or two after the conference, it is a good idea to send a follow-up note to the parents. In this note, briefly and concisely reiterate the plan or step agreed to in the conference. Be polite and professional; avoid the temptation to be too informal or chatty. If the issue is a long term one such as the behavior or on-going work performance of the student, make periodic follow-up contacts to keep the parents informed of the progress.

Skill 2.9   Community resources to assist families

The Community as a Resource

The community is a vital link to increasing learning experiences for students. Community resources can supplement the educational resources of school communities. With state and federal educational funding becoming increasingly subject to legislative budget cuts, school communities welcome the financial support that community resources can provide in terms of discounted prices on high end supplies (e.g. computers, printers, and technology supplies), along with providing free notebooks, backpacks and student supplies for low income students who may have difficulty obtaining the basic supplies for school.

Community stores can provide cash rebates and teacher discounts for educators in struggling school districts and compromised school communities. Both professionally and personally, communities can enrich the student learning experiences by including the following support strategies:

- Provide programs that support student learning outcomes and future educational goals
- Create mentoring opportunities that provide adult role models in various industries to students interested in studying in that industry
- Provide financial support for school communities to help low-income or homeless students begin the school year with the basic supplies
- Develop paid internships with local university students to provide tutorial services for identified students in school communities who are having academic and social difficulties processing various subject areas.
- Providing parent-teen-community forums to create public voice of change in communities
- Offer parents without computer or Internet connection, stipends to purchase technology to create equitable opportunities for students to do research and complete word.doc paper requirements.
- Stop in classrooms and ask teachers and students what's needed to promote academic progress and growth.

Community resources are vital in providing additional support for students, school communities and families struggling to remain engaged in declining educational institutions competing for federal funding and limited District funding. The commitment that a community shows to its educational communities is a valuable investment in the future. Community resources that are able to provide additional funding for tutors in marginalized classrooms or help schools reduce classrooms of students needing additional remedial instruction directly impact educational equity and facilitation of teaching and learning for both teachers and students.

Promoting a Sense of Community

The bridge to effective learning for students begins with a collaborative approach by all stakeholders that support the educational needs of students. Underestimating the power and integral role of the community institutions in impacting the current and future goals of students can carry high stakes for students beyond the high school years who are competing for college access, student internships, and entry level jobs in the community. Researchers have shown that school involvement and connections with community institutions have greater retention rates of students graduating and seeking higher education experiences. The current disconnect and autonomy that has become commonplace in today's society must be reevaluated in terms of promoting tomorrow's citizens.

When community institutions provide students and teachers with meaningful connections and input, the commitment is apparent in terms of volunteering, loyalty and professional promotion. Providing students with placements in leadership positions such as the ASB (Associated Student Body); the PTSA (Parent Teacher Student Association); School Boards; neighborhood sub-committees addressing political or social issues; or government boards that impact and influence school communities creates an avenue for students to explore ethical, participatory, collaborative, transformational leadership that can be applied to all areas of a student's educational and personal life.

Community liaisons provide students with opportunities to experience accountability and responsibility so that students learn about life and how organizations work with effective communication and teams working together to accomplish goals and objectives. Teaching students skills of inclusion, social and environmental responsibility and creating public forums that represent student voice and vote foster student interest and access to developing and reflecting on individual opinions and understanding the dynamics of the world around them.

When a student sees that the various support systems are in place and consistently working as a team to effectively provide resources and avenues of academic promotion and accountability, students have no fear of taking risks to grow by becoming a teen voice on a local committee about "Teen Violence" or volunteering in a local hospice for young children with terminal diseases. The linkages of community institutions provide role-models of a world in which the student will soon become an integral and vital member, so being a part of that world as a student makes the transition easier as a young adult.

Skill 2.10   Child protection laws (e.g., mandated reporting)

SEE Skills 2.6 and 2.7

SUBAREA II. KNOWLEDGE OF CHILDREN'S LITERATURE AND THE WRITING PROCESS

Competency 003 Understand children's literature, including genres, literary elements, and literary techniques

Skill 3.1 Major works and authors of nineteenth- and twentieth-century literature for young children; genres of children's literature and the characteristics of different genres

Children's literature is a genre of its own and emerged as a distinct and independent form in the second half of the 18th century. *The Visible World in Pictures* by John Amos Comenius, a Czech educator, was one of the first printed works and the first picture book. For the first time, educators acknowledged that children are different from adults in many respects. Modern educators acknowledge that introducing elementary students to a wide range of reading experiences plays an important role in their mental/social/psychological development. Some of the most common forms of literature specifically for children follow:

- **Traditional Literature:** Traditional literature opens up a world where right wins out over wrong, where hard work and perseverance are rewarded, and where helpless victims find vindication—all worthwhile values that children identify with even as early as kindergarten. In traditional literature, children will be introduced to fanciful beings, humans with exaggerated powers, talking animals, and heroes that will inspire them. For younger elementary children, these stories in Big Book format are ideal for providing predictable and repetitive elements that can be grasped by these children.

- **Folktales/Fairy Tales:** Some examples: The Three Bears, Little Red Riding Hood, Snow White, Sleeping Beauty, Puss-in-Boots, Rapunzel and Rumpelstiltskin. Adventures of animals or humans and the supernatural characterize these stories. The hero is usually on a quest and is aided by other-worldly helpers. More often than not, the story focuses on good and evil and reward and punishment.

- **Fables:** Animals that act like humans are featured in these stories and usually reveal human foibles or sometimes teach a lesson. Example: Aesop's Fables.

- **Myths:** These stories about events from the earliest times, such as the origin of the world, are considered true in their own societies.

- **Legends:** These are similar to myths except that they tend to deal with events that happened more recently. Example: Arthurian legends.

- **Tall tales:** Examples: Paul Bunyan, John Henry, and Pecos Bill. These are purposely exaggerated accounts of individuals with superhuman strength.

- **Modern Fantasy:** Many of the themes found in these stories are similar to those in traditional literature. The stories start out based in reality, which makes it easier for the reader to suspend disbelief and enter worlds of unreality. Little people live in the walls in The Borrowers and time travel is possible in The Trolley to Yesterday. Including some fantasy tales in the curriculum helps elementary-grade children develop their sense of imagination. These often appeal to ideals of justice and issues having to do with good and evil; and because children tend to identify with the characters, the message is more likely to be retained.

- **Science Fiction:** Robots, spacecraft, mystery, and civilizations from other ages often appear in these stories. Most presume advances in science on other planets or in a future time. Most children like these stories because of their interest in space and the "what if" aspect of the stories.
  <u>Examples:</u> *Outer Space and All That Junk* and *A Wrinkle in Time*.

- **Modern Realistic Fiction:** These stories are about real problems that real children face. By finding that their hopes and fears are shared by others, young children can find insight into their own problems. Young readers also tend to experience a broadening of interests as the result of this kind of reading. It's good for them to know that a child can be brave and intelligent and can solve difficult problems.

- **Historical Fiction:** Rifles for Watie is an example of this kind of story. Presented in a historically-accurate setting, it's about a young boy (16 years) who serves in the Union army. He experiences great hardship but discovers that his enemy is an admirable human being. It provides a good opportunity to introduce younger children to history in a beneficial way.

- **Biography:** Reading about inventors, explorers, scientists, political and religious leaders, social reformers, artists, sports figures, doctors, teachers, writers, and war heroes help children to see that one person can make a difference. They also open new vistas for children to think about when they choose an occupation to fantasize about.

- **Informational Books:** These are ways to learn more about something you are interested in or something that you know nothing about. Encyclopedias are good resources, of course, but a book like *Polar Wildlife* by Kamini Khanduri shows pictures and facts that will capture the imaginations of young children.

Note: Books marked with an asterisk (*) have won the Caldecott medal which is explained in the section on picture books.

Earliest Literature

Fine children's literature opens up each child to vicarious experiences that enrich his/her world. From being read to by parents and caregivers from the earliest ages, children during toddlerhood can handle **board books** with sturdy pages such as Kit Allen's *Sweater*, Donald Crews's **Freight Train,* and Margaret Wise Brown's *Goodnight, Moon.* Children ages two and three enjoy what are called "**toy books**," i.e. those that have flaps to lift up, textures to touch, or holes to peek through. Examples include Dorothy Kunhardt's *Pat the Bunny* and Eric Hill's *Where's Spot?*

From ages three to seven children enjoy a variety of nonfiction **concept books**. These books combine language and pictures to show concrete examples of abstract concepts. Hundreds of beautiful books comprise this genre, such as Lois Ehlert's **Color Zoo* (animals, shapes, and colors), counting books such as Eric Carle's **10 Little Rubber Ducks* (directions, numbers, and up and down) Tana Hoban's *Count and See* (numbers and sets of l0 up to l00), and Molly Bang's **Ten, Nine, Eight* (a gentle lullaby as an African-American father readies his daughter for bed).

Another category of concept books is **alphabet books**, popular with children from preschool through grade 2. Outstanding examples include the Lobels's **On Market Street* (every item purchased from the market is in alphabetical order); Ehlert's *Eating the Alphabet: Fruits and Vegetables From A to Z*; Bowen's *Antler, Bear, Canoe: A Northwoods Alphabet Year*; Musgrove's *Ashanti to Zulu: African Traditions*; and Lara Rankin's *The Handmade Alphabet* (this gives the American Sign Language signal for each alphabet letter in sequence).

In grades K, 1, and 2 when children are becoming early readers, two other genres of literature become salient: **wordless picture books** and **easy-to-read books**. The first of these, the wordless picture book, is excellent for children just breaking into reading. The books accommodate readers and nonreaders alike, for there is no text. Children must be capable of "reading" the pictures and creative enough to supply the dialogue and descriptive language to accompany them. Many children have enjoyed Mercer Mayer's *Frog Goes to Dinner*, Emily Arnold McCully's *Picnic*, Peter Sis's *Dinosaur!* and Mitsumasa Anno's *Anno's Journey.* The teacher should be discriminating about easy-to-read books because some are of questionable literary quality. Among the best are such familiars as Arnold Lobel's *Frog and Toad Are Friends*, Cynthis Rylant's *Henry and Mudge* books, and Else Minarik's **Little Bear* books illustrated by Maurice Sendak.

From the preschool years onward, the **picture book**, characterized by illustrations and a plot that are closely interrelated (one usually cannot exist independently of the other) are suitable for children. With the explosion of picture books in the last fifteen years, there are some that may even be used with children in grade 6 and above. Each year a medal is awarded in the U.S. to the best-illustrated picture book by the Caldecott committee. They also choose one or two honor books. Teachers of children ages 4-8 should be intimately familiar with the Caldecott list which can be found in any children's library or on the Internet, as these books are exemplary reading choices. In this discussion those books which are Caldecott winners have been marked with an asterisk (*).Well-illustrated children's books show sensitivity to line, color, shape, texture, and overall composition.

Illustrators use various artistic media from watercolor (David Wiesner's *Tuesday*), to oil painting (Paul Zelinsky's *Rapunzel* and Lane Smith's illustrations of Jon Scieszka's The True Story of the 3 Little Pigs!), collage (used extensively by Eric Carle (The Very Hungry Caterpillar) and Ezra Jack Keats (*The Snowy Day and *Goggles!), to pastels (Ed Young's *Lon Po Po: A Red-Riding Hood Story from China). Other outstanding picture books include Sendak's *Where the Wild Things Are, Vera B. Williams's *More More More Said the Baby, Barbara Joosse's Mama, Do You Love Me? Jane Yolen's *Owl Moon and Leo Lionni's *Swimmy.

Early Elementary Levels

Chapter books are appropriate for readers in grades 2, 3, and 4 and beyond. They are characterized by occasional illustrations, relatively short chapters to begin with, and interesting plots that appeal to children ages 8 and up. High quality chapter books include the following for children ages 8-10: Patricia McKissack's, Porch Lies: Tales of Slicksters, Tricksters, and Other Wily Characters; Kate DiCamillo's Because of Winn-Dixie, and E.B. White's Charlotte's Web.

It seems that in every generation, there is one writer or one book that tends to dominate children's literature—the most recent one being the Harry Potter books. There is always a lot of discussion about what is appropriate for children and at what age. The criticism about the themes in the Harry Potter books is that it revolves around witchery and witchcraft, which has upset some communities enough that the books have been abolished in the curricula and libraries of the schools.

Following are some authors who are making significant contributions to early elementary children's literature and some examples of their works:

Enid Blyton, British author, *The Famous Five, The Secret Seven* series.

J.K. Rowling, British author, *Harry Potter* series.

Jacqueline Wilson, British author, *Tracy Beaker* series.

Jane Yolen, American author, <u>*Owl Moon*</u>, <u>*Devil's Arithmetic*</u>.

Betsy Byars, American author, <u>*Summer of the Swans*</u>.

Skill 3.2   Major themes associated with literature for young children

In general, children's literature does indeed focus greatly on themes that pertain to choices, morals, and values. Children's literature is intended to instruct students through entertaining stories, while also promoting an interest in the very act of reading, itself.

Young readers respond to themes that reflect their lives. Some simplistic examples of themes with appeal to children are:

- The world is black or white (there are no gray areas).
- Different is fine, but hard.
- Good guys always win and bad guys are simply bad.
- Body functions are gross, but funny.
- Magic and adventure are natural.
- Being good is nice.

The major themes of works written by well-known authors can be classified under the following genre headings:

- Science Fiction: relies on the suspension of disbelief to create worlds beyond today that are sometimes surreal. Sci-fi takes scientific knowledge to the planets and beneath the sea to create imaginary life worlds.
- Fantasy: readers must suspend belief to enter into a world that includes mythical creatures and fairies that are dealing with parallel issues in the current world. The stories have origins and themes from old traditions and stories that have been handed down historically.
- Horror and ghost stories: sometimes grounded in reality, these stories and books are developed upon the fears and phobias of the reader. They are designed to make the reader second guess reality and they are created to perpetuate and heighten the things in life that frighten and create physical reactions.

- Action and Adventure: elicit the adventure spirit of the reader with plots that are busy and dangerous. The protagonist is self-reliant and conquers a dangerous situation alone using mental and physical acuity to assess and problem solve issues. Crime solving adventures are popular with middle readers and detective novels with younger characters. Using wit and brains to problem solve is popular with young juvenile readers.
- Historical fiction: based on real-life events and people who have overcome adversity and left a mark on society in deeds and events. The themes are based in historical events and constructed to engage the reader and also teach the reader something about history.
- Biography: takes true-life people who have existed at some point on the planet and creates real life drama about their lives or relevant segments of their lives.
- Educational books: every school has a curriculum of core subject books used in teaching students academic facts and required knowledge.

Skill 3.3   Analysis of rhetorical and literary devices (e.g., analogies, metaphors, symbolism, repetition) in literature for young children

Children's literature is likely to contain the same types of literary devices as you would find in more advanced, adult literature. Literary devices are techniques that writers use to convey meaning or to frame an artistic work. They are tools that the author uses to add layers of meaning, tell a better story, appeal to the senses or help the reader to better visualize the story.

Small children may or may not grasp the full significance of these literary devices, although they will be appreciated by more advanced readers. Many of us read books as children in which the symbolism and themes and metaphors escaped us. We merely enjoyed the stories, focusing on the literal meaning of the story and missing more sophisticated layers of meaning. However, when we reread them as parents to our own children, we were able to see and appreciate different levels of meaning.

Literary devices used by children's authors may include:

Analogies. This is when one thing is compared to another using the word "like" or "as." Example: "She walked slowly along, like a sad, wet puppy." Analogies are a form of description that help young readers to learn about something new by comparing it to something they already understand.

Metaphors. These are like analogies, only without the comparison word is left out, so one thing stands for another. Example: "His unhappiness was a prison, holding him inside it." Because metaphors are not meant to be taken entirely literally, they are a form of abstraction. Young readers are more literal and may have difficulty with abstraction. (The ability to engage in abstract thinking typically does not emerge until later childhood, according to Piaget.)

Symbolism is when something comes to stand for something else. For example, a black cat has come to be understood as standing for "bad luck." In literature, the color white often stands for goodness or holiness or purity and a burning candle may stand for hope or life.

Repetition may be used by a writer to underscore the importance of a part of a work or to point to the central theme. Repetition is very helpful to young readers.

It is sufficient if the young child grasps only the literal meaning of a written work. As children grow and read more, they should begin to recognize and appreciate subtler elements such as foreshadowing, references to darkness to indicate possible danger or evil, the way the good guys wear white and the bad guys wear black, and so on. While these elements are not explicitly pointed out by the author, they are important parts of the story and if children do not learn to notice these details, they will eventually be missing important parts of the story. Noticing and appreciating these artistic elements enriches the reader's experience with the story.

It is helpful, when children are young, to explicitly point out and explain these literary devices to children. This helps them to gain a fuller appreciation of the story and will heighten their abilities to notice details.

Teachers can help children develop the ability to notice and appreciate literary devices by reading sections of a story to them and see if you can get them to predict what will happen next. (Ideally, the section chosen should contain symbolic foreshadowing.) Then, ask the students why they make this prediction. This could lead to a discussion of the ways in which the writer gives clues to what is going to happen through the use of symbolism.

Skill 3.4   Comparison of different styles and communicative purposes in children's literature

When students approach a work of literature, they will need to be able to understand the author's style, the theme of the work, and the author's voice. Does the teacher jump right into the book? Or does the teacher use a simple piece of literature to first teach the concepts so that when they get into more complex novels, for example, they will already know what the concepts mean?

Consider this: A fairy tale may involve a character telling the story of his friend. There is no doubt that if the author had the friend's mother tell the story, the novel would come across quite differently. So, the teacher presents *The Three Bears*. This is a story that is told in third person. The teachers ask students to re-design the story as if Goldilocks had told the story. Then the teacher asks the students to re-design the story once more as if Papa Bear had told the story. Students will quickly see that while the plot does not change, the way the plot is presented changes slightly.

Children's literature can similarly enlighten students on the various aspects of theme and style, as well as many other literary elements. The more they learn literary elements through simple children's stories, the easier it will be for them to make connections to more complex literature.

In comparing fiction to nonfiction, students need to learn about the conventions of each. In fiction, students can generally expect to see plot, characters, setting, and themes. In nonfiction, students may see a plot, characters, settings, and themes, but they will also experience interpretations, opinions, theories, research, and other elements.

Overall, students can begin to see patterns that identify fiction apart from nonfiction. Often, the more fanciful or unrealistic a text or story is, the more likely it is fiction.

Skill 3.5   Criteria for evaluating children's literature (e.g., reading level, literary quality, cultural diversity, interesting information, vocabulary richness, appealing plot, gender preferences, variety in settings and character types)

In selecting appropriate literature for children, teachers must consider several factors. Primary among these factors is the composition of the class (including diversity) and the preferences of the children. Other factors to consider are the children's reading ability, interests, and the recognized quality level of the book which can be partially determined by referring to professional reviews.

Books should be chosen at an appropriate reading level. They should be challenging enough to promote vocabulary growth and learning new information. It might be helpful to think of Lev Vygotsky's "Zone of Proximal Development" in selecting reading material for children: books should neither be to easy as to lead to boredom nor so difficult as to lead to frustration. This means that teachers may have to provide a wide selection of suitable reading materials and then allow students to choose.

Librarians are an excellent resource in choosing appropriate reading material for children. A good librarian regularly reads and evaluates children's books and can offer up-to-date information on current, high-quality books for children.

A quality children's book will have an engaging plot with skillful use of literary devices and will convey interesting and worthwhile information (often as a matter of course while telling a larger story).

Probably one of the most important elements in writing a book that will capture a child's imagination is character development. The most beloved and enduring books have well-developed central characters with whom generations of children can identify. Series books are often developed around compelling central characters, which children come to know and love.

Children love to identify with the characters in books, so it is important to select books with characters that provide positive role models for children. For a long time, children's books provided very limited role models especially for females and minorities. Today, publishers have a greater awareness of the need to provide more diverse characters in their stories and teachers should provide access to books from a wide range of cultural backgrounds for children.

One of the best criteria for evaluating children's literature is how well it compels children to want to read. By this measure, the *Harry Potter* books and other popular series score very high indeed.

Children should gain in knowledge and understanding through reading. Their vocabularies enriched and enlarged. Ideally, teachers should pre-read and evaluate books to assess their appropriateness before recommending them to students. If this is not possible, teachers should consult librarians or refer to professionally published reviews. Avid child readers can also be a good source of information on new books that may be appropriate, so teachers should ask for and consider their suggestions. However, it is important to evaluate these suggestions before adding them to a list of required or recommended classroom reading list.

Skill 3.6   **Analysis of excerpts of literature for young children in relation to style, theme, or point of view**

In both fiction and non-fiction, authors portray ideas in very subtle ways through their skillful use of language. Style, tone, and point of view are the most basic of ways in which authors do this.

Style is the artful adaptation of language to meet various purposes. For example, authors can modify their word choice, sentence structure, and organization in order to convey certain ideas. For example, an author may write on a topic (the environment, for example) in many different styles. In an academic style, the author would use long, complex sentences, advanced vocabulary, and very structured paragraphing. However, in an informal explanation in a popular magazine, the author may use a conversational tone where simple words and simple sentence structures are utilized.

Tone is the attitude an author takes toward his or her subject. That tone is exemplified in the language of the text. For example, consider the environment once again. One author may dismiss the idea of global warming; his tone may be one of derision against environmentalists. A reader might notice this through the style (word choice, for example), the details the author decides to present, and the order in which details are presented. Another author may be angry about global warming and therefore might use harsh words and other tones that indicate anger. Finally, yet another author may not care one bit about the issue of the environment, either way. Let's say this author is a comedian who likes to poke fun at political activists. Her tone is humorous, therefore, she will adjust her language accordingly, as well. All types of tones are about the same subject—they simply reveal, through language, different opinions and attitudes about the subject. In a fictional work, the author may reveal his/her attitude toward the characters or about certain events through the use of tone.

Point of view is the perspective through which the story is told. While most of us think of point of view in terms of first or third person (or even the points of view of various characters in stories), point of view also helps explain a lot of language and presentation of ideas in non-fiction and fiction texts. The above environmentalism example proves this. Three points of view are represented, and each creates a different style of language. In fictional works, the point of view from which the story is told will change the story fundamentally. A story that is told from the point of view of the hero will be vastly different from one that is told from the point of view of the villain. Works that are told from the point of view of an all-knowing voice are said to have an "omniscient" point of view.

Students need to learn that language and text is changed dramatically by tone, style, and point of view. They can practice these concepts by exploring these elements in everything they read. Students can explore these elements for each non-fiction or fiction text they have to read in class.

Themes in children's literature may be revealed when a character encounters a situation that he or she must make a decision about. Often, that very decision is directly related to the theme. Typically, characters will not choose the most moral of decisions, and for the rest of the story, they will face various consequences. By the end of the story, there may be some reconciliation and an acknowledgement from the character that the wrong decision has been made.

Of course, not all children's literature follows that pattern; however, when themes are presented in children's literature, typically, they are much easier to pick up on. For example, more and more children's literature is focusing on elements of multiculturalism. The theme is made evident through very explicit characters, plot events, or situations.

Children's literature often contains themes related to moral issues. In a way, children's literature has been a vehicle for various cultures, including our own, to instill proper values in children. Therefore, it is not uncommon to find such themes in children's literature as the nature between good and evil, multiculturalism, sharing, or following advice given by parents or other adults.

Skill 3.7   Uses of literature for young children (e.g., providing exposure to high quality literary prose, enhancing other areas of the curriculum, promoting children's understanding of themselves and others)

The use of literature enhances learning for young children in many ways. By providing exposure to high quality literary prose, children enlarge their understanding of the world. They can hear about far away places and learn about different types of people. They can have "experiences" they could not possibly have in real life, by being transported through the magic of literature. Quality literature will expand both their imagination and creativity.

As a byproduct of their exposure to literature, children gain information about diverse activities that might otherwise be unavailable to them. Literature expands their world. Children may learn about ancient times, scientific discoveries, undersea animals, or space travel. Reading is an accessible way in which one person can enter the mind of another and share in the knowledge possessed by that person. "Learning across the curriculum" can be enhanced by using literature as another means to convey essential information. Thus, a history lesson is enhanced by reading a literary account of what it must have felt like to travel on the Mayflower, or a science lesson may be given life by reading a biography of a great scientist.

Learning about literary characters and their experiences is one of the first ways in which a child considers the human condition and the emotions we all experience. Children gain insight into people's behavior and motivations, and develop empathy, through following stories in literature. Following the stories of others allows a child to better understand him or herself.

Exposing young children to literature also builds a child's essential communication skills—both written and verbal. Hearing and reading great prose gives children an "ear" for the proper use of the English language, and a sense for how it may sound when used in its highest form. When children are exposed to a steady diet of high quality literature, their excellent use of language becomes second nature to them.

Students also expand their ability to properly use vocabulary, idiom, and descriptive language by becoming familiar with these things through literary exposure. It is very difficult for teachers to impart the ability to communicate well directly. This ability is generally acquired indirectly through steady and frequent exposure to well-written and well-spoken language—modeling. The use of literature to improve the use of language is particularly important for students who come from homes where communication skills are limited.

Even very young children who cannot yet read can enjoy the benefits of quality literature when their parents and teachers read to them. One of the side benefits of using literature in this way is that it promotes togetherness and bonding. Many adults have fond memories of family story times and of reading circle time when they were young. The habit of becoming a lifelong reader begins in early childhood, which is why it is so important to expose children to quality literature during these impressionable years.

Competency 004   Understand principles and concepts of writing for various purposes

Skill 4.1   The developmental continuum of writing

Children develop writing skills through a series of steps. The steps and their characteristics are:

- Role Play Writing

In this stage, the child writes in scribbles and assigns a message to the symbols. Even though an adult would not be able to read the writing, the child can read what is written although it may not be the same each time the child reads it. S/he will be able to read back the writing because of prior knowledge that print carries a meaning. The child will also dictate to adults who can write a message or story.

- Experimental Writing

In this stage the child writes in simple forms of language. They usually write with letters according to the way they sound, for example, the word "are" may be written as "r". However, the child does display a sense of sentence formation and writes in groups of words with a period at the end. S/he is aware of a correspondence between written words and oral language.

- Early Writing

Children start to use a small range of familiar text forms and sight words in their writing. The topics they choose for writing are ones that have some importance for them, such as their family, friends or pets. Because they are used to hearing stories, they do have a sense of how a story sounds and begin to write simple narratives. They learn that they do have to correct their writing so that others can easily read it.

- Conventional Writing

By the time students reach this stage of writing, they have a sense of audience and purpose for writing. They are able to proofread their writing and edit it for mistakes. They have gained the ability to transfer between reading and writing so that they can get ideas for writing from what they read. By this time students also have a sense of what correct spelling and grammar look like and they can change the order of events in the writing so that it makes sense for the reader.

Development of fine motor skills is an important first step for a child to write correctly. Before being required to manipulate a pencil, children should have dexterity and strength in their fingers, which helps them to gain more control of small muscles.

Instructional Strategies

The primary grip

Beginning writers with undeveloped fine motor skills should be taught the primary grip. First, have the child join the tips of the thumb and middle finger. Then place the pen in the space between them. Finally, have the child lay the index finger on top of the pen. This way, the index finger pushes against the thumb and middle finger. As children grow, the proportions of their hands change. This allows them to hold the pen differently and write faster.

Paper position

Right-handed children should place the paper directly in front of them and hold it in place with the left hand. The light should come from the left. Otherwise, the child's' hand will cast a shadow just where they need to see what they are writing. With the paper slightly to the right of the writer, their line of vision is clear. Teachers should check to see if the students are sitting upright. Make sure they are not gripping the pen too hard, and the paper in the right position.

Beginning strokes

A teacher may need to teach a student the direction of the pencil strokes. A good word to practice with is their first name. Identify one letter at a time. Show the beginning point right on the top line and the ending point on the bottom line. Slowly write their name on one line, one letter at a time, so the child can clearly see it. Have the child write directly under your sample, not to the side. Write your sample in straight, easy to copy letters.

Problems To Look For:

Gripping the pencil too tightly

A common problem for all young children learning to write is gripping the pencil too tightly, which makes writing tiresome. Usually the student learns to relax their grip as writing skill develops, but teachers can remind students to hold the instrument gently.

Holding the pencil incorrectly

If the child tends to hold the pencil too close to the point, make a mark on the pencil at the correct spot, to remind the student where to grip the pencil.

Left-handed writers

In languages that are written left-to-right; like the English language, it is more difficult to write with the left hand. A right-hander writes away from their body and pulls the pencil, while a left-hander must write toward their body and push the pencil. Left-handed students should place their paper at an angle and to the left.

Skill 4.2   Knowledge and use of prewriting and drafting strategies, including techniques for generating topics and developing ideas (e.g., brainstorming, semantic mapping, outlining, reading and research)

Prewriting strategies assist students in a variety of ways. Listed below are the most common prewriting strategies students can use to explore, plan and write on a topic. It is important to remember when teaching these strategies that not all prewriting must eventually produce a finished piece of writing. In fact, in the initial lesson of teaching prewriting strategies, it might be more effective to have students practice prewriting strategies without the pressure of having to write a finished product. Here are some suggested prewriting strategies:

- Keep an idea book so that they can jot down ideas that come to mind.
- Write in a daily journal.
- Write down whatever comes to mind; this is called "free writing." Students do not stop to make corrections or interrupt the flow of ideas.

A variation of this technique is focused free writing - writing on a specific topic - to prepare for an essay.

- Make a list of all ideas connected with their topic; this is called brainstorming
- Make sure students know that this technique works best when they let their mind work freely. After completing the list, students should analyze the list to see if a pattern or way to group the ideas emerges.
- Ask the questions Who? What? When? Where? When? and How? Help the writer approach a topic from several perspectives.
- Create a visual map on paper to gather ideas. Cluster circles and lines to show connections between ideas. Students should try to identify the relationship that exists between their ideas. If they cannot see the relationships, have them pair up, exchange papers and have their partners look for some related ideas.
- Observe details of sight, hearing, taste, touch, and taste.
- Visualize by making mental images of something and write down the details in a list.

After they have practiced with each of these prewriting strategies, ask them to pick out the ones they prefer and ask them to discuss how they might use the techniques to help them with future writing assignments. It is important to remember that they can use more than one prewriting strategy at a time. Also they may find that different writing situations may suggest certain techniques.

Skill 4.3 **Formal elements of good writing (e.g., paragraphing, topic sentences, cohesive transitions)**

Organization

In studies of professional writers and how they produce their successful works, it has been revealed that writing is a process that can be clearly defined although in practice it must have enough flexibility to allow for creativity. The teacher must be able to define the various stages that a successful writer goes through in order to make a statement that has value. There must be a discovery stage when ideas, materials, supporting details, etc., are deliberately collected. These may come from many possible sources: the writer's own experience and observations, deliberate research of written sources, interviews of live persons, television presentations, or the internet.

The next stage is organization where the purpose, thesis, and supporting points are determined. Most writers will put forth more than one possible thesis and in the next stage, the writing of the paper, settle on one as the result of trial and error. Once the paper is written, the editing stage is necessary and is probably the most important stage. This is not just the polishing stage. At this point, decisions must be made regarding whether the reasoning is cohesive—does it hold together? Is the arrangement the best possible one or should the points be rearranged? Are there holes that need to be filled in? What form will the introduction take? Does the conclusion lead the reader out of the discourse or is it inadequate or too abrupt, etc.

It's important to remember that the best writers engage in all of these stages recursively. They may go back to discovery at any point in the process. They may go back and rethink the organization, etc. To help students become effective writers, the teacher needs to give them adequate practice in the various stages and encourage them to engage deliberately in the creative thinking that makes writers successful.

Recognizing the Main Idea

A **topic** of a paragraph or story is what the paragraph or story is about.

The **main idea** of a paragraph or story states the important idea(s) that the author wants the reader to know about a topic.

The topic and main idea of a paragraph or story are sometimes directly stated. There are times; however, that the topic and main idea are not directly stated, but simply implied. Look at this paragraph.

> Henry Ford was an inventor who developed the first affordable automobile. The cars that were being built before Mr. Ford created his Model-T were very expensive. Only rich people could afford to have cars.

The topic of this paragraph is Henry Ford. The main idea is that Henry Ford built the first affordable automobile.

Identifying Supporting Details

The **supporting details** are sentences that give more information about the topic and the main idea.

The supporting details in the aforementioned paragraph about Henry Ford would be that he was an inventor and that before he created his Model-T, only rich people could afford cars because they were too expensive.

Reading an essay should not take extraordinary effort. Particularly if the concepts are not too complex, reading an essay should not require extensive re-reading. The ideas should be clear and straightforward. Anyone who has tried to write an essay knows that this sounds much easier than it really is! So, how do teachers actually help students to become proficient with writing multi-paragraph essays in ways that allow them to clearly communicate their ideas? The trick is to help them understand that various conventions of writing serve the purpose of making comprehension easier for their readers. Those conventions include good paragraphing, transitions between paragraphs, ideas, and sentences, topic sentences, concluding sentences, appropriate vocabulary, and sufficient context.

Paragraphing

Good paragraphing entails dividing up ideas into bite-sized chunks. A good paragraph typically includes a topic sentence that explains the content of the paragraph. A good paragraph also includes sufficient explanation of that topic sentence. So, for example, if a topic sentence suggests that the paragraph will be about the causes of the Civil War, the rest of the paragraph should actually explain specific causes of the Civil War.

As writers transition from one paragraph to another—or sentence to another—they will usually provide transitional phrases that give sign-posts to readers about what is coming next. Words like "however," "furthermore," "although," "likewise," etc., are good ways of communicating intention to readers. When ideas are thrown together on a page, it is hard to tell what the writer is actually doing with those ideas. Therefore, students need to become familiar with using transitional phrases.

Concluding sentences can often be unnecessary, but when done right, they provide a nice "farewell" or closing to a piece of writing. Students do not always need to use concluding sentences in paragraphs, however, they should be alerted to their potential benefits.

When writers use appropriate vocabulary, they are sensitive to the audience and purpose of what they are writing. For example, if writing an essay on a scientific concept to a group of non-scientists, I will not use specialized vocabulary to explain concepts. However, if I were writing for a group of scientists, not using that vocabulary may not look so good. It depends on what the writer intends with the piece of writing. Therefore, students need to learn early on that all writing has purpose and that because of that purpose, good writers will make conscious decisions about how to arrange their texts, which words to use, and which examples and metaphors to include.

Finally, when writers provide sufficient context, they ensure that readers do not have to extensively question the text to figure out what is going on. Again, this has a lot to do with knowing the audience. Using the scientific concept example from above, I would need to provide more context if my audience was a group of non-scientists than I would if my audience were scientists. In other words, I would have to provide more background so that the non-scientists could understand the concepts.

Writing Introductions

It is important to remember that in the writing process, the introduction should be written last. Until the body of the paper has been determined—thesis, development—it's difficult to make strategic decisions regarding the introduction. The Greek rhetoricians called this part of a discourse *exordium*, a "leading into." The basic purpose of the introduction, then, is to lead the audience into the discourse. It can let the reader know what the purpose of the discourse is and it can condition the audience to be receptive to what the writer wants to say. An introduction can be very brief or it can take up a large percentage of the total word count. Aristotle said that the introduction could be compared to the flourishes that flute players make before their performance—an overture in which the musicians display what they can play best in order to gain the favor and attention of the audience for the main performance.

In order to do this, we must first of all know what we are going to say; who the readership is likely to be; what the social, political, economic, etc., climate is; what preconceived notions the audience is likely to have regarding the subject; and how long the discourse is going to be.

There are many ways to do this:

- Show that the subject is important.
- Show that although the points we are presenting may seem improbable, they are true.
- Show that the subject has been neglected, misunderstood, or misrepresented.
- Explain an unusual mode of development.
- Forestall any misconception of the purpose.
- Apologize for a deficiency.
- Arouse interest in the subject with an anecdotal lead-in.
- Ingratiate oneself with the readership.
- Establish one's own credibility.

The introduction often ends with the thesis, the point or purpose of the paper. However, this is not set in stone. The thesis may open the body of the discussion, or it may conclude the discourse. The most important thing to remember is that the purpose and structure of the introduction should be deliberate if it is to serve the purpose of "leading the reader into the discussion."

Writing Conclusions

It is easier to write a conclusion after the decisions regarding the introduction have been made. Aristotle taught that the conclusion should strive to do five things:

1. Inspire the reader with a favorable opinion of the writer.
2. Amplify the force of the points made in the body of the paper.
3. Reinforce the points made in the body.
4. Rouse appropriate emotions in the reader.
5. Restate in a summary way what has been said.

The conclusion may be short or it may be long depending on its purpose in the paper. Recapitulation, a brief restatement of the main points or certainly of the thesis is the most common form of effective conclusions. A good example is the closing argument in a court trial.

Skill 4.4   Revising written texts to improve unity, coherence, and logical organization

Revise comes from the Latin word revidere, meaning, "to see again." Revision is probably the most important step for the writer in the writing process. Here, students examine their work and make changes in wording, details and ideas. So many times, students write a draft and then feel they're done. On the contrary – students must be encouraged to develop, change, and enhance their writing as they go, as well as once they've completed a draft.

Therefore, effective teachers realize that revision and editing go hand-in-hand and that students often move back and forth between these stages during the course of one written work. Also, these stages can be practiced in small groups, pairs and/or individually. Students must learn to analyze and improve their own work as well as the works of their peers. Some methods to use include:

1. Students, working in pairs, analyze sentences for variety.

2. Students work in pairs or groups to ask questions about unclear areas in the writing or to help students add details, information, etc.

3. Students perform final edit.

Many teachers introduce a Writer's Workshop to their students to maximize learning about the writing process. Writer's Workshops vary across classrooms, but the main idea is for students to become comfortable with the writing process to produce written work. A basic Writer's Workshop will include a block of classroom time committed to writing various projects (i.e., narratives, memoirs, book summaries, fiction, book reports, etc). Students use this time to write, meet with others to review/edit writing, make comments on writing, revise their own work, proofread, meet with the teacher, and publish their work.

Teachers who facilitate effective Writer's Workshops are able to meet with students one at a time and can guide that student in his/her individual writing needs. This approach allows the teacher to differentiate instruction for each student's writing level.

Students need to be trained to become effective at proofreading, revising and editing strategies. Begin by training them using both desk-side and scheduled conferences. Listed below are some strategies to use to guide students through the final stages of the writing process (and these can easily be incorporated into a Writer's Workshop).

- Provide some guide sheets or forms for students to use during peer responses.
- Allow students to work in pairs and limit the agenda.
- Model the use of the guide sheet or form for the entire class.
- Give students a time limit or number of written pieces to be completed in a specific amount of time.
- Have the students read their partners' papers and ask at least three who, what, when, why, how questions. The students answer the questions and use them as a place to begin discussing the piece.
- At this point in the writing process, a mini-lesson that focuses on some of the problems your students are having would be appropriate.

To help students revise, provide students with a series of questions that will assist them in revising their writing.

1. Do the details give a clear picture? Add details that appeal to more than just the sense of sight.

2. How effectively are the details organized? Reorder the details if it is needed.

3. Are the thoughts and feelings of the writer included? Add personal thoughts and feelings about the subject.

As you discuss revision, begin by discussing the definition of "revise." Also, state that all writing must be revised to improve it. After students have revised their writing, it is time for the final editing and proofreading.

There are a number of approaches that involve grammar instruction in the context of the writing.

1. Sentence Combining—try to use the student's own writing as much as possible. The theory behind combining ideas and the correct punctuation should be emphasized.
2. Sentence and paragraph modeling—provide students with the opportunity to practice imitating the style and syntax of professional writers.
3. Sentence transforming—give students an opportunity to change sentences from one form to another, i.e. from passive to active, inverting the sentence order, change forms of the words used.
4. Daily Language Practice—introduce or clarify common errors using daily language activities. Use actual student examples whenever possible. Correct and discuss the problems with grammar and usage.

Good paragraphing entails dividing up ideas into bite-sized chunks. A good paragraph typically includes a topic sentence that explains the content of the paragraph. A good paragraph also includes sufficient explanation of that topic sentence. So, for example, if a topic sentence suggests that the paragraph will be about the causes of the Civil War, the rest of the paragraph should actually explain specific causes of the Civil War.

As writers transition from one paragraph to another—or one sentence to another—they will usually provide transitional phrases that give sign-posts to readers about what is coming next. Words like "however," "furthermore," "although," "likewise," etc., are good ways of communicating intention to readers. When ideas are thrown together on a page, it is hard to tell what the writer is actually doing with those ideas. Therefore, students need to become familiar with using transitional phrases.

Concluding sentences can often be unnecessary, but when done right, they provide a nice "farewell" or closing to a piece of writing. Students do not always need to use concluding sentences in paragraphs; however, they should be alerted to their potential benefits.

Skill 4.5   Editing written work according to the conventions of edited American English

Sentence completeness
Avoid fragments and run-on sentences

Subject-verb agreement
A verb agrees in number with its subject. Making them agree relies on the ability to properly identify the subject.

One of the boys *was playing* too rough.

No one in the class, not the teacher nor the students, was listening to the message from the intercom.

The candidates, including a grandmother and a teenager, are debating some controversial issues.

If two singular subjects are connected by *and* the verb must be plural.

A *man* and his *dog* were jogging on the beach.

If two singular subjects are connected by *or* or *nor,* a singular verb is required.

Neither Dot nor Joyce has missed a day of school
this year.

If one singular subject and one plural subject are connected by *or* or *nor,* the verb agrees with the subject nearest to the verb.

Neither the coach nor the players were able to sleep on the bus.

If the subject is a collective noun, its sense of number in the sentence determines the verb: singular if the noun represents a group or unit and plural if the noun represents individuals.

The House of Representatives has adjourned for the holidays.

The House of Representatives have failed to reach agreement on the subject of adjournment.

Students should proofread the draft for punctuation and mechanical errors. There are a few key points to remember when helping students learn to edit and proofread their work.

- It is crucial that students are not taught grammar in isolation, but in context of the writing process.
- Ask students to read their writing and check for specific errors like using a subordinate clause as a sentence.
- Provide students with a proofreading checklist to guide them as they edit their work.

Spelling

Concentration in this section will be on spelling plurals and possessives. The multiplicity and complexity of spelling rules based on phonics, letter doubling, and exceptions to rules - not mastered by adulthood - should be replaced by a good dictionary. As spelling mastery is also difficult for adolescents, our recommendation is the same. Learning the use of a dictionary and thesaurus will be a more rewarding use of time.

Most plurals of nouns that end in hard consonants or hard consonant sounds followed by a silent e are made by adding s. Some words ending in vowels only add s.

fingers, numerals, banks, bugs, riots, homes, gates, radios, bananas

Nouns that end in soft consonant sounds s, j, x, z, ch, and sh, add es. Some nouns ending in o add es.

dresses, waxes, churches, brushes, tomatoes, potatoes

Nouns ending in y preceded by a vowel just add s.

boys, alleys

Nouns ending in y preceded by a consonant change the y to i and add es.

babies, corollaries, frugalities, poppies

Some nouns plurals are formed irregularly or remain the same.

sheep, deer, children, leaves, oxen

Capitalization

Capitalize all proper names of persons (including specific organizations or agencies of government); places (countries, states, cities, parks, and specific geographical areas); and things (political parties, structures, historical and cultural terms, and calendar and time designations); and religious terms (any deity, revered person or group, sacred writings).

> Percy Bysshe Shelley, Argentina, Mount Rainier National Park, Grand Canyon, League of Nations, the Sears Tower, Birmingham, Lyric Theater, Americans, Midwesterners, Democrats, Renaissance, Boy Scouts of America, Easter, God, Bible, Dead Sea Scrolls, Koran

Capitalize proper adjectives and titles used with proper names.

> California gold rush, President John Adams, French fries, Homeric epic, Romanesque architecture, Senator John Glenn

Note: Some words that represent titles and offices are not capitalized unless used with a proper name.

Capitalized	Not Capitalized
Congressman McKay	the congressman from Florida
Commander Alger	commander of the Pacific Fleet
Queen Elizabeth	the queen of England

Capitalize all main words in titles of works of literature, art, and music. The candidate should be cognizant of proper rules and conventions of punctuation, capitalization, and spelling. Competency exams will generally test the ability to apply the more advanced skills; thus, a limited number of more frustrating rules is presented here. Rules should be applied according to the American style of English, i.e. spelling theater instead of theatre and placing terminal marks of punctuation almost exclusively within other marks of punctuation.

Skill 4.6 **Factors to consider in writing for various audiences and purposes (e.g., narration, expression, information, persuasion)**

Discourse, whether in speaking or writing, falls naturally into four different forms: narrative, descriptive, expository, and persuasive. The first question to be asked when reading a written piece, listening to a presentation, or writing is "What's the point?" This is usually called the thesis. If you are reading an essay, when you've finished, you want to be able to say, "The point of this piece is that the foster-care system in America is a disaster." If it's a play, you should also be able to say, "The point of that play is that good overcomes evil." The same is true of any written document or performance. If it doesn't make a point, the reader/listener/viewer is confused or feels that it's not worth the effort. Knowing this is very helpful when you are sitting down to write your own document, be it essay, poem, or speech. What point do you want to make? We make these points in the forms that have been the structure of western thinking since the Greek Rhetoricians.

Persuasion is a piece of writing, a poem, a play, a speech whose purpose is to change the minds of the audience members or to get them to do something. This is achieved in many ways: (1) The credibility of the writer/speaker might lead the listeners/readers to a change of mind or a recommended action. (2) Reasoning is important in persuasive discourse. No one wants to believe that he accepts a new viewpoint or goes out and takes action just because he likes and trusts the person who recommended it. Logic comes into play in reasoning that is persuasive. (3) The third and most powerful force that leads to acceptance or action is emotional appeal. Even if a person has been persuaded logically, reasonably, that he should believe in a different way, he is unlikely to act on it unless he is moved emotionally. A man with resources might be convinced that people suffered in New Orleans after Katrina, but he will not be likely to do anything about it until he is moved emotionally, until he can see elderly people stranded on houses. Sermons are good examples of persuasive discourse.

Persuasive writing often uses all forms of discourse. The introduction may be a history or background of the idea being presented—exposition. Details supporting some of the points may be stories—narrations. Descriptive writing will be used to make sure the point is established emotionally.

Exposition is discourse whose only purpose is to inform. Expository writing is not interested in changing anyone's mind or getting anyone to take a certain action. It exists to give information. Some examples are driving directions to a particular place or the directions for putting together a toy that arrives unassembled. The writer doesn't care whether you do or don't follow the directions. She only wants to be sure you have the information in case you do decide to use them.

Narration is discourse that is arranged chronologically—something happened, and then something else happened, and then something else happened. It is also called a story. News reports are often narrative in nature as are records of trips, etc.

Description is discourse whose purpose is to make an experience available through one of the five senses—seeing, smelling, hearing, feeling (as with the fingers), and tasting. Descriptive words are used to make it possible for the reader to "see" with her own mind's eye, hear through her own mind's ear, smell through her own mind's nose, taste with her mind's tongue, and feel with her mind's fingers. This is how language moves people. Only by experiencing an event can the emotions become involved. Poets are experts in descriptive language.

In the past, teachers have assigned reports, paragraphs and essays that focused on the teacher as the audience with the purpose of explaining information. However, for students to be meaningfully engaged in their writing, they must write for a variety of reasons. Writing for different audiences and aims allows students to be more involved in their writing. If they write for the same audience and purpose, they will continue to see writing as just another assignment. Listed below are suggestions that give students an opportunity to write in more creative and critical ways.

- Write letters to the editor, to a college, to a friend, to another student that would be sent to the intended audience.
- Write stories that would be read aloud to a group (the class, another group of students, to a group of elementary school students) or published in a literary magazine or class anthology.
- Write plays that would be performed.
- Discuss the parallels between the different speech styles we use and writing styles for different readers or audiences.
- Write a particular piece for different audiences.
- Expose students to writing that is on the same topic but with a different audience and have them identify the variations in sentence structure and style.
- As part of the prewriting have students identify the audience. Make sure students consider the following when analyzing the needs of their audience.
    1. Why is the audience reading my writing? Do they expect to be informed, amused or persuaded?
    2. What does my audience already know about my topic?
    3. What does the audience want or need to know? What will interest them?
    4. What type of language suits my readers?

Remind your students that it is not necessary to identify all the specifics of the audience in the initial stage of the writing process but that at some point they must make some determinations about audience.

Skill 4.7   Formats and genres of writing (e.g., letter, poem, story, play)

Elements of Nonfiction

Nonfiction comes in a variety of styles. While many students simplify nonfiction as being true (as opposed to fiction, which is make-believe), nonfiction is much deeper. Nonfiction can include opinion and perspective. The following are various types of nonfiction, all of which students should be exposed to:

- Informational texts: These types of books explain concepts or phenomena. An informational text might explain the history of a state or the idea of photosynthesis. These types of text usually are based on research.
- Newspaper articles: These short texts rely completely on factual information and are presented in a very straightforward, sometimes choppy manner. The purpose of these texts simply is to present information to readers in a quick and efficient manner.
- Essays: Usually, essays take an opinion (whether it is about a concept, a work of literature, a person, or an event) and describe how the opinion was arrived at or why the opinion is a good one.
- Biographies: These texts explain the lives of individuals. They usually are based on extensive research.
- Memoirs: In a way, a memoir like an autobiography, but usually based on a specific idea, concept, issue, or event in life. For example, most Presidents of the United States write memoirs about their time in office.
- Letters: When letters are read and analyzed in the classroom, students generally are studying the writer's style or the writer's true, deep-down opinions and feelings about certain events. Often, students will find letters of famous individual in history reprinted in textbooks.
- Journals: Similar to letters, journals present very personal ideas. They give students, when available (as most people never want their journals published), an opportunity to see peoples' thought processes about various events or issues.

The key in teaching students about nonfiction is to expose them to a variety of types of nonfiction and discuss how those types are similar and different from one another. But, again, the key is exposure. How will students ever know about these types of literature in a deep and analytical sense without getting the chance to read them and study them academically in the classroom?

Elements of Fiction

Most works of fiction contain a common set of elements that make them come alive to readers. In a way, even though writers do not consciously think about each of these elements as story elements when they sit down to write, all stories essentially contain these "markers" that make them the stories that they are. But, even though all stories have these elements, they are a lot like fingerprints: Each story's story elements are just a bit different.

Let's look at a few of the most commonly discussed elements. The most commonly discussed story element in fiction is plot. Plot is the series of events in a story. Typically, but not always, plot moves in a predictable fashion:

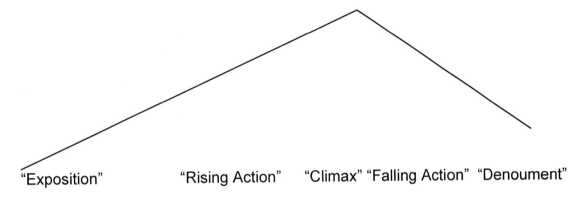

"Exposition"   "Rising Action"   "Climax" "Falling Action" "Denoument"

Exposition is where characters and their situations are introduced. *Rising action* is the point at which conflict starts to occur. *Climax* is the highest point of conflict, often a turning point. *Falling action* is the result of the climax. *Denoument* is the final resolution of the plot.

Character is another commonly studied story element. We will often find in stories heroes, villains, comedic characters, dark characters, etc. When we examine the characters of a story, we look to see who they are and how their traits contribute to the story. Often, because of their characteristics, plot elements become more interesting. For example, authors will pair unlikely characters together somehow that, in turn, creates specific conflict.

The setting of a story is the place or location where it occurs. Often, the specific place is not as important as some of the specifics about the setting. For example, the setting of *The Great Gatsby*, New York, is not as significant as the fact that it takes place amongst incredible wealth. Conversely, *The Grapes of Wrath*, although taking place in Oklahoma and California, has a more significant setting of poverty. In fact, as the story takes place *around* other migrant workers, the setting is even more significant. In a way, the setting serves as a reason for various conflicts to occur.

Themes of stories are the underlying messages, above and beyond all plot elements, that writers want to convey. Very rarely will one find that good literature is without a theme—or a lesson, message, or ideal. The best writers in the English language all seem to want to convey something about human nature or the world, and they turn to literature in order to do that. Common themes in literature are jealousy, money, love, human against corporation or government, etc. These themes are never explicitly stated; rather, they are the result of the portrayal of characters, settings, and plots. Readers get the message even if the theme is not directly mentioned.

Finally, the mood of a story is the atmosphere or attitude the writer conveys through descriptive language. Often, mood fits in nicely with theme and setting. For example, in Edgar Allen Poe's stories, we often find a mood of horror and darkness. We get that from the descriptions of characters and the setting, as well as from specific plot elements. Mood simply helps us better understand the writer's theme and intentions through descriptive, stylistic language.

Elements of Drama

In both drama and fiction, various dramatic events occur in a fairly predictable fashion. For example, all dramatic action begins with some sort of introductory scene where characters are introduced, basic premises are covered, and the plot is set so that action can occur. Rising action begins as the plot ramps up. It occurs as elements in the plot move toward some sort of problematic circumstance, whether comedic or tragic. If the plot is tragic, something bad will happen; if the plot is comedic, something good or humorous will happen. Let's take this difference one step further: Classically, a tragedy would end with a funeral and a comedy would end in a wedding. Today, however, there are greater variations, but generally, most works fit into one of those two categories.

As the rising action continues to move toward some ultimate fate, whether comedic or tragic, eventually it will hit a climax. The climax is the major turning point or significant event in the work. Everything that occurs after the climax is considered falling action, and the general idea is that once a work has hit the climax, the work is now moving toward conclusion. Falling action is generally the response to the climax (or the result of it). Often, though, most works of fiction and drama will not provide too much falling action, as that might be considered giving away too much. After the climax, most works like to allow readers/viewers to imagine some of the consequences. Conclusion is the final event or the moment when the work entirely finishes. After that, everything else is left to the readers'/viewers' imagination.

In drama, particularly, certain devices enhance the viewers' understanding of the plot. We will discuss three of these devices:

Suspense occurs at any moment where the audience knows something that a character on stage does not—and the "thing" the character does not know will cause him or her adverse affects. Now, suspense does not always equal tragedy. Often, the result is comedic. But the point is that the audience will have possibly heard something in a previous scene and a character comes on stage and has no idea that something is going to occur. Or, within a scene, something suspenseful is going to occur, and the audience has a sense that the plot in the scene will not be so docile.

Soliloquy is a speech to oneself. This is where a character possibly shares his or her feelings to the audience, almost as if the character is thinking out loud. This gives the audience clues as to what may happen, how the character is handling something, etc. Usually, soliloquies occur in an aside, but not all asides contain soliloquies. An aside is any time where "real" time in the drama stops for a moment so that a character can address the audience or his/her thoughts so that the audience hears them (and the other characters do not).

Elements of Poetry

People read poetry for many reasons, and they are often the very same reasons poets would give for writing it. Just the feel and sounds of the words that are turned by the artistic hands and mind of a poet into a satisfying and sometimes delightful experience is a good reason to read a poem. Good poetry constantly surprises.

However, the major purpose a writer of poetry has for creating this work of art is the sharing of an experience, a feeling, an emotion, and that is also the reason a reader turns to poetry rather than prose in his search for variety, joy, and satisfaction.

Poets are also interpreters of life. Poets feel deeply and they have the skill and inspiration to recreate those feelings and interpret them in such a way that understanding and insight may come from the experience. They often bring understanding to life's big (or even not-so-big) questions.

Children can respond to poetry at very early stages. Elementary students are still at the stage where the sounds of unusual words intrigue them and entertain them. They are also very open to emotional meanings of passages. Teaching poetry to 5th graders can be an important introduction to seeking meaning in literature. If a 5th grader enjoys reading poetry both silently and aloud, a habit may be formed that will last a lifetime.

The structure of a poem is defined by:
1. The pattern of the sound and rhythm
2. The visible shape it takes
3. Rhyme or free verse

1. The pattern of the sound and rhythm
It helps to know the history of this peculiarity of poetry. Until the invention of the printing press, History was passed down in oral form almost exclusively and was often set to music. A rhymed story is much easier to commit to memory. Adding a tune makes it even easier to remember, so it's not a surprise that much of the earliest literature—epics, odes, etc., are rhymed and were probably sung. When we speak of the pattern of sound and rhythm, we are referring to two things: verse form and stanza form.

The verse form is the rhythmic pattern of a single verse. An example would be any meter: blank verse, for instance, is iambic pentameter. A stanza is a group of a certain number of verses (lines), having a rhyme scheme. If the poem is written, there is usually white space between the verses although a short poem may be only one stanza. If the poem is spoken, there will be a pause between stanzas.

2. The visible shape it takes
In the seventeenth century, some poets shaped their poems to reflect the theme. A good example is George Herbert's Easter Wings. Since that time, poets have occasionally played with this device; it is, however, generally viewed as nothing more than a demonstration of ingenuity. The rhythm, effect, and meaning are often sacrificed to the forcing of the shape.

3. Rhyme and free verse

Poets also use devices to establish form that will underscore the meanings of their poems. A very common one is alliteration. When the poem is read (which poetry is usually intended to be), the repetition of a sound may not only underscore the meaning, it may also pleasure to the reading. Following a strict rhyming pattern can add intensity to the meaning of the poem in the hands of a skilled and creative poet. On the other hand, the meaning can be drowned out by the steady beat-beat-beat of it. Shakespeare very skillfully used the regularity of rhyme in his poetry, breaking the rhythm at certain points to very effectively underscore a point. For example, in Sonnet #130, "My mistress' eyes are nothing like the sun," the rhythm is primarily iambic pentameter. It lulls the reader (or listener) to accept that this poet is following the standard conventions for love poetry, which in that day reliably used rhyme and more often than not iambic pentameter to express feelings of romantic love along conventional lines. However, in Sonnet #130, the last two lines sharply break from the monotonous pattern, forcing reader or speaker to pause:

> And yet, by heaven, I think my love as rare
> As any she belied with false compare

Shakespeare's purpose is clear: he is not writing a conventional love poem; the object of his love is not the red-and-white conventional woman written about in other poems of the period. This is a good example where a poet uses form to underscore meaning.

Poets eventually began to feel constricted by the rhyming conventions and began to break away and make new rules for poetry. When poetry was only rhymed, it was easy to define it. When free verse, or poetry written in a flexible form, came upon the scene in France in the 1880s, it quickly began to influence English-language poets such as T. S. Eliot, whose memorable poem, The Wasteland, had an alarming but desolate message for the modern world. It's impossible to imagine that it could have been written in the soothing, lulling rhymed verse of previous periods. Those who first began writing in free verse in English were responding to the influence of the French vers libre. However, it should be noted that it could be loosely applied to the poetry of Walt Whitman, writing in the mid-nineteenth century, as can be seen in the first stanza of Son of Myself:

> I celebrate myself, and sing myself,
> And what I assume you shall assume,
> For every atom belonging to me as good belongs to you.

When poetry was no longer defined as a piece of writing arranged in verses that had a rhyme-scheme of some sort, distinguishing poetry from prose became a point of discussion. Merriam Webster's Encyclopedia of Literature defines poetry as follows: "Writing that formulates a concentrated imaginative awareness of experience in language chosen and arranged to create a specific emotional response through its meaning, sound and rhythm."

A poet chooses the form of his poetry deliberately, based upon the emotional response he hopes to evoke and the meaning he wishes to convey. Robert Frost, a twentieth-century poet who chose to use conventional rhyming verse to make his point is a memorable and often-quoted modern poet. Who can forget his closing lines in "Stopping by Woods"?

> And miles to go before I sleep,
> And miles to go before I sleep.

Would they be as memorable if the poem had been written in free verse?

Slant Rhyme: Occurs when the final consonant sounds are the same, but the vowels are different. This occurs frequently in Irish, Welsh, and Icelandic verse. Examples include: green and gone, that and hit, ill and shell.

Alliteration: Alliteration occurs when the initial sounds of a word, beginning either with a consonant or a vowel, are repeated in close succession. Examples include: Athena and Apollo, Nate never knows, People who pen poetry.

Note that the words only have to be close to one another: Alliteration that repeats and attempts to connect a number of words is little more than a tongue-twister.

The function of alliteration, like rhyme, might be to accentuate the beauty of language in a given context, or to unite words or concepts through a kind of repetition. Alliteration, like rhyme, can follow specific patterns. Sometimes the consonants aren't always the initial ones, but they are generally the stressed syllables. Alliteration is less common than rhyme, but because it is less common, it can call our attention to a word or line in a poem that might not have the same emphasis otherwise.

Assonance: If alliteration occurs at the beginning of a word and rhyme at the end, assonance takes the middle territory. Assonance occurs when the vowel sound within a word matches the same sound in a nearby word, but the surrounding consonant sounds are different. "Tune" and "June" are rhymes; "tune" and "food" are assonant. The function of assonance is frequently the same as end rhyme or alliteration; all serve to give a sense of continuity or fluidity to the verse. Assonance might be especially effective when rhyme is absent: It gives the poet more flexibility, and it is not typically used as part of a predetermined pattern.

Onomatopoeia: Word used to evoke the sound in its meaning. The early Batman series used pow, zap, whop, zonk and eek in an onomatopoetic way.

Rhythm in poetry refers to the recurrence of stresses at equal intervals. A stress (accent) is a greater amount of force given to one syllable in speaking than is given to another. For example, we put the stress on the first syllable of such words as father, mother, daughter, children. The unstressed or unaccented syllable is sometimes called a slack syllable. All English words carry at least one stress except articles and some prepositions such as by, from, at, etc. Indicating where stresses occur is to scan; doing this is called scansion. Very little is gained in understanding a poem or making a statement about it by merely scanning it. The pattern of the rhythm—the meter—should be analyzed in terms of its overall relationship to the message and impression of the poem.

Slack syllables, when they recur in pairs cause rhythmic trippings and bouncings; on the other hand, recurrent pairs of stresses will create a heavier rocking effect. The rhythm is dependent on words to convey meaning. Alone, they communicate nothing. When examining the rhythm and meaning of a poem, a good question to ask is whether the rhythm is appropriate to the theme. A bouncing rhythm, for example, might be dissonant in a solemn elegy.

Stops are those places in a poem where the punctuation requires a pause. An end-stopped line is one that ends in a pause whereas one that has no punctuation at its end and is, therefore, read with only a slight pause after it is said to be run-on and the running on of its thought into the next line is called enjambment. These are used by a poet to underscore, intensify, communicate meaning.

Rhythm, then, is a pattern of recurrence and in poetry is made up of stressed and relatively unstressed syllables. The poet can manipulate the rhythm by making the intervals between his stresses regular or varied, by making his lines short or long, by end-stopping his lines or running them over, by choosing words that are easier or less easy to say, by choosing polysyllabic words or monosyllables. The most important thing to remember about rhythm is that it conveys meaning.

The basic unit of rhythm is called a foot and is usually one stressed syllable with one or two unstressed ones or two stressed syllables with one unstressed one. A foot made up of one unstressed syllable and one stressed one is called an iamb. If a line is made of five iambs, it is iambic pentameter. A rhymed poem typically establishes a pattern such as iambic pentameter, and even though there will be syllables that don't fit the pattern, the poem, nevertheless, will be said to be in iambic pentameter. In fact, a poem may be considered weak if the rhythm is too monotonous.

Skill 4.8   Use of various techniques to convey meaning (e.g., precise vocabulary, figurative language)

When students delve deep into a writing task, they can quickly forget that the writing has to convey meaning to a particular audience. Because they often know that the teacher is their only audience, tailoring vocabulary, illustrations, and other writing elements to meet the needs of a particular audience may be ignored. So, teachers, as much as possible, should specify other audiences for whom students are writing to. These audiences could be real (sending letters to an elected official) or fake (pretending to write a newspaper article). But by doing this, students get the opportunity to practice changing their language to meet specific needs.

Ask students to do the following:
Explain to a friend what you did last night. Tell all the details.

Then, ask students to do this:
Explain the same thing to your grandmother—tell all the details of what you did last night.

Students will most likely note that they will use different words, sentence structures, and details in the two explanations.

So, the basics of writing to a particular audience would include the following:

- Precise Vocabulary: While students may not know all the best words that could summarize their thoughts (they'll learn new words that will help make their writing more concise), whenever one very precise word can take the place of a variety of words, students should use that one precise word. Also, it is important that students realize that their vocabulary choice must truly convey the proper intention of the word meaning. However, depending on audience, certain word changes can help relate more to the readers; but there is no doubt that the words still need to be precise.
- Figurative language: Often, images, figures of speech, analogies, similes, and metaphors help to convey meaning to readers. Writers choose elements of figurative language depending on their audiences, but they certainly do use figurative language as a way to help convey meaning that straightforward language may not so easily do.
- Illustrations: Illustrations are examples, however, they are usually more detailed. Illustrations can help make abstract ideas more concrete. Again, the use of illustration depends on the audience. While one audience may quickly connect to an illustration, another audience may have no idea what the illustration even means.

SEE also Skill 3.3 and the poetry section of Skill 4.7

SUBAREA III.   CORE KNOWLEDGE IN THE CONTENT AREAS

Competency 005   Understand principles and concepts of mathematics

Skill 5.1   Mathematical terminology, symbols, and representations

As with other subjects, it is important to provide explicit instruction for students as to the relationship between the oral numbers and their written form. Typically, this begins by showing students examples of numbers in their written format. Then by providing students with direct instruction in the mechanical formation of the numbers.

There are many different instructional procedures for both numerical identification and the formation of the numbers. Children may look at number books that connect numerals with sets of objects or work with puzzles that do the same. There are also math mats with print numbers and the same number of dots on which students must match manipulatives to each dot. No matter the procedure used, students need specific, explicit instruction in this area. One example of a format for teaching students to identify numbers is based on a direct instructional model. In this format, students are shown the number to be taught more times than other numbers. As skills build, the newly introduced numbers are shown more times than those previously learned (some recommend at least seven representations of the new information). Consistent review and direct instruction with specific correction procedures are hallmarks of the direct instruction model.

It is important to expose children to various ways numbers can be represented. For example, the number ten can be represented in the following ways (and more):

    10   ten   12-2   6+4   X

Teaching students from the beginning that there are different ways to represent a number helps to build their number sense and helps them begin to see the relationships and patterns of numbers.

In teaching students to mechanically create the numbers, there are again many different procedures. Some handwriting programs provide specific procedures for this process. There are also poems available to help the students remember the strokes and order in which they can be combined to form the numbers. A reversal of numbers is common in young children and should not be reprimanded harshly. It is appropriate to correct and provide additional models to demonstrate the correct formation in a positive manner.

Traditionally, it is universal to:

- Provide clear consistent directions and models
- Practice and provide guidance often
- Introduce the numbers individually
- Provide review often

Students learn terminology that indicates a needed operation:

Addition: total, sum, in all, join, how many
Subtraction: difference, how many more than, how many less than, left
Multiplication: in all, each, of
Division: in each group, per, divide

Younger students learn that **+** is the symbol for addition and **–** is the symbol for subtraction. Older students learn that division is symbolized by **÷, /,** or **–** and multiplication is symbolized by **X, ·,** and **( )**.

As they progress, students will learn the symbols for less than (**<**), greater than (**>**), equal to (**=**), less than or equal to (**≤**), greater than or equal to (**≥**), and plus or minus (**±**).

Rational numbers can be expressed as the ratio of two integers, $\frac{a}{b}$ where b ≠ 0, for example $\frac{2}{3}$, $-\frac{4}{5}$, 5 = $\frac{5}{1}$.

The rational numbers include integers, fractions and mixed numbers, terminating and repeating decimals. Every rational number can be expressed as a repeating or terminating decimal and can be shown on a number line.

Integers are positive and negative whole numbers and zero.
        ...-6, -5, -4, -3, -2, -1, 0, 1, 2, 3, 4, 5, 6, ...

Whole numbers are natural numbers and zero.
        0, 1, 2, 3, 4, 5, 6...

Natural numbers are the counting numbers.
        1, 2, 3, 4, 5, 6...

Irrational numbers are real numbers that cannot be written as the ratio of two integers. These are infinite non-repeating decimals.
        <u>Examples</u>: $\sqrt{5}$ = 2.2360.., pi =∏ = 3.1415927...

Skill 5.2 Number properties and number representations (e.g., cardinal and ordinal numbers)

	Word Name	Standard Numeral	Pictorial Model
Decimal	Three-tenths	0.3	
Fraction	One-half	$\frac{1}{2}$	
Integer or Whole Number	Three	3	

Cardinal numbers are also known as "counting" numbers because they indicate quantity. Examples of cardinal numbers are 1, 2, and 10.

Ordinal numbers indicate the order of things in a set; for ex. 1st, 2nd, 10th. They do not show quantity, only position.

Skill 5.3   Properties of real numbers

The real number system includes all rational and irrational numbers.

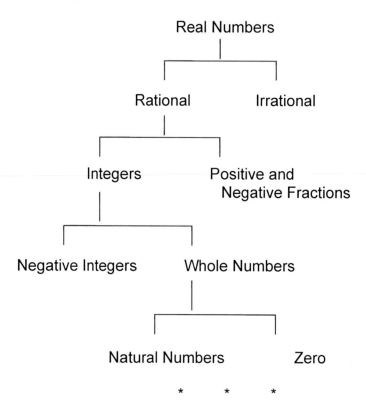

Real Numbers

Rational   Irrational

Integers   Positive and
                  Negative Fractions

Negative Integers   Whole Numbers

Natural Numbers   Zero

*   *   *

Properties are rules that apply for addition, subtraction, multiplication, or division of real numbers. These properties are:

Commutative: You can change the order of the terms or factors as follows.

For addition: $a + b = b + a$
For multiplication: $ab = ba$

Since addition is the inverse operation of subtraction and multiplication is the inverse operation of division, no separate laws are needed for subtraction and division.

Example: $5 + 8 = 8 + 5 = 13$

Example: $2 \times 6 = 6 \times 2 = 12$

Associative: You can regroup the terms as you like.

For addition: $a + (b + c) = (a + b) + c$
For multiplication: $a(bc) = (ab)c$

This rule does not apply for division and subtraction.

Example: $(2 + 7) + 5 = 2 + (7 + 5)$
$9 + 5 = 2 + 12 = 14$

Example: $(3 \times 7) \times 5 = 3 \times (7 \times 5)$
$21 \times 5 = 3 \times 35 = 105$

Identity: Finding a number so that when added to a term results in that number (additive identity); finding a number such that when multiplied by a term results in that number (multiplicative identity).

For addition: $a + 0 = a$ (zero is additive identity)
For multiplication: $a \cdot 1 = a$ (one is multiplicative)

Example: $17 + 0 = 17$

Example: $34 \times 1 = 34$
The product of any number and one is that number.

Inverse: Finding a number such that when added to the number it results in zero; or when multiplied by the number results in 1.

For addition: $a + (-a) = 0$
For multiplication: $a \cdot (1/a) = 1$

$(-a)$ is the additive inverse of a; $(1/a)$, also called the reciprocal, is the multiplicative inverse of a.

Example: Additive Inverse: $25 - 25 = 0$

Example: Multiplicative Inverse: $5 \times \frac{1}{5} = 1$ The product of any number and its reciprocal is one.

Distributive: This technique allows us to operate on terms within parentheses without first performing operations within the parentheses. This is especially helpful when terms within the parentheses cannot be combined.

$$a (b + c) = ab + ac$$

<u>Example</u>: $6 \times (4 + 9) = (6 \times 4) + (6 \times 9)$
$6 \times 5 = 24 + 54 = 78$

To multiply a sum by a number, multiply each addend by the number, then add the products.

Skill 5.4   The base ten number system

Place value is the basis of our entire number system. A place value system is one in which the position of a digit in a number determines its value. In the standard system, called base ten, each place represents ten times the value of the place to its right. You can think of this as making groups of ten of the smaller unit and combining them to make a new unit.

Ten ones make up one of the next larger unit, tens. Ten of those units make up one of the next larger unit, hundreds. This pattern continues for greater values (ten hundreds = one thousand, ten thousands = one ten thousand, etc.), and lesser, decimal values (ten tenths = one one, ten hundredths = one tenth, etc.).

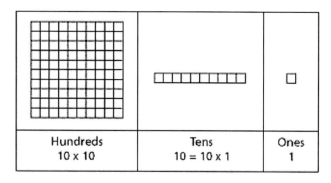

Hundreds	Tens	Ones
10 x 10	10 = 10 x 1	1

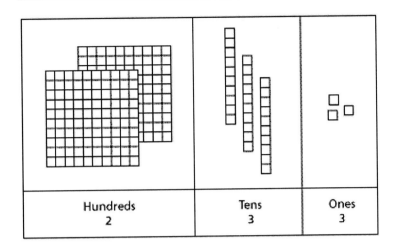

Hundreds 2	Tens 3	Ones 3

In standard form, the number modeled above is 233.

A place-value chart is a way to make sure digits are in the correct places. The value of each digit depends on its position or "place".. A great way to see the place-value relationships in a number is to model the number with actual objects (place-value blocks, bundles of craft sticks, etc.), write the digits in the chart, and then write the number in the usual, or standard form.

Place value is vitally important to later mathematics. Without it, keeping track of greater numbers rapidly becomes impossible. (Can you imagine trying to write 999 with only ones?) A thorough mastery of place value is essential to learning the operations with greater numbers. It is the foundation for regrouping ("borrowing" and "carrying") in addition, subtraction, multiplication, and division

Pre-K and K students learn about the base ten system when counting (and grouping) straws during calendar to count the number of school days or when they are working with unifix cubes. Children learn that there are ten pennies in a dime and ten dimes in a dollar when learning about and playing with money.

Skill 5.5   Fractions, decimals, and percents

A **fraction** is an expression of numbers in the form of x/y, where x is the numerator and y is the denominator, which cannot be zero.

Example: $\dfrac{3}{7}$ 3 is the numerator; 7 is the denominator

If the fraction has common factors for the numerator and denominator, divide both by the common factor to reduce the fraction to its lowest form.

Example:

$$\frac{13}{39} = \frac{1 \times 13}{3 \times 13} = \frac{1}{3} \qquad \text{Divide by the common factor 13}$$

A **mixed** number has an integer part and a fractional part.

Example: $2\dfrac{1}{4}, \ ^{-}5\dfrac{1}{6}, \ 7\dfrac{1}{3}$

There are two main kinds of manipulatives that can be used to teach fractions in the early grades. Length models, such as paper strips and Cuisenaire® rods, help to illustrate fractions on a number line. Area models are usually portions of a circle or a rectangle and are particularly helpful in demonstrating operations with fractions. Example of area models are pies, pizzas, and Geoboards.

Percent = per 100 (written with the symbol %). Thus $10\% = \dfrac{10}{100} = \dfrac{1}{10}$.

Example: Find 23% of 1000.

$$= \frac{23}{100} \times \frac{1000}{1} = 23 \times 10 = 230$$

Example: Convert 6.25% to a fraction and to a mixed number.

$$6.25\% = 0.0625 = 0.0625 \times \frac{10000}{10000} = \frac{625}{10000} = \frac{1}{16}$$

Decimals = deci = part of ten. To find the decimal equivalent of a fraction, use the denominator to divide the numerator as shown in the following examples.

Example: Find the decimal equivalent of $\dfrac{7}{10}$.

$$\begin{array}{r} .7 \\ 10\overline{)7.0} \\ \underline{70} \\ 00 \end{array}$$

Since 10 cannot divide into 7 evenly, put a decimal point in the answer row on top; put a 0 behind 7 to make it 70. Continue the division   process. If a remainder occurs, put a 0 by the last digit of the remainder and continue the division.

Thus $\dfrac{7}{10} = 0.7$

It is a good idea to write a 0 before the decimal point so that the decimal point is emphasized.

Example: Find the decimal equivalent of $\dfrac{7}{125}$.

$$\begin{array}{r} .056 \\ 125\overline{)7.000} \\ \underline{625} \\ 750 \\ \underline{750} \\ 0 \end{array}$$

Example: Convert 0.056 to a fraction.
Multiplying 0.056 by $\dfrac{1000}{1000}$ to get rid of the decimal point:

$$0.056 \times \dfrac{1000}{1000} = \dfrac{56}{1000} = \dfrac{7}{125}$$

A **decimal** can be converted to a **percent** by multiplying by 100, or merely moving the decimal point two places to the right. A **percent** can be converted to a **decimal** by dividing by 100, or moving the decimal point two places to the left.

Examples:

$$0.375 = 37.5\%$$
$$0.7 = 70\%$$
$$0.04 = 4\%$$
$$3.15 = 315\%$$

$$84\% = 0.84$$
$$3\% = 0.03$$
$$60\% = 0.6$$
$$110\% = 1.1$$
$$\tfrac{1}{2}\% = 0.5\% = 0.005$$

A **percent** can be converted to a **fraction** by placing it over 100 and reducing to simplest terms.

Examples: $32\% = \frac{32}{100} = \frac{8}{25}$

$6\% = \frac{6}{100} = \frac{3}{50}$

$111\% = \frac{111}{100} = 1\frac{11}{100}$

Common Equivalents

$$\tfrac{1}{2} = 0.5 = 50\%$$
$$\tfrac{1}{3} = 0.33\tfrac{1}{3} = 33\tfrac{1}{3}\%$$
$$\tfrac{1}{4} = 0.25 = 25\%$$
$$\tfrac{1}{5} = 0.2 = 20\%$$
$$\tfrac{1}{6} = 0.16\tfrac{2}{3} = 16\tfrac{2}{3}\%$$
$$\tfrac{1}{8} = 0.12\tfrac{1}{2} = 12\tfrac{1}{2}\%$$
$$\tfrac{1}{10} = 0.1 = 10\%$$
$$\tfrac{2}{3} = 0.66\tfrac{2}{3} = 66\tfrac{2}{3}\%$$
$$\tfrac{5}{6} = 0.83\tfrac{1}{3} = 83\tfrac{1}{3}\%$$
$$\tfrac{3}{8} = 0.37\tfrac{1}{2} = 37\tfrac{1}{2}\%$$
$$\tfrac{5}{8} = 0.62\tfrac{1}{2} = 62\tfrac{1}{2}\%$$
$$\tfrac{7}{8} = 0.87\tfrac{1}{2} = 87\tfrac{1}{2}\%$$
$$1 = 1.0 = 100\%$$

Skill 5.6   Standard arithmetical operations

Recognition and understanding of the relationships between concepts and topics is of great value in mathematical problem solving and the explanation of more complex processes.

For instance, multiplication is simply repeated addition. This relationship explains the concept of variable addition. We can show that the expression $4x + 3x = 7x$ is true by rewriting 4 times x and 3 times x as repeated addition, yielding the expression $(x + x + x + x) + (x + x + x)$. Thus, because of the relationship between multiplication and addition, variable addition is accomplished by coefficient addition.

SEE also Skill 5.7

Skill 5.7   Number operations and computational techniques

Addition of Whole Numbers

The properties in Skill 5.3 and others lay the groundwork for a child's understanding of addition. Once children know these properties, they can use them as thinking strategies to help them remember addition facts for 0 through 9. If we think of these facts in terms of a table, there are 100 addition facts that a child has to learn.

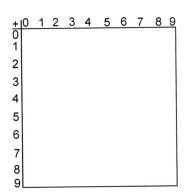

Here is how the properties help that process:

1. Commutativity: If children understand commutativity, once they learn the first 55 addition facts, they will automatically know the remaining 45 facts; i.e., that 4 + 1 = 5 just as 1 + 4 = 5.
2. Adding zero: Teaching children that $a + 0 = a$ adds another 10 addition facts; i.e., 0 + 0 = 0, 1 + 0 = 1 . . . 9 + 0 = 9.
3. Counting on by 1 and 2: Children find close sums, that is, sums obtained by adding 1 or 2, by counting. This would account for 17 more addition facts—2–10 and 4–11.
4. Combinations to ten: Children use combinations of their ten fingers to find sums such as 7 + 3, 6 + 4, 5 + 5, and so on.
5. Doubles: These are addition facts such as 1 + 1 = 2, 2 + 2 = 4, 3 + 3 = 6, etc. Children easily learn these facts because they are also the results of counting by twos.
6. Associativity: When children understand associativity as regrouping, they can understand that 8 + 7 = 15 is the same as 8 + (2 + 5) = 15 is the same as (8 + 2) + 5 = 15 is the same as 10 + 5 = 15.
7. Doubles $\pm$ 1 and $\pm$ 2: As an example, 7 + 8 = 7 + 7 + 1 = 14 + 1 = 15.

Example: At the end of a day of shopping, a shopper had $24 remaining in his wallet. He spent $45 on various goods. How much money did the shopper have at the beginning of the day?

The total amount of money the shopper started with is the sum of the amount spent and the amount remaining at the end of the day.

$$\begin{array}{r} \$24 \\ +\ 45 \\ \hline \$69 \end{array}$$ The original total was $69.

Example: A race took the winner 1 hr. 58 min. 12 sec. on the first half of the race and 2 hr. 9 min. 57 sec. on the second half of the race. How much time did the entire race take?

$$\begin{array}{ll} \quad\ 1 \text{ hr. } 58 \text{ min. } 12 \text{ sec.} & \\ +\ 2 \text{ hr. }\ 9 \text{ min. } 57 \text{ sec.} & \text{Add these numbers} \\ \hline \quad\ 3 \text{ hr. } 67 \text{ min. } 69 \text{ sec.} & \\ \qquad\qquad +\ 1 \text{ min } -60 \text{ sec.} & \text{Change 60 seconds to 1 min.} \\ \hline \quad\ 3 \text{ hr. } 68 \text{ min. }\ 9 \text{ sec.} & \\ +\ 1 \text{ hr.} -60 \text{ min.}\qquad & \text{Change 60 minutes to 1 hr.} \\ \hline \quad\ 4 \text{ hr. }\ \ 8 \text{ min. }\ 9 \text{ sec.} & \leftarrow \text{final answer} \end{array}$$

Subtraction of Whole Numbers

Subtraction is expressed as $a - b$, read "a minus b," where a is the minuend and b is the subtrahend. Just as there are properties and methods that aid students in understanding addition, there are conceptual models that aid students with subtraction:

1. Take-Away:
   Start with 10 objects.
   Take away 4 objects.
   How many objects are left?
2. Missing Addend:
   Start with 4 objects.
   How many more objects are needed to give a total of 10 objects?
3. Comparison:
   Start with two sets of objects, with 10 objects in one set and 4 in the other set.
   How many more objects are in the larger set?
4. Number–Line:
   Move forward (to the right) 10 units.
   Move backward (to the left) 4 units.

What is the distance from 0?

Example: At the end of his shift, a cashier has $96 in the cash register. At the beginning of his shift, he had $15. How much money did the cashier collect during his shift?

The total collected is the difference of the ending amount and the starting amount.

$$
\begin{array}{r}
\$96 \\
-15 \\
\hline
\$81
\end{array}
$$

The total collected was $81.

Multiplication of Whole Numbers

Multiplication is one of the four basic number operations. In simple terms, multiplication is the addition of a number to itself a certain number of times. For example, 4 multiplied by 3 is the equal to $4 + 4 + 4$ or $3 + 3 + 3 + 3$. Another way of conceptualizing multiplication is to think in terms of groups. For example, if we have 4 groups of 3 students, the total number of students is 4 multiplied by 3. We call the solution to a multiplication problem the product.

The basic algorithm for whole number multiplication begins with aligning the numbers by place value with the number containing more places on top.

172
x 43   Note that we placed 122 on top because it has more
                    places than 43 does.

Next, we multiply the ones' place of the second number by each place value of the top number sequentially.

(2)
172
x 43 ──→ {3 x 2 = 6, 3 x 7 = 21, 3 x 1 = 3}
516   Note that we had to carry a 2 to the hundreds' column
               because 3 x 7 = 21. Note also that we add, not
               multiply, carried numbers to the product.

Next, we multiply the number in the tens' place of the second number by each place value of the top number sequentially. Because we are multiplying by a number in the tens' place, we place a zero at the end of this product.

(2)
172
x 43   {4 x 2 = 8, 4 x 7 = 28, 4 x 1 = 4}
516
6880

Finally, to determine the final product we add the two partial products.

172
x 43
516
+ 6880
7396   The product of 172 and 43 is 7396.

Example: A student buys 4 boxes of crayons. Each box contains 16 crayons. How many total crayons does the student have?

The total number of crayons is 16 x 4.

16
x 4
64   Total number of crayons equals 64 crayons.

Division of Whole Numbers

Division, the inverse of multiplication, is another of the four basic number operations. When we divide one number by another, we determine how many times we can multiply the divisor (number divided by) before we exceed the number we are dividing (dividend). For example, 8 divided by 2 equals 4 because we can multiply 2 four times to reach 8 (2 x 4 = 8 or 2 + 2 + 2 + 2 = 8). Using the grouping conceptualization we used with multiplication, we can divide 8 into 4 groups of 2 or 2 groups of 4. We call the answer to a division problem the quotient.

If the divisor does not divide evenly into the dividend, we express the leftover amount either as a remainder or as a fraction with the divisor as the denominator. For example, 9 divided by 2 equals 4 with a remainder of 1 or 4 ½.

The basic algorithm for division is long division. We start by representing the quotient as follows.

$$14\overline{)293}$$ ⟶ 14 is the divisor and 293 is the dividend.

This represents 293 ÷ 14.

Next, we divide the divisor into the dividend starting from the left.

$$14\overline{)293}^{\,2}$$ ⟶ 14 divides into 29 two times with a remainder.

Next, we multiply the partial quotient by the divisor, subtract this value from the first digits of the dividend, and bring down the remaining dividend digits to complete the number.

$$\begin{array}{r} 2 \\ 14\overline{)293} \\ -28\downarrow \\ \hline 13 \end{array}$$ ⟶ 2 x 14 = 28, 29 – 28 = 1, and bringing down the 3 yields 13.

Finally, we divide again (the divisor into the remaining value) and repeat the preceding process. The number left after the subtraction represents the remainder.

$$\begin{array}{r} 20 \\ 14\overline{)293} \\ -28 \\ \hline 13 \\ -0 \\ \hline 13 \end{array}$$ ⟶ The final quotient is 20 with a remainder of 13. We can also represent this quotient as 20 13/14.

Example: Each box of apples contains 24 apples. How many boxes must a grocer purchase to supply a group of 252 people with one apple each?

The grocer needs 252 apples. Because he must buy apples in groups of 24, we divide 252 by 24 to determine how many boxes he needs to buy.

$$
\begin{array}{r}
10 \\
24\overline{)252} \\
-24 \\
\hline
12 \\
-\ 0 \\
\hline
12
\end{array}
$$

$12 \longrightarrow$ The quotient is 10 with a remainder of 12.

Thus, the grocer needs 10 boxes plus 12 more apples. Therefore, the minimum number of boxes the grocer can purchase is 11 boxes.

Example: At his job, John gets paid $20 for every hour he works. If John made $940 in a week, how many hours did he work?

This is a division problem. To determine the number of hours John worked, we divide the total amount made ($940) by the hourly rate of pay ($20). Thus, the number of hours worked equals 940 divided by 20.

$$
\begin{array}{r}
47 \\
20\overline{)940} \\
-80 \\
\hline
140 \\
-140 \\
\hline
0
\end{array}
$$

$0 \longrightarrow$ 20 divides into 940, 47 times with no remainder.

John worked 47 hours.

Addition and Subtraction of Decimals

When adding and subtracting decimals, we align the numbers by place value as we do with whole numbers. After adding or subtracting each column, we bring the decimal down, placing it in the same location as in the numbers added or subtracted.

Example: Find the sum of 152.3 and 36.342.

$$
\begin{array}{r}
152.300 \\
+\ \ 36.342 \\
\hline
188.642
\end{array}
$$

Note that we placed two zeroes after the final place value in 152.3 to clarify the column addition.

Example: Find the difference of 152.3 and 36.342.

$$
\begin{array}{cc}
2\ 9\ 10 & (4)11(12) \\
152.300 & 152.300 \\
-\ \ 36.342 & -\ 36.342 \\
\hline
58 & 115.958
\end{array}
$$

Note how we borrowed to subtract from the zeroes in the hundredths' and thousandths' place of 152.300.

Skill 5.8   **Patterns, relations, and functions (e.g., recognizing and analyzing patterns in numbers, shapes, and data, the translation of problem-solving situations into expressions and equations involving variables and unknowns)**

This is a place where we are trying to introduce some of the ideas of algebra into the lower grades. Many of the traditional ways of talking about this in algebra would certainly not be appropriate. For example, we would not want to introduce the technical definition of the word "function." However, there are many types of patterns and relationships that we could address.

It is common in arithmetic to teach students to count by 2's, 5's and 10's. By introducing a different number such as, telling students to count by 5's beginning with 3, students can begin to develop pattern recognition. Larger numbers can be used as addition skills improve.. Students can then be asked to identify the pattern by providing the first few numbers in a sequence. Students will progress to developing some sequences on their own.

There are also many patterns that can be devised using geometric shapes. A great deal of material is readily available on the internet or in workbooks or in software for the computer. By encouraging students to create problems for others to solve, students begin to feel that they are part of the world of adults.

Students can also begin to recognize patterns within statistical analysis. Data can be presented or collected as part of a class exercise. Students can begin to identify patterns from the data. Material is available on this topic on the internet.

As the children progress in their mathematical education, the concept of relationships can be introduced. For example, given that you were looking at a group of bicycles parked in front of the school, how could we calculate how many wheels there are? How could we express the relationship of the number of wheels to the number of bicycles? What if they were tricycles instead of bicycles? Try to think of other situations that your students encounter where relationships like this might enter in.

Measurement exercises lend themselves well to learning about relationships. If you have a measurement for an object expressed in centimeters, how can you use that number to figure out how many millimeters that would be? Also, if they are beginning to learn about fractions and/or decimals, you could reverse it: how can we get from millimeters to centimeters?

Of course there is always money. Children are quick to realize the importance of money in our society, and relevant problems about money will usually find an interesting audience. Using coins of different denominations as examples, you can make up many questions and exercises to illustrate patterns and relationships. In kindergarten, students learn to recognize a penny, nickel, dime, quarter, and one-dollar bill. In 1st grade, they learn how different combinations of coins have equivalent values, for example, that 10 pennies are the same as 1 dime. Teaching children that money has value can start with a simple exercise of counting pennies to understand their monetary value. From here, students can advance to counting nickels, dimes, and so on. The next step might be to have students combine different coins and compute the value of the combination. As students advance in their understanding of the value of money, shopping math can be introduced where students see that money has value in exchange for goods. They can also learn to make change and count change.

Look for ways to link mathematics to other subjects. This is very easy in science. It is also possible in geography and history (many numbers occur in reading about these subjects). Music has an important mathematical component. Art can also be related to mathematics, particularly geometry. Try to help your students make as many connections as possible between mathematics and other subjects, and between all the things they are studying in school and the real world they live in.

Skill 5.9   Types and properties of geometric figures

A **triangle** is a polygon with three sides.

Triangles can be classified by the types of angles or the lengths of their sides.

Classifying by angles:

An **acute** triangle has exactly three *acute* angles.
A **right** triangle has one *right* angle.
An **obtuse** triangle has one *obtuse* angle.

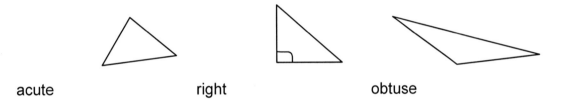

acute   right   obtuse

Classifying by sides:

All *three* sides of an **equilateral** triangle are the same length.
Two sides of an **isosceles** triangle are the same length.
None of the sides of a **scalene** triangle are the same length.

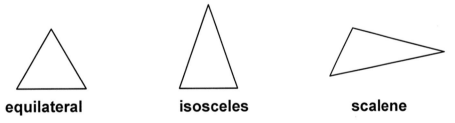

equilateral   **isosceles**   **scalene**

A **polygon** is a simple closed figure composed of line segments. In a **regular polygon** all sides are the same length and all angles are the same measure.

The union of all points on a simple closed surface and all points in its interior form a space figure called a **solid**. The five regular solids, or **polyhedra**, are the cube, tetrahedron, octahedron, icosahedron, and dodecahedron. A **net** is a two-dimensional figure that can be cut out and folded up to make a three-dimensional solid. Below are models of the five regular solids with their corresponding face polygons and nets.

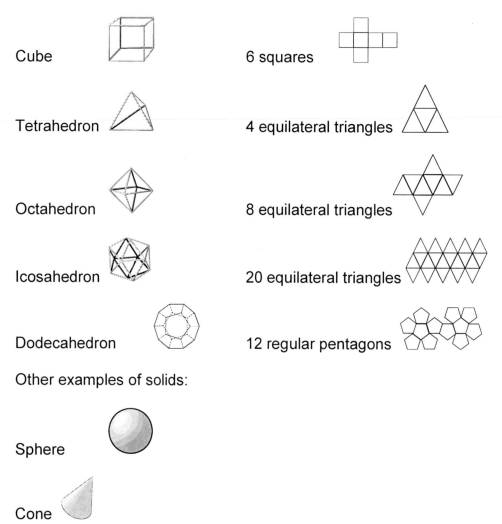

Cube   6 squares

Tetrahedron   4 equilateral triangles

Octahedron   8 equilateral triangles

Icosahedron   20 equilateral triangles

Dodecahedron   12 regular pentagons

Other examples of solids:

Sphere

Cone

Skill 5.10   Basic geometric concepts (e.g., symmetry)

Tangrams, or puzzle pieces, are excellent manipulatives for children to use to explore geometric shapes and relationships. They allow students to transform shapes through flips and rotations as well as to take them apart and put them together in different formations. Tangrams can be tangible pieces that students manipulate with their hands or they can be virtual pieces on the computer that students manipulate to visualize geometric shape changes.

A **Tessellation** is an arrangement of closed shapes that completely covers the plane without overlapping or leaving gaps. Unlike **tilings**, tessellations do not require the use of regular polygons. In art the term is used to refer to pictures or tiles mostly in the form of animals and other life forms, which cover the surface of a plane in a symmetrical way without overlapping or leaving gaps. M. C. Escher is known as the "father" of modern tessellations. Tessellations are used for tiling, mosaics, quilts, and art.

If you look at a completed tessellation, you will see the original motif repeats in a pattern. There are 17 possible ways that a pattern can be used to tile a flat surface, or "wallpaper."

A **transformation** is a change in the position, shape, or size of a geometric figure. **Transformational geometry** is the study of manipulating objects by flipping, twisting, turning and scaling.

Symmetry is exact similarity between two parts or halves, as if one were a mirror image of the other.

A **translation** is a transformation that "slides" an object a fixed distance in a given direction. The original object and its translation have the same shape and size, and they face in the same direction.

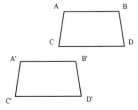

An example of a translation in architecture would be stadium seating. The seats are the same size and the same shape and face in the same direction.

A **rotation** is a transformation that turns a figure about a fixed point called the center of rotation. An object and its rotation are the same shape and size, but the figures may be turned in different directions. Rotations can occur in either a clockwise or a counterclockwise direction.

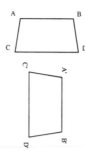

Rotations can be seen in wallpaper and art, and a Ferris wheel is an example of rotation.

An object and its **reflection** have the same shape and size, but the figures face in opposite directions.

The line (where a mirror may be placed) is called the **line of reflection**. The distance from a point to the line of reflection is the same as the distance from the point's image to the line of reflection.

Skill 5.11 Relationship between standard algorithms and fundamental concepts of algebra and geometry

In the early primary grades, the concept of algebra is significantly different than what an adult remembers as algebra class. As adults, we typically recall the letters being used to hold the place of a number and solving various equations to find the answer for a variable. However, for young children the basis for this concept is developed through learning about patterns, the attributes of objects and how to describe objects in detail. These ideas help students to develop the fundamental thinking and concepts behind algebraic reasoning. These patterns may begin through concrete objects, but will be further developed into counting patterns and other recognition of the patterns of numbers.

Beginning with the basic understanding of the symbols used throughout math (numerical representations) students can investigate things around them. They can gather this information and begin to report it in a way that means something to others who look at it. These facts related to their own thinking can be expanded. As students look at a variety of situations and manipulate the objects to draw new conclusions, their problem solving skills are advanced. These skills will allow students to begin to solve missing number problems or solve for unknown pieces to a situation. This can be done with the youngest students as well. An example of a preschool missing object problem might be:

Red   yellow   red   _____   red   yellow   red   yellow   red

In this case, the students would be shown real objects of two colors set in a pattern and need to determine which one is missing from the center of the pattern. This type of thinking is more complex. As children begin to compare, sort, order and demonstrate seriating of objects using various characteristics their thinking changes. These changes are the beginning of algebraic thought. As they add on to patterns, make changes to patterns, build their own patterns, or convert patterns into new formats, they are thinking in more complex ways. Connecting this new thinking with the understanding of the number system is the beginning of using variables to define the relationships between mathematical concepts. This method of problem solving is then defined further into the expression of these relationships in a more traditional mathematical manner.

Pre-K children should be able to recognize and extend simple repeating patterns using objects and pictures. By patterns, we mean a sequence of symbols, sounds, movements, or objects that follow a simple rule, such as ABBABBABB. Students should be presented with a simple pattern that they try to understand. Once they have an understanding of the pattern, they should copy and extend it. Students at this age are capable of assigning letters to their patterns to verbalize how the pattern repeats. This is the very early fundamental stages of algebra.

SEE also Skill 5.10

Skill 5.12   Measurement instruments, units, and procedures for problems involving length, area, angles, volume, mass, and temperature

Prior to introducing measurement with standard tools such as a ruler, it is appropriate to teach children how to measure with non-standard units such as paper clips. Students are taught to use the paper clip as a unit and by laying the paper clips end to end, they measure an object longer than the paper clip (repetition of a single unit to measure something larger than the unit).

Students should be able to determine what unit of measurement is appropriate for a particular problem, as indicated by the following table:

Problem Type	Unit (Customary System)	Unit (Metric System)
Length	Inch Foot Yard	Millimeter Centimeter Meter
Distance	Mile	Kilometer
Area	Square inches Square feet Square yards Square miles	Square millimeters Square centimeters Square meters Square kilometers
Volume	Cubic inches Cubic feet Cubic yards	Cubic millimeters Cubic centimeters Cubic meters
Liquid volume	Fluid ounces Cups Pints Quarts Gallons	Milliliters Liters
Mass		Milligrams Centigrams Grams Kilograms
Weight	Ounces Pounds Tons	Milligrams Centigrams Grams Kilograms
Temperature	Degrees Fahrenheit	Degrees Celsius or Kelvin

After you have decided that there is some object you want to measure, the first question to be answered is what attributes can be measured on this object. Most physical objects would have a length, although even here there are choices to be made. Since the world is three-dimensional, you have to choose which dimension will be the length, which the width, and which the height. We use those words to distinguish the three dimensions from each other, but of course all three would be measured in length units. Other measurable attributes of common physical objects are their weight, surface area, volume and temperature.

In Pre K-3 volume is not an appropriate topic, except as it might enter into a discussion of liquid measure. Also the time spent on area concepts will probably be short. Measurement of temperature will normally be confined to air temperature for this age group.

When it comes to choosing between standard and nonstandard units of measurement, it depends on what country you are in. In the United States English units are still considered standard, while metric are nonstandard. It would be nice if the world could agree on a single system. If we ever did, the most natural and easiest to use would have to be metric. Children should be introduced to metric units right along with English units. The only way the change will ever be made in this country is if young children grow up knowing the metric system. By using it and seeing how easy it converts from one unit to another because it goes in powers of 10, they should be convinced that it is the better way to go.

With the advent of good and inexpensive digital cameras, math teachers have some wonderful opportunities to show students how pervasive mathematics and measuring are in their lives. The teacher can go around the immediate area of the school taking pictures of physical objects that illustrate various things they are studying. For example, if you are working on length measures and also geometric figures, before having them measure the length and width of a bunch of rectangles on paper, show them pictures (a powerpoint demonstration would be ideal here) of different rectangles around the neighborhood. For example, walls of the classroom, tiles on the floor or ceiling, sidewalks, exteriors of buildings, etc.

Do the same for other geometric figures. Bridges are good to get triangles. Church windows are often circular. Children are usually quite familiar with circles, but circles introduce some very real problems. With younger students the perimeter can be approximated (remember that all measurements are approximate anyway). Using a piece of string and fitting it around a circle on a piece of paper, then measuring the length of the string that seems to fit, makes a nice little exercise.

Every math classroom should be equipped with various measuring devices-- a set of rulers, a few meter sticks, some thermometers, a few different scales for weighing objects, clocks and perhaps a stopwatch and protractors. Hands-on exercises are most effective. When showing pictures of objects we want to measure in the immediate environment, ask the students how we could measure these objects and what would be an appropriate instrument to use. What units would be best to express the measurement. Have them guess the result of measuring the object. Where could they go to find out if their guess was a good approximation to the reported measurement of this object?

Angles are difficult to teach to young children. They can be introduced by having them stand up, face front, then turn to face sideways right. What if we turned only part way to the right? How could we measure this? Don't be too fast to tell them how we adults talk about and measure angles for this. You might have some interesting ideas presented for solving this problem. Eventually, you will tell them about angles and how they are measured. Draw some angles and talk about what exactly is being measured here. Point out that the angle is no bigger if you extend the sides indefinitely. Actual measuring with protractors could be introduced if you feel the children are ready, but getting the idea of what we mean by the concept of angle is more important at first.

Skill 5.13   Collection, organization, and analysis of data

Collecting, describing, and analyzing data are fun activities in the early childhood classroom. There are numerous exciting and playful methods for collecting data to be used in various classroom lessons. Some fun ways to collect data include:

- Have students drop a piece of cereal into a bowl that is their favorite color.
- Have students draw a tally mark under their lunch choice on a bulletin board.
- Utilize a thumbs up or thumbs down approach for students' response when asking whole group questions.
- Use wipe boards
- Have the students themselves stand in lines to form a human graph to show a particular set of data

Ideas for collecting data to organize describe and analyze:

- Favorite colors
- Birthdays
- Hair/eye/clothing colors
- Favorite foods
- Favorite books
- Ending to a story (like/don't like)
- Shoe size (type/color/style)
- Favorite songs

Once the data has been collected, it needs to be organized into a format easily analyzed by the students. This can involve: tables, tally charts, and graphs. Using the real objects to form the bars of the graphs can provide the students with immediate results. This can be very important to young children. It also provides a concrete representation; whereas, transferring the data to paper to create the graph/table or chart is more abstract of a concept.

Once the graph, table or chart is completed it is important to utilize mathematical language to describe and analyze the information. Comparing two different bars on the graph, finding the greatest, finding the smallest/least or other types of analysis help students to develop their critical thinking skills. The students need to be exposed to vocabulary terms which mean the same thing (such as smallest and least).

Gathering, organizing and analyzing data is an easy to incorporate daily routine into the early childhood classroom. An entire activity can be completed in five to ten minutes of the math class on a regular basis and provide students with a fun, real-life, critical thinking activity which increases not only mathematical understanding and skills, but builds vocabulary skills as well. It is also an area of math which can help to tie together many other subject areas in an easy way.

Bar, Line, Picto-, and Circle Graphs

	Test 1	Test 2	Test 3	Test 4	Test 5
Evans, Tim	75	66	80	85	97
Miller, Julie	94	93	88	97	98
Thomas, Randy	81	86	88	87	90

Bar graphs are used to compare various quantities.

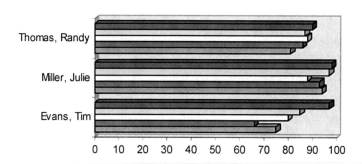

Line graphs are used to show trends, often over a period of time.

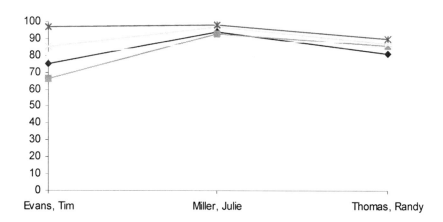

A **pictograph** shows comparison of quantities using symbols. Each symbol represents a number of items.

Skill 5.14 The application of mathematical reasoning to analyze and solve problems.

For very young children, almost any mathematical question posed is a problem to be solved. Too often, the term problem solving is misrepresented as word problems. In fact, any problem presented to a child where they are unaware of the answer, is a problem to be solved. From the very beginning, children need to experience a variety of mathematical situations across all subject areas. Exposing children to a variety of contexts in which to solve problems allows the child to develop their own constructs upon which they can build new learning.

Problem solving is not about one strategy or right way, but rather is about allowing students of varying mathematical skills and abilities to look at the same situation presented and find a way to solve it. In a group of five, it may be reasonable to expect five different methods to reach the solution. Providing students with the means to investigate a problem allows them to be flexible in their approach. Often times, teachers limit the abilities of their students to solve problems by restricting them to one mode of reaching a solution. Parents can also be guilty of this as well.

For example, the kindergartener who is presented with a problem where there are three pies and twelve people to feed may easily use pieces of real pie to work out an appropriate solution. However, the parent or teacher who indicates you must use the division algorithm to solve the problem may automatically set this same student up for failure.

Problem solving needs to be incorporated in a real way for students to understand appreciate and value the process. Using daily activities or problems can help make problem solving a regular part of a child's day. As situations arise, in any subject area, it is important for the teacher to incorporate problem solving activities. Having the students help with lunch count, attendance, counting the number of days left in the school year, calculating the time left until recess, or other daily types of activities are examples of ways to include realistic problem solving in the classroom.

Additionally, problem solving activities should be incorporated into all subject areas. In science, children can graph the daily temperatures and make predictions for the future temperatures. In social studies, they can gather, tabulate and calculate the data related to the topic presented (how many classmates agree that drugs are bad for your body). In language arts, children can solve problems find in all types of children's literature. Charting favorite books, calculating ages of characters in stories, and drawing maps of the setting(s) of books are some beginning examples of ways to connect the two subjects. There are also numerous exciting books written with a mathematical basis which can be used to cover both subjects in a fun manner.

It is important for the teacher to be a role model. Thinking aloud as you come across a problem in the course of the day will help the students begin to realize the necessity and real-world implications of solving problems. Encouraging students to be reflective will also help in building the necessary mathematical language. Also, students can begin to share their ideas and methods with each other, which is an excellent strategy for learning about problem solving.

Typically, there are four steps to problem solving. Teachers will need to teach each of the steps explicitly and model them regularly. The steps are:

1. Understand the problem

   This involves, among other things, understanding all the words in the problem, understanding what you are being asked to find, possibly being able to draw a picture or diagram, knowing if there is enough information, and knowing if there is too much information.

2. Devise a plan

   This involves being able to choose an appropriate strategy to solve the problem. These strategies include, but are not limited to, guessing and checking, looking for a pattern, using a model, and working backward.

3. Carry out the plan

   This is the actual solving of the problem using whatever strategy you have chosen.

4. Look back

   Included in this step is checking the answer, if possible, to make sure it is correct. This step may be extended to include determining if there might have been an easier way to find the solution.

When assessing problem solving, the most effective method is direct observation. Teachers need to observe students to determine what strategies are being implemented. Watching students solve problems presented can provide teachers with insight into future teaching opportunities and skills mastered already by the students. Problem solving alone is difficult to assign a grade, but the information gained from the process is critical to future teaching.

Competency 0006   Understand principles and concepts of history and social science.

Skill 6.1   Basic knowledge of major developments in the history of Massachusetts, the United States, and the world

Massachusetts

Of all of the original thirteen states of America, Massachusetts is the one most commonly associated with the early history of the nation. Plymouth Rock, the Pilgrims and Puritans, Salem and its witchcraft, the Boston Tea Party, Paul Revere, Lexington and Concord are all names and events that leap to mind.

Legend says Saint Brendan visited the coast of Massachusetts about 550; there is indication the coast was visited by the Vikings about 1000; it was explored in 1602 by Bartholomew Gosnold who was searching for sassafras roots; it was mapped by John Smith in 1614. Yet the real history of Massachusetts began in 1620 with the arrival of 102 pilgrims who arrived in search of a place that allowed them to worship as they chose. The *Mayflower* brought them to Plymouth, where they struggled against the elements to survive with little food. Almost half of the pilgrims died during their first winter in Massachusetts. The spring and summer allowed a bountiful harvest, and the first Thanksgiving Day was a great celebration.

Soon other settlers arrived, and within 20 years Massachusetts had 8 towns and more than 2,500 settlers. In 1629 a royal charter was granted to the "Puritan colony" of Massachusetts Bay, which had developed near Salem. This colony grew rapidly over the next ten years. Plymouth colony was finally granted a charter in 1692. This Massachusetts Bay Colony insisted on political freedom and was unexplainably intolerant of other religious practices. In fact, religious intolerance led to the banishment of Roger Williams and Anne Hutchinson and the founding of Rhode Island and Connecticut. Quakers were persecuted and several persons were hanged. The so-called Salem witch trials also reflected the religious intolerance within the colony. In addition, the early colonists were frequently threatened by the Native American people, and seemed constantly to be at war with them.

Struggles with England to control life in the colonies continued into the 18th century. It continued even when the colonists were helping England during the French and Indian Wars. This long history of unhappiness with English rule set the stage for Massachusetts to play a leading role when dissatisfaction began to crystallize throughout the English colonies. The Boston Tea Party occurred within the boundaries of Massachusetts, as did the first battles of the Revolutionary War. Paul Revere's famous ride announcing the arrival of British troops also occurred in Massachusetts.

In 1780, the state constitution was written, and after the Revolution, Massachusetts was one of the first states to ratify the U.S. Constitution. In the early days of statehood, Massachusetts was clearly anti-Federalist, but by 1797 this attitude changed. Residents bitterly opposed the war of 1812, but did their part in supplying soldiers and money.

The constitution prohibited slavery, but the radicals led the way as Massachusetts became the birthplace of the abolition movement. The first issue of William Lloyd Garrison's *Liberator* was published in Boston in 1831. The residents of Massachusetts were strongly supportive of the Union in the Civil War.

Since the Civil War, the state has continuously grown and developed. Due to the amount of industry in Massachusetts, questions of labor have been of vital importance throughout these years. In 1920 women were permitted to hold public office.

Massachusetts has also been historically a center of learning and artistic expression. Harvard University was one of the first colleges founded in the United States and continues to be widely respected as a leader in higher education. The Massachusetts Institute of Technology is certainly one of the strongest scientific and technical schools in the nation.

Some of the Massachusetts natives who became very famous, making important contributions in learning, technology and the arts include:
- Henry James
- James Otis
- Rufus Choate
- Horace Mann
- G. Stanley Hall
- Mary Lyon
- Phillips Brooks
- Alexander Graham Bell
- Charles William Eliot

The United States

An understanding of the history of the United States for an early childhood educator should include many of the topics listed below. Although these are not all covered in an early childhood curriculum, it is important for the teacher to have a thorough understanding of this history.

- Native American civilization prior to European influence
- Exploration and early settlement by Europeans
  - Christopher Columbus discovered the Bahamas and Cuba in 1492
  - John Cabot explored the Labrador coast of North America in 1497
  - Balboa discovered the Pacific Ocean in 1513
  - Ponce de Leon searched for the fountain of youth in Florida in 1513
  - Cortez conquered Mexico in 1521
  - Fernando de Soto discovered the Mississippi River in 1541
  - Coronado explored the southern part of the U.S. in 1541
  - Other early explorers were Narvaez, Verrazano, and Magellan.
- Earliest Permanent settlements
  - Jacques Cartier established Montreal in 1540
  - Jean Ribault and the French Huguenots established a colony in Florida that was demolished by Spanish troops in 1565. The Spanish built a fort on the same site, which grew into the town of Saint Augustine. (Believed to be the first permanent settlement)
- Colonial America
  - The original 13 colonies and their similarities and differences
  - Struggles with Native Americans
  - Relations with European countries
  - Agriculture and Manufacturing; Trade
- The Revolutionary War
  - Causes
  - Major developments of the war
  - Outcomes
- The formation of governments
  - The Articles of Confederation
  - The U.S. Constitution
  - State governments and constitutions
  - The Nullification Controversy
- The Mexican War: Causes and Outcomes
- Conflicts over Slavery
  - Missouri Compromise
  - Dred Scott Decision
  - John Brown's Raid at Harper's Ferry
- The Civil War
  - Causes and results
  - Broad outline of the war
  - Reconstruction

- Westward Expansion and Manifest Destiny
- The Spanish-American War
- Progressivism
- The California Gold Rush and the Trans-Continental Railroad
- Industrialization and the Labor Movement
- World War I
- The Great Depression
- World War II
- The Korean Conflict
- The Civil Rights Movement and other Freedom and Equality Efforts
- The Viet Nam War
- The First Gulf War
- September 11 and the rise of Terrorism
- The Second Gulf War and Afghanistan

World History

An understanding of World History for an early childhood educator should include many of the topics listed below. Although these are not all covered in an early childhood curriculum, it is important for the teacher to have a thorough understanding of this history. Major periods and events in World History that should be understood include:

- The Pre-historic period
  - Populating the world
  - Development of agriculture and animal husbandry
  - Development and growth of communities and cities
  - Division and specialization of labor
  - Development of trade
- Major Early Civilizations
  - Mesopotamia
  - Egypt
  - The Indus River Basin
  - China
  - Israel
  - Greece
  - The Roman Republic
  - The Persian Empire
- Second Age of Empires
  - The Roman Empire
  - The Byzantine Empire
  - Charlemagne and the Carolingian Empire
  - The Islamic Empire
  - Tang and Song Dynasties in China
  - Independence of Japan and Korea
  - Mayan Culture

- o European Expansion
    - o Expansion of the Muslim world into Asia and Africa
    - o The Crusades
    - o The Mongol Empire
    - o The Rise of Western Christendom
    - o Ottoman Empire and Safavid Persia
    - o The Spice Trade
    - o European Impact on Africa
    - o European Empires and the beginning of colonization
- o The Protestant Reformation and the Catholic Counter-Reformation
- o The Enlightenment and the age of Revolutions
    - o The French Revolution
    - o The American Revolution
    - o The Mexican Revolution
    - o The Napoleonic Wars
    - o The Bolshevik Revolution
- o European Hegemony
    - o Nationalism
    - o Colonialism in Africa, India, Asia and the Americas
    - o The end of Imperial China and the Rise of Japan
    - o India under the Raj
- o Life-changing and Mind-changing thought and technology
    - o The scientific revolution
    - o The industrial revolution
    - o The agricultural revolution
    - o The rise of modern industries
- o Twentieth-Century Conflict
    - o World War I
    - o World War II
    - o The Rise of the State of Israel
    - o The Cold War
    - o The Korean Conflict
    - o The Cuban Revolution
    - o The Vietnam Conflict
    - o Development of the Third World
    - o The Iranian Revolution and the Rise of Islamism
    - o Arab-Israeli Conflicts
    - o The Fall of the Soviet Union
    - o The Information Revolution
    - o Globalization
    - o Terrorism

Skill 6.2   Origins, fundamental concepts, and historical development of western civilization (e.g., the political, philosophic, religious, intellectual, and aesthetic values of ancient Israel, Greece and Rome and their political and historical influence

The classical civilization of **Greece** reached the highest levels in human achievement based on the foundations already laid by such ancient groups as the Egyptians, Phoenicians, Minoans, and Mycenaeans.

Among the more important contributions of Greece were the Greek alphabet derived from the Phoenician letters, which formed the basis for the Roman alphabet and our present-day alphabet. Extensive trading and colonization resulted in the spread of the Greek civilization. The love of sports, with emphasis on a sound body, led to the tradition of the Olympic Games. Greece was responsible for the rise of independent, strong city-states. Note the complete contrast between independent, freedom-loving Athens with its practice of pure democracy, i.e. direct, personal, active participation in government by qualified citizens, and the rigid, totalitarian, militaristic Sparta. Other important areas that the Greeks are credited with influencing include drama, epic and lyric poetry, fables, myths centered on the many gods and goddesses, science, astronomy, medicine, mathematics, philosophy, art, architecture, and recording historical events. The conquests of Alexander the Great spread Greek ideas to the areas he conquered and brought to the Greek world many ideas from Asia including the value of ideas, wisdom, curiosity, and the desire to learn as much about the world as possible.

A most interesting and significant characteristic of the Greek, Hellenistic, and Roman civilizations was "secularism" where emphasis shifted away from religion to the state. Men were not absorbed in or dominated by religion as had been the case in Egypt and the nations located in Mesopotamia. Religion and its leaders did not dominate the state and its authority was greatly diminished.

The **Israelites** came from Ur in Mesopotamia, where the patriarch Abraham made a "covenant" with their god, Yahweh. The Israelites were in Canaan around 1900 B.C.E. They were taken into captivity in Egypt and declared their freedom and left for the Sinai desert in about 1280 BCE. There, they became God's chosen people in a new "covenant." A loosely affiliated group of clans that shared a common religion then formed themselves into the Kingdom of Israel. The kings during this period were Saul, David and Solomon. After Solomon's death the kingdom divided into Israel in the north and Judah in the south. The northern kingdom (Israel) was defeated by the Assyrians in about 705 BCE. Judah (the southern kingdom) fell to the Babylonians under Nebuchadnezzar II in about 562. When the Persian Empire emerged, the Jews were permitted to return to Palestine where they lived under religious law.

The primary contribution of the Israelites was their religion, perhaps the earliest form of monotheism. This religion regulated every aspect of the life of the people with an encompassing legal code, preserved in Scripture, which regulated all aspects of human interaction, both within the community and with outsiders. Their alphabet is a few steps beyond picture writing (hieroglyphics), and is still used today. Until the 1940s, the Israelite (Jewish) people have lived scattered throughout the world. The formation of the nation of Israel gave them a "land" and a political existence.

Rome became an independent community in about 500 BCE and began an internal strengthening and external expansion that controlled the entire Italian peninsula by 272 BCE. Through numerous wars of conquest, their control included most of the known world.

Rome was originally organized as a **Republic**, in which power was held by a Senate, elected by the people, and appointed magistrates. As the influence and control of the government came to include larger areas and more people, the Republic was overwhelmed. A series of power struggles between rival leaders brought civil war. The power struggles ended when Octavian, renamed Augustus) set up an empire that led to the Pax Romana (Roman Peace), lasting from about 27 BCE to 180 CE.

Rome's major contributions include government structure, the organization and operation of their army, the construction of a series of roads connecting all parts of their empire, their system of centralized government and imperial control of conquered territories. Roman philosophers and artists continued the trends in philosophy and artistic expression begun by the Greeks.

Skill 6.3   The development and influence of science and technology in western societies

The **Scientific Revolution** was characterized by a shift in scientific approach and ideas. Near the end of the sixteenth century Galileo Galilei introduced a radical approach to the study of motion. He moved from attempts to explain why objects move the way they do and began to use experiments to describe precisely how they move. He also used experimentation to describe how forces affect non-moving objects. Other scientists continued in the same approach. Outstanding scientists of the period included Johannes Kepler, Evangelista Torricelli, Blaise Pascal, Isaac Newton and Leibniz. This was the period when experiments dominated scientific study. This method was particularly applied to the study of physics.

The **Agricultural Revolution** occurred first in England. It was marked by experimentation that resulted in increased production of crops from the land and a new and more technical approach to the management of agriculture. The revolution in agricultural management and production was hugely enhanced by the industrial revolution and the invention of the steam engine. The introduction of steam-powered tractors greatly increased crop production and significantly decreased labor costs. Developments in Agriculture were also enhanced by the scientific revolution and the learning from experimentation that led to philosophies of crop rotation and soil enrichment. Improved systems of irrigation and harvesting also contributed to the growth of agricultural production.

The **Industrial Revolution**, which began in Great Britain and spread elsewhere, was the development of power-driven machinery (fueled by coal and steam) leading to the accelerated growth of industry with large factories replacing homes and small workshops as work centers. The lives of people changed drastically, and a largely agricultural society changed to an industrial one. In Western Europe, the period of empire and colonialism began. The industrialized nations seized and claimed parts of Africa and Asia in an effort to control and provide the raw materials needed to feed the industries and machines in the "mother country". Later developments included power based on electricity and internal combustion, replacing coal and steam.

The Information Revolution refers to the sweeping changes during the latter half of the twentieth century as a result of technological advances and a new respect for the knowledge or information provided by trained, skilled and experienced professionals in a variety of fields. This approach to understanding a number of social and economic changes in global society arose from the ability to make computer technology both accessible and affordable. In particular, the development of the computer chip has led to such technological advances as the Internet, the cell phone, Cybernetics, wireless communication, and the related ability to disseminate and access a massive amount of information quite readily.

Skill 6.4 Basic concepts of geography and global features (e.g., continents, hemispheres, latitude and longitude, poles)

The six themes of geography are:

Location - including relative and absolute location. A relative location refers to the surrounding geography, e.g., "on the banks of the Mississippi River." Absolute location refers to a specific point, such as 41 degrees North latitude, 90 degrees West longitude, or 123 Main Street.

Spatial organization is a description of how things are grouped in a given space. In geographical terms, this can describe people, places, and environments anywhere and everywhere on Earth. The most basic form of spatial organization for people is where they live. The vast majority of people live near other people, in villages and towns and cities and settlements. These people live near others in order to take advantage of the goods and services that naturally arise from cooperation. These villages and towns and cities and settlements are, to varying degrees, near bodies of water. Water is a staple of survival for every person on the planet and is also a good source of energy for factories and other industries, as well as a form of transportation for people and goods. For example, in a city, where are the factories and heavy industry buildings? Are they near airports or train stations? Are they on the edge of town, near major roads? What about housing developments? Are they near these industries, or are they far away? Where are the other industry buildings? Where are the schools and hospitals and parks? What about the police and fire stations? How close are homes to each of these things? Towns and especially cities are routinely organized into neighborhoods, so that each house or home is near most things that its residents might need on a regular basis. This means that large cities have multiple schools, hospitals, grocery stores, fire stations, etc.

Place - A place has both human and physical characteristics. Physical characteristics include features such as mountains, rivers, deserts, etc. Human characteristics are the features created by human interaction with their environment such as canals and roads.

Human-Environmental Interaction - The theme of human-environmental interaction has three main concepts: humans adapt to the environment (wearing warm clothing in a cold climate, for instance,) humans modify the environment (planting trees to block a prevailing wind, for example,) and humans depend on the environment (for food, water and raw materials.)

Movement - The theme of movement covers how humans interact with one another through trade, communications, emigration and other forms of interaction.

Regions - A region is an area that has some kind of unifying characteristic, such as a common language, a common government, etc. There are three main types of regions. Formal regions are areas defined by actual political boundaries, such as a city, county, or state. Functional regions are defined by a common function, such as the area covered by a telephone service. Vernacular regions are less formally defined areas that are formed by people's perception, e.g. "the Middle East," and "the South."

Geography involves studying location and how living things and earth's features are distributed throughout the earth. It includes where animals, people, and plants live and the effects of their relationship with earth's physical features. Geographers also explore the locations of earth's features, how they got there, and why it is so important. Another way to describe where people live is by the **geography** and **topography** around them. The vast majority of people on the planet live in areas that are very hospitable. Yes, people live in the Himalayas and in the Sahara, but the populations in those areas are small indeed when compared to the plains of China, India, Europe, and the United States. People naturally want to live where they won't have to work really hard just to survive, and world population patterns reflect this.

The earth's physical environment is divided into three major parts: the atmosphere, the hydrosphere, and the lithosphere: The atmosphere is the layer of air that surrounds the earth. The hydrosphere is the water portion of the planet (70% of the earth is covered by water) and the lithosphere is the solid portion of the earth.

Climate is average weather or daily weather conditions for a specific region or location over a long or extended period of time. Studying the climate of an area includes information gathered on the area's monthly and yearly temperatures and its monthly and yearly amounts of precipitation. In addition, a characteristic of an area's climate is the length of its growing season.

Continents – the major divisions of land on the earth

Hemispheres – The two parts of the earth defined when the sphere is divided in half by the equator or by a line of longitude.

Latitude and Longitude – Latitude is the angular distance north or south from the earth's equator measured in degrees. Longitude is angular distance usually expressed in degrees east or west from the Prime Meridian, which passes through Greenwich, England.

Poles – the ends of the earth's axis.

Skill 6.5 **Major physical features and regions of Massachusetts, the United States, and world areas**

Common Physical Features

Mountains are landforms with rather steep slopes at least 2,000 feet or more above sea level. Mountains are found in groups called mountain chains or mountain ranges. At least one range can be found on six of the earth's seven continents. North America has the Appalachian and Rocky Mountains; South America the Andes; Asia the Himalayas; Australia the Great Dividing Range; Europe the Alps; and Africa the Atlas, Ahaggar, and Drakensburg Mountains. Mountains are commonly formed by volcanic activity, or when land is thrust upward where two tectonic plates collide.

Hills are elevated landforms rising to an elevation of about 500 to 2000 feet. They are found everywhere on earth including Antarctica where they are covered by ice.

Plateaus are elevated landforms usually level on top. Depending on location, they range from being an area that is very cold to one that is cool and healthful. Some plateaus are dry because they are surrounded by mountains that keep out any moisture. Some examples include the Kenya Plateau in East Africa, which is very cool. The plateau extending north from the Himalayas is extremely dry while those in Antarctica and Greenland are covered with ice and snow. Plateaus can be formed by underground volcanic activity, erosion, or colliding tectonic plates.
Plains are described as areas of flat or slightly rolling land, usually lower than the landforms next to them. Sometimes called lowlands (and sometimes located along **seacoasts)** they support the majority of the world's people. Some are found inland and many have been formed by large rivers. This resulted in extremely fertile soil for successful cultivation of crops and numerous large settlements of people. In North America, the vast plains areas extend from the Gulf of Mexico north to the Arctic Ocean and between the Appalachian and Rocky Mountains. In Europe, rich plains extend east from Great Britain into central Europe on into the Siberian region of Russia. Plains in river valleys are found in China (the Yangtze River valley), India (the Ganges River valley), and Southeast Asia (the Mekong River valley).

Valleys are land areas that are found between hills and mountains. Some have gentle slopes containing trees and plants; others have very steep walls and are referred to as canyons. One famous example is Arizona's Grand Canyon of the Colorado River, which was formed by erosion.

Deserts are large dry areas of land receiving ten inches or less of rainfall each year. Among the better known deserts are Africa's large Sahara Desert, the Arabian Desert on the Arabian Peninsula, and the desert Outback covering roughly one third of Australia. Deserts are found mainly in the tropical latitudes, and are formed when surrounding features such as mountain ranges extract most of the moisture from the prevailing winds

Deltas are areas of lowlands formed by soil and sediment deposited at the mouths of rivers. The soil is generally very fertile and most fertile river deltas are important crop-growing areas. One well-known example is the delta of Egypt's Nile River, known for its production of cotton.

Mesas are the flat tops of hills or mountains usually with steep sides. Mesas are similar to plateaus, but smaller.

Basins are considered to be low areas drained by rivers or low spots in mountains.

Foothills are generally considered a low series of hills found between a plain and a mountain range.

Marshes and swamps are wet lowlands providing growth of such plants as rushes and reeds.

Oceans are the largest bodies of water on the planet. The four oceans of the earth are the **Atlantic Ocean**, one-half the size of the Pacific and separating North and South America from Africa and Europe; the **Pacific Ocean**, covering almost one-third of the entire surface of the earth and separating North and South America from Asia and Australia; the **Indian Ocean**, touching Africa, Asia, and Australia; and the ice-filled **Arctic Ocean,** extending from North America and Europe to the North Pole. The waters of the Atlantic, Pacific, and Indian Oceans also touch the shores of Antarctica.

Seas are smaller than oceans and are surrounded by land. Some examples include the Mediterranean Sea found between Europe, Asia, and Africa; and the Caribbean Sea, touching the West Indies, South and Central America. A lake is a body of water surrounded by land. The Great Lakes in North America are a good example.

Rivers, considered a nation's lifeblood, usually begin as very small streams, formed by melting snow and rainfall, flowing from higher to lower land, emptying into a larger body of water, usually a sea or an ocean. Examples of important rivers for the people and countries affected by and/or dependent on them include the Nile, Niger, and Zaire Rivers of Africa; the Rhine, Danube, and Thames Rivers of Europe; the Yangtze, Ganges, Mekong, Hwang He, and Irrawaddy Rivers of Asia; the Murray-Darling in Australia; and the Orinoco in South America. River systems are made up of large rivers and numerous smaller rivers or tributaries flowing into them. Examples include the vast Amazon Rivers system in South America and the Mississippi River system in the United States.

Canals are man-made water passages constructed to connect two larger bodies of water. Famous examples include the **Panama Canal** across Panama's isthmus connecting the Atlantic and Pacific Oceans and the **Suez Canal** in the Middle East between Africa and the Arabian peninsulas connecting the Red and Mediterranean Seas.

World weather patterns are greatly influenced by ocean surface currents in the upper layer of the ocean. These current continuously move along the ocean surface in specific directions. Ocean currents that flow deep below the surface are called sub-surface currents. These currents are influenced by such factors as the location of landmasses in the current's path and the earth's rotation.

Surface currents are caused by winds and classified by temperature. Cold currents originate in the Polar Regions and flow through surrounding water that is measurably warmer. Those currents with a higher temperature than the surrounding water are called warm currents and can be found near the equator. These currents follow swirling routes around the ocean basins and the equator.

The Gulf Stream and the California Current are the two main surface currents that flow along the coastlines of the United States. The Gulf Stream is a warm northern part of the Atlantic Ocean. Benjamin Franklin studied and named the Gulf Stream. The California Current is a cold current that originates in the Artic regions and flows southward along the west coast of the United States.

The United States

The continental United States is bordered by the Pacific Ocean on the west and the Atlantic Ocean on the east. The country is divided into two main sections by the Rocky Mountains, which extend from New Mexico in the south through the Canadian border on the north. The western portion of the country contains forested, mountainous areas in the Pacific Northwest and Northern California, including Mt. St. Helens, an active volcano in the Cascade Range. Dryer, warmer regions in the south include the Mojave Desert in the Southwest. The Great Salt Lake in Utah is at the foot of the Wasatch Mountains.

The Rocky Mountains slope down in the east to the Great Plains, a large, grassy region drained by the Mississippi River, the nation's largest river, and one of the largest rivers in the world. The Great Plains give way in the east to hilly, forested regions. The Appalachian Mountain chain runs along the eastern coast of the U.S. Along the border with Canada between Minnesota and New York are Lake Huron, Lake Ontario, Lake Michigan, Lake Erie and Lake Superior, known as the Great Lakes.

Alaska is located in northwestern North America and contains Mt. McKinley, also called Denali, which is the highest mountain on the continent. Hawaii is a series of volcanic islands in the South Pacific.

Physical Features of Massachusetts

Massachusetts is one of the fifty states located in the northeastern portion of the contiguous forty-eight states. This portion of the United States is also referred to as New England. The name Massachusetts was taken from the name of an Indian tribe which had lived in the region before European settlers arrived. The name is believed to mean "at the Great Hills." Massachusetts is called the Bay State – appropriate because in addition to the Massachusetts Bay there are also Plymouth Bay Cape Cod Bay and Buzzards Bay.

Historically, Massachusetts was covered by glaciers. Glaciation is responsible for:
- Smoothing the topographical features of the state
- Incorporating thin and acidic rocks into the soil
- Creating aquifers
- Altering the course of rivers

Massachusetts is a relatively small state of only about 8500 square miles. As a point of comparison, it is roughly about the same size as the country of Israel. Massachusetts may be quite small, but it has a large variety of physical landscape features. In very general terms there are ten geographical defined areas of Massachusetts. These are:
- Cape and Islands
- Boston Basin
- Coastal Plains and Hills
- Worcester Uplands
- Hill Towns Transition Zone
- Taconic Mountains
- Housatonic or Marble Valleys
- Berkshires
- Connecticut Valley
- Bristol Lowland

The eastern section is low and level, with a gradual rise toward the west and northwest. The eastern portion of the state provides a north-south flow of water flow. The rivers of Massachusetts are small and can be utilized for some limited power, but are not appropriate for transportation uses. The coastal waters provide access to rich fishing opportunities as well as being accessible for importing and exporting goods.

The rest of the state can be divided into three main surface regions. Just west of the eastern sandy lowland is a plateau about 1,100 feet in height. Then the Connecticut Valley from which hills rise up to 1200 feet. The valley is broad and fertile. In the extreme west is the Berkshire country, with the Berkshire Hills running north to south. These hills are extensions of the Green Mountains of Vermont.

Massachusetts offers an average growing season of between one hundred thirty and two hundred and twenty days, with a relatively even amount of precipitation throughout the year. Most of this precipitation comes from storms which develop in the west and travel east.

Skill 6.6   Basic economic and political concepts (e.g., representative government, popular sovereignty, supply and demand, market economy)

Economics is the study of how a society allocates its scarce resources to satisfy what are basically unlimited and competing wants. A fundamental fact of economics is that resources are scarce and that wants are infinite. The fact that scarce resources have to satisfy unlimited wants means that choices have to be made. If society uses its resources to produce good A then it doesn't have those resources to produce good B. More of good A means less of good B. This trade-off is referred to as the opportunity cost, or the value of the sacrificed alternative.

Economic systems refer to the arrangements a society has devised to answer what are known as the Three Questions: What goods to produce, How to produce the goods, and For Whom are the goods being produced, or how is the allocation of the output determined. Different economic systems answer these questions in different ways. These are the different "isms" that exist that define the method of resource and output allocation.

A **market economy** answers these questions in terms of demand and supply and the use of markets. **Demand** is based on consumer preferences and satisfaction and refers to the quantities of a good or service that buyers are willing and able to buy at different prices during a given period of time. **Supply** is based on costs of production and refers to the quantities that sellers are willing and able to sell at different prices during a given period of time. The determination of market equilibrium price is where the buying decisions of buyers coincide with the selling decision of sellers

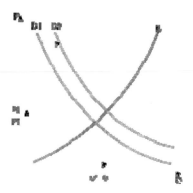

Consumers vote for the products they want with their dollar spending. Goods acquiring enough dollar votes are profitable, signaling to the producers that society wants their scarce resources used in this way. This is how the "What" question is answered. The producer then hires inputs in accordance with the goods consumers want, looking for the most efficient or lowest cost method of production. The lower the firm's costs for any given level of revenue, the higher the firm's profits. This is the way in which the "How" question is answered in a market economy. The "For Whom" question is answered in the marketplace by the determination of the equilibrium price. Price serves to ration the good to those who can and will transact at the market price of better. Those who can't or won't are excluded from the market. This mechanism results in market efficiency or obtaining the most output from the available inputs that are consistent with the preferences of consumers. Society's scarce resources are being used the way society wants them to be used.

Popular sovereignty grants citizens the ability to directly participate in their own government by voting and running for public office. This ideal is based on a belief of equality that holds that all citizens have an equal right to engage in their own governance, and is established in the United States Constitution. The Constitution also contains a list of specific rights that citizens have, and which the government cannot infringe upon. Popular sovereignty also allows for citizens to change their government if they feel it is necessary. This was the driving ideal behind the Declaration of Independence and is embodied in the governmental structure laid out in the Constitution.

The **rule of law** is the ideal that the law applies not only to the governed, but to the government as well. This core value gives authority to the justice system, which grants citizens protection from the government by requiring that any accusation of a crime be proved by the government before a person is punished. This is called due process and ensures that any accused person will have an opportunity to confront his accusers and provide a defense. Due process follows from the core value of a right to liberty. The government cannot take away a citizen's liberty without reason or without proof. The correlating ideal is also a core value - that someone who does harm another or break a law will receive justice under the democratic system. The ideal of justice holds that a punishment will fit the crime, and that any citizen can appeal to the judicial system if he feels he has been wronged.

Citizens' duties also vary from nation to nation. Duties demanded by law (also considered civic responsibilities) include paying taxes, obeying laws, and defending the country. Although some governments require jury duty, in the United States this would be a duty not required by law along with voting, doing volunteer work to help others, and becoming aware of public problems.

Citizenship is granted one of two ways: either by birth or by naturalization. Some Americans hold dual citizenship.

Skill 6.7   Purposes of government, and the functions of federal, state, and local government in the United States

Purposes of Government

The American nation was founded upon the idea that people would have a large degree of liberty, and autonomy. The famous maxim, "no taxation without representation," was a rallying cry for the Revolution. Although the colonists strained under the increasingly oppressive taxes British taxes, they principally objected to their lack of say in the matter. No American colonist had a seat in Parliament , and no American colonist could vote for members of Parliament.

One of the most famous words in the Declaration of Independence is "liberty," the pursuit of which all people should be free to attempt. That idea, that a people should be free to pursue their own course, even to the extent of making their own mistakes, has dominated political thought in the 200-plus years of the American republic.

Representation, the idea that a people can vote—or even replace—their lawmakers was a new idea in the British colonies. What the Sons of Liberty and other revolutionaries were asking for was to stand on an equal footing with the

Mother Country. Along with the idea or representation comes the idea that key ideas and concepts can be deliberated and discussed, with theoretically everyone having a chance to voice their views. This applied to both lawmakers and the people who elected them. Lawmakers wouldn't just pass bills that became laws; rather, they would debate the particulars and go back and forth on the strengths and weaknesses of proposed laws before voting on them. Members of both houses of Congress had the opportunity to speak out on the issues, as did the people at large, who could contact their lawmakers and express their views. This idea ran very much counter to the experience that the Founding Fathers had before the Revolution—that of taxation without representation. The different branches of government were designed to serve as a mechanism of checks and balances on each other so that no one branch could become too powerful. They would each have their own specific powers.

Another key concept in the American ideal is **equality**, the idea that every person shares the same rights and responsibilities as every other, under the law. Great Britain, as American colonists had come to know it, was a stratified society, with social classes firmly in place. Not everyone was equal under the law or in the coffers: it was clear to see that the that money meant entitlement; one could avoid inscription of buy ones way out of a crime. The goal of American's Declaration of Independence and her Constitution was to provide equality for all who read these documents. The reality, though, was vastly different for large sectors of society, including women and non-white Americans.

Due process under the law was also a big concern of the founders. Various amendments protect the rights of people. Amendments five through eight protect citizens who are accused of crimes and are brought to trial. Every citizen has the right to due process of law, (due process as defined earlier, and being that the government must follow the same fair rules for everyone brought to trial.) These rules include the right to a trial by an impartial jury, the right to be defended by a lawyer, and the right to a speedy trial. The last two amendments limit the powers of the federal government to those that are expressly granted in the Constitution, any rights not expressly mentioned in the Constitution, thus, belong to the states or to the people.

This feeds into the idea of basic opportunity. The so-called "American Dream" is that every individual has an equal change to make his or her fortune in the new land, and that the United States will welcome, and even encourage. initiative. The system is based on individual freedom of choice. The history of the country is filled with stories of people who ventured to America and made their fortunes in the Land of Opportunity. Unfortunately for anyone who wasn't a white male, that basic opportunity was sometimes a difficult thing to achieve.

The American Government

The American governmental system is a **federal system**—fifty individual states federated or forming or uniting as one nation. The national and state governments share the powers of government. This federal system required decentralization, which makes it impossible to coexist with totalitarianism. Both national and state governments exist and govern by the will of the people who are the source of their authority. Local governmental systems operate under the same guidelines.

The American political system is a **two-party system**, consisting of the Democratic and Republican parties. Political parties in America have approximately five major functions: (1) Choose candidates who will run for public office; (2) assist in organizing the government; (3) formulate political platforms and policies; (4) obtain the funds needed to conduct election campaigns; and (5) take the initiative to make sure voters are aware of issues, problems to be solved, and any other information about public affairs. The two-party system in America operates at the national, state, and local levels.

At the United States Federal level:

Legislative – Article I of the Constitution established the legislative or law-making branch of the government called the Congress. It is made up of two houses, the House of Representatives and the Senate. Voters in all states elect the members who serve in each respective House of Congress. The Legislative branch is responsible for making laws, raising and printing money, regulating trade, establishing the postal service and federal courts, approving the President's appointments, declaring war and supporting the armed forces. The Congress also has the power to change the Constitution itself, and to *impeach* (bring charges against) the President. Charges for impeachment are brought by the House of Representatives, and are then tried in the Senate.

Executive – Article II of the Constitution created the Executive branch of the government, headed by the President, who leads the country, recommends new laws, and can veto bills passed by the Legislative branch. As the chief of state, the President is responsible for carrying out the laws of the country and the treaties and declarations of war passed by the Legislative branch. The President also appoints federal judges and is commander-in-chief of the military when it is called into service. Other members of the Executive branch include the Vice-President, also elected, and various cabinet members as he might appoint: ambassadors, presidential advisors, members of the armed forces, and other appointed and civil servants of government agencies, departments and bureaus. Though the President appoints them, the Legislative branch must approve them.

Judicial – Article III of the Constitution established the Judicial branch of government headed by the Supreme Court. The Supreme Court has the power to rule that a law passed by the legislature, or an act of the Executive branch is illegal and unconstitutional. Citizens, businesses, and government officials can in an appeal capacity, ask the Supreme Court to review a decision made in a lower court if someone believes that the ruling by a judge is unconstitutional. The Judicial branch also includes lower federal courts known as federal district courts that have been established by the Congress. These courts try lawbreakers and review cases referred from other courts.

Powers delegated to the federal government:	Powers reserved to the states:
1. To tax.	1. To regulate intrastate trade.
2. To borrow and coin money	2. To establish local governments.
3. To establish postal service.	3. To protect general welfare.
4. To grant patents and copyrights.	4. To protect life and property.
5. To regulate interstate & foreign commerce.	5. To ratify amendments.
6. To establish courts.	6. To conduct elections.
7. To declare war.	7. To make state and local laws.
8. To raise and support the armed forces.	
9. To govern territories.	
10. To define and punish felonies and piracy on the high seas.	
11. To fix standards of weights and measures.	
12. To conduct foreign affairs.	

Concurrent powers of the federal government and states.
1. Both Congress and the states may tax.
2. Both may borrow money.
3. Both may charter banks and corporations.
4. Both may establish courts.
5. Both may make and enforce laws.
6. Both may take property for public purposes.
7. Both may spend money to provide for the public welfare.

Implied powers of the federal government.

1. To establish banks or other corporations implied from delegated powers to tax, borrow, and to regulate commerce.
2. To spend money for roads, schools, health, insurance, etc. implied from powers, to establish post roads, to tax to provide for general welfare and defense, and to regulate commerce.
3. To create military academies, implied from powers to raise and support an armed force.
4. To locate and generate sources of power and sell surplus implied from powers to dispose of government property, commerce, and war powers.
5. To assist and regulate agriculture implied from power to tax and spend for general welfare and regulate commerce.

State governments are mirror images of the federal government, with a few important exceptions: Governors are not technically commanders in chief of armed forces; state supreme court decisions can be appealed to federal courts; terms of state representatives and senators vary; judges, even of the state supreme courts, are elected by popular vote; governors and legislators have term limits that vary by state.

Local governments vary widely across the country. Some local governments consist of a city council, of which the mayor is a member and has limited powers; in other cities, the mayor is the head of the government and the city council are the chief lawmakers. Local governments also have less strict requirements for people running for office than do the state and federal governments.

Skill 6.8   How laws are enacted and enforced

Federal laws are passed by the Congress, and can originate in either the House of Representatives or the Senate. The first step in the passing of a law is for the proposed law to be introduced in one of the houses of Congress. A proposed law is called a **bill** while it is under consideration by Congress. A bill can be introduced, or sponsored, by a member of Congress by giving a copy to the clerk or by placing a copy in a special box called a hopper.

Once a bill is introduced, copies are printed and it is assigned to one of several standing committees of the house in which it was introduced. The committee studies the bill and performs research on the issues it would cover. Committees may call experts to testify on the bill and gather public comments. The committee may revise the bill. Finally, the committee votes on whether to release the bill to be voted on by the full body. A committee may also lay aside a bill so that it cannot be voted on. Once a bill is released, it can be debated and amended by the full body before being voted on. If it passes by a simple majority vote, the bill is sent to the other house of Congress, where the process begins again.

Once a bill has passed both the House of Representatives and the Senate, it is assigned to a conference committee that is made up of members of both houses. The conference committee resolves differences between the House and Senate versions of a bill, if any, and then sends it back to both houses for final approval. Once a bill receives final approval, it is signed by the Speaker of the House and the Vice President, who is also the President of the Senate, and sent to the President for consideration. The President may either sign the bill or **veto** it. If he vetoes the bill, his veto may be overruled if two-thirds of both the Senate and the House vote to do so. Once the President signs it the bill becomes a law.

Federal laws are enforced by the executive branch and its departments. The Department of Justice, led by the United States Attorney General is the primary law enforcement department of the federal government. The Justice Department is aided by other investigative and enforcement departments such as the Federal Bureau of Investigation (FBI) and the U.S. Postal Inspectors.

The U.S. Constitution and Congressional laws provide basic as well as additional rights to American citizens. These civil rights include freedom of religion, assembly, speech, voting, holding public office, and traveling throughout the country. U.S. citizens have the right to live in America and cannot be forced to leave. American citizenship is guaranteed and will not be taken away for any reason, unless one commits certain serious actions. Civil rights have limitations such as minimum age for voting and limited free speech, forbidding the damage to someone's reputation by slander and lying.

Skill 6.9 **Democratic principles and values contained in the Declaration of Independence, the U.S. Constitution, and the Constitution of the Commonwealth of Massachusetts (e.g., the rule of law, due process, equal protection of the laws, majority rule, protection of minority rights)**

The Commonwealth of Massachusetts is governed under a constitution which dates from 1780. It provides for an executive branch including a Governor and Lieutenant Governor, who are elected to four year terms. The governor is assisted by a council of 8 members. There is a legislative branch made up of two houses, a senate of forty members and a house of representatives of 240 members. The judiciary is made up of a supreme judicial court, a superior court, district and municipal courts and land courts.

Each county has its own probate court. All judges are appointed by the governor, with the approval of the council. The unit of local government is the **township**, or the town. This form of government originated in Massachusetts. Selectmen, elected at the town meetings, are at the head of affairs in towns. Limited town-meeting governments may be established in towns of 6,000 or more. Although only members of the limited town meeting have a vote, all citizens of the town may speak on any subject before the meeting. City governments may be established in towns of 12,000 or more. Yet many of the larger towns has chosen to retain the township form of government.

The Declaration of Independence was the founding document of the United States of America. The Articles of Confederation were the first attempt of the newly independent states to reach a new understanding amongst their selves. The Declaration was intended to demonstrate the reasons the colonies were seeking separation from Great Britain. Conceived by and written for the most part by **Thomas Jefferson,** it is not only important for what it says, but also for how it says it. The Declaration is in many respects a poetic document. Instead of a simple recitation of the colonists' grievances, it set out clearly the reasons why the colonists were seeking their freedom from Great Britain. They had tried all means to resolve the dispute peacefully. It was the right of a people, when all other methods of addressing their grievances have been tried and failed, to separate themselves from that power that was keeping them from fully expressing their rights to **"life, liberty, and the pursuit of happiness"**.

A convention met under the presidency of George Washington, with fifty-five of the sixty-five appointed members present. A constitution was written in four months. The Constitution of the United States is the fundamental law of the republic. It is a precise, formal, written document of the *extraordinary*, or *supreme*, type of constitution. The founders of the Union established it as the highest governmental authority. There is no national power superior to it. The foundations were so broadly laid as to provide for the expansion of national life and to make it an instrument which would last for all time.

To maintain its stability, the framers created a difficult process for making any changes to it. No amendment can become valid until it is ratified by three-fourths of all of the states. The British system of government was part of the basis of the final document. But significant changes were necessary to meet the needs of a partnership of states that were tied together as a single federation, yet sovereign in their own local affairs. This constitution established a system of government that was unique and advanced far beyond other systems of its day.

The constitution binds the states in a governmental unity in everything that affects the welfare of all. At the same time, it recognizes the right of the people of each state to independence of action in matters that relate only to them. Since the Federal Constitution is the law of the land, all other laws must conform to it.

The debates conducted during the Constitutional Congress represent the issues and the arguments that led to the compromises in the final document. The debates also reflect the concerns of the Founding Fathers that the rights of the people be protected from abrogation by the government itself and the determination that no branch of government should have enough power to continually dominate the others. There is a **system of checks and balances.**

Bill Of Rights - The first ten amendments to the United States Constitution dealing with civil liberties and civil rights. James Madison was credited with writing a majority of them. They are in brief:

1. Freedom of Religion.
2. Right To Bear Arms.
3. Security from the quartering of troops in homes.
4. Right against unreasonable search and seizures.
5. Right against self-incrimination.
6. Right to trial by jury, right to legal council.
7. Right to jury trial for civil actions.
8. No cruel or unusual punishment allowed.
9. These rights shall not deny other rights the people enjoy.
10. Powers not mentioned in the Constitution shall be retained by the states or the people.

The rule of law is the ideal that the law applies not only to the governed, but to the government as well. This core value gives authority to the justice system, which grants citizens protection from the government by requiring that any accusation of a crime be proved by the government before a person is punished. This is called **due process** and ensures that any accused person will have an opportunity to confront his accusers and provide a defense.

Due process follows from the core value of a right to liberty. The government cannot take away a citizen's liberty without reason or without proof. The correlating ideal is also a core value - that someone who does harm another or break a law will receive **justice** under the democratic system. The ideal of justice holds that a punishment will fit the crime, and that any citizen can appeal to the judicial system if he feels he has been wronged.

Skill 6.10   The responsibilities of U.S. Citizens (e.g., respecting others' rights, obeying laws and rules, paying taxes, jury duty, voting)

Massachusetts residents have a host of rights and responsibilities as part of their contract with the state. The state constitution protects residents from harm, from unfair government and from violence from outside sources. The state government protects rights to a legal job at a fair wage as well.

Massachusetts residents are expected to obey state, local, and national laws and to pay their taxes and vote in elections at all three levels of government. Voting is an approach to decision-making that permits each entitled individual to express a view or opinion on a matter or a person seeking political leadership office. It is generally considered a hallmark of democratic government. They are expected to represent the state well when they travel outside its borders. Additionally the legal system requires citizens to be available to serve on juries as necessary.

Respect is an attitude toward other people or groups that recognizes and values feelings, interests and beliefs, without necessarily agreeing with them. The idea of the rights of individuals and groups is a socially normalized outgrowth of respect.

Obedience is essentially submissive compliance with the orders or instructions, laws or rules of others. Obedience generally involves some recognition of social or legal dominance and submission. It is thus unlike "compliance" which is generally influenced by one's peers, and unlike "conformity" which is generally a willingness to match the behavior of the majority. Obedience includes obedience to social norms, laws, government, political organizations, religion, church or synagogue, God, self-imposed constraints, philosophical ethical codes, etc.

Dissent is a belief or opinion in opposition to an accepted ideology or to those who hold particular beliefs, powers, or policies. Dissent may be expressed in a number of ways, some of which are socially and politically acceptable while others are not.

Competency 0007   **Understand principles and concepts of science and technology/engineering**

Skill 7.1   **Foundations of scientific thought (e.g., reliance on verifiable evidence, reasoning, and logical arguments, avoidance of bias)**

Observations, however general they may seem, lead scientists to create a viable question and an educated guess (hypothesis) about what to expect. It is always important to be open-minded and to look at all of the information. An open-minded approach to science provides room for more questioning, and, hence, more learning. A central concept in science is that all evidence is empirical. This means that all evidence must be is observed by the five senses. The phenomenon must be both observable and measurable, with reproducible results.

The question stage of scientific inquiry involves repetition. By repeating the experiment you can discover whether or not you have reproducibility. If results are reproducible, the hypothesis is valid. If the results are not reproducible, one has more questions to ask. It is also important to recognize that one experiment is often a stepping-stone for another. It is possible that data will be re-tested (by the same scientist or by another), and that a different conclusion may be found. In this way, scientific competition acts as a system of checks and balances.

Scientific research can be biased in the choice of what data to consider, in the reporting or recording of the data, and/or in how the data are interpreted. The scientist's emphasis may be influenced by his/her nationality, sex, ethnic origin, age, or political convictions. For example, when studying a group of animals, male scientists may focus on the social behavior of the males and typically male characteristics.

Although bias related to the investigator, the sample, the method, or the instrument may not be completely avoidable in every case, it is important to know the possible sources of bias and how bias could affect the evidence. Moreover, scientists need to be attentive to possible bias in their own work as well as that of other scientists.

Objectivity may not always be attained. However, one precaution that may be taken to guard against undetected bias is to have many different investigators or groups of investigators working on a project. By different, it is meant that the groups are made up of various nationalities, ethnic origins, ages, and political convictions and composed of both males and females. It is also important to note one's aspirations, and to make sure to be truthful to the data, even when grants, promotions, and notoriety are at risk.

SEE also Skill 7.7

Skill 7.2   Major scientific discoveries and technological innovations

Anton van Leeuwenhoek is known as the father of microscopy. In the 1650s, Leeuwenhoek began making tiny lenses that yielded magnifications up to 300x. He was the first to see and describe bacteria, yeast plants, and the microscopic life found in water. Over the years, light microscopes have advanced to produce greater clarity and magnification. The scanning electron microscope (SEM) was developed in the 1950s. Instead of light, a beam of electrons passes through the specimen. Scanning electron microscopes have a resolution about one thousand times greater than light microscopes. The disadvantage of the SEM is that the chemical and physical methods used to prepare the sample result in the death of the specimen.

Carl Von Linnaeus (1707-1778), a Swedish botanist, physician and zoologist is well known for his contributions in ecology and taxonomy. Linnaeus is famous for his binomial system of nomenclature in which each living organism has two names, a genus and a species name. He is considered as the father of modern ecology and taxonomy.

In the late 1800s, Pasteur discovered the role of microorganisms in the cause of disease, pasteurization, and the rabies vaccine. Koch took this observations one step further by formulating that specific diseases were caused by specific pathogens. **Koch's postulates** are still used as guidelines in the field of microbiology: the same pathogen must be found in every diseased person, that pathogen must be isolated and grown in culture, the disease is induced in experimental animals from the culture, and the same pathogen must be isolated from the experimental animal.

In the 18th century, many fields of science like botany, zoology and geology began to evolve as scientific disciplines in the modern sense.

In the 20th century, the rediscovery of Mendel's work led to the rapid development of genetics by Thomas Hunt Morgan and his students.

DNA structure was another key event in biological study. In the 1950s, James Watson and Francis Crick discovered the structure of a DNA molecule as that of a double helix. This structure made it possible to explain DNA's ability to replicate and to control the synthesis of proteins.

The use of animals in biological research has expedited many scientific discoveries. Animal research has allowed scientists to learn more about animal biological systems, including the circulatory and reproductive systems. One significant use of animals is for the testing of drugs, vaccines, and other products (such as perfumes and shampoos) before use or consumption by humans. Along with the pros of animal research, the cons are also very significant. The debate about the ethical treatment of animals has been ongoing since the introduction of animals in research. Many people believe the use of animals in research is cruel and unnecessary. Animal use is federally and locally regulated. The purpose of the Institutional Animal Care and Use Committee (IACUC) is to oversee and evaluate all aspects of an institution's animal care and use program.

DNA sequencing has aroused lot of interest among the science community during the last century. Nucleic acid research is both exciting and challenging. PCR (Polymerase Chain Reaction) is a molecular biological technique for enzymatically replicating DNA without using a living organism (such as E.coli or yeast). A small amount of DNA is amplified exponentially and this technique is widely used in experiments involving gene manipulations. The PCR technique is used in paternity testing and DNA fingerprinting.

Genetic manipulation has been intensely studied since the 1970's. Scientists have aided humans through the use of medical gene therapy, the creation of healthy, disease resistant crops, and most recently reproductive cloning. Before extensive application in humans, the cloning technology was attempted with animals. To date, many have been produced, and some have gone on to reproduce successfully without intervention.

The goal of the human genome project is to map and sequence the three billion nucleotides in the human genome, and to identify all of the genes on it. The project was launched in 1986 and an outline of the genome was finished in 2000 through international collaboration. In May 2006, the sequence of the last chromosome was published. While the map and sequencing are complete, scientists are still studying the functions of all the genes and their regulation. Humans have successfully decoded the genome of other mammals as well.

Skill 7.3 The relationship between science and technology

The combination of biology and technology has improved the human standard of living in many ways. However, the negative impact of increasing human life expectancy and population on the environment is problematic. In addition, advances in biotechnology (e.g. genetic engineering, cloning) produce ethical dilemmas that society must consider.

Science attempts to investigate and explain the natural world, while technology attempts to solve human adaptation problems. Technology often results from the application of scientific discoveries, and advances in technology can increase the impact of scientific discoveries. For example, Watson and Crick used science to discover the structure of DNA and their discovery led to many biotechnological advances in the manipulation of DNA. These technological advances greatly influenced the medical and pharmaceutical fields. The success of Watson and Crick's experiments, however, was dependent on the technology available. Without the necessary technology, the experiments would have failed.

SEE also Skill 7.6

Skill 7.4   Basic concepts and principles of life science (e.g., as related to cells, the human body, heredity, ecosystems)

All organisms are adapted to life in their unique habitat. The habitat includes all the components of their physical environment and is a necessity for the species' survival. Below are several key components of a complete habitat that all organisms require.

Food and Water

Because all biochemical reactions take place in aqueous environments, all organisms must have access to clean water, even if only infrequently. Organisms also require two types of food: a source of energy (fixed carbon) and a source of nutrients. Autotrophs can fix carbon for themselves, but must have access to certain inorganic precursors. These organisms must also be able to obtain other nutrients, such as nitrogen, from their environment. Heterotrophs, on the other hand, must consume other organisms for both energy and nutrients. The species these organisms use as a food source must be present in their habitat.

Sunlight and Air

This need is closely related to that for food and water because almost all species derive some needed nutrients from the sun and atmosphere. Plants require carbon dioxide to photosynthesize and oxygen is required for cellular respiration. Sunlight is also necessary for photosynthesis and is used by many animals to synthesize essential nutrients (i.e. vitamin D).

Shelter and Space

The need for shelter and space vary greatly between species. Many plants do not need shelter, per se, but must have adequate soil to spread their roots and acquire nutrients. Certain invasive species can threaten native plants by out-competing them for space. Other types of plants and many animals also require protection from environmental hazards. These locations may facilitate reproduction (for instance, nesting sites) or provide seasonal shelter (for examples, dens and caves used by hibernating species).

Cells

Life is highly organized. The organization of living systems builds on levels from small to increasingly more large and complex. All aspects, whether it is a cell or an ecosystem, have the same requirements to sustain life. Life is organized from simple to complex in the following way:

Atoms→molecules→organelles→cells→tissues→organs→organ systems→organism

The cell is the basic unit of all living things. There are three types of cells. They are prokaryotes, eukaryotes, and archaea. Archaea have some similarities with prokaryotes, but are as distantly related to prokaryotes as prokaryotes are to eukaryotes.

Prokaryotes consist only of bacteria and cyanobacteria (formerly known as blue-green algae). These cells have no defined nucleus or nuclear membrane. The DNA, RNA, and ribosomes float freely within the cell. The cytoplasm has a single chromosome condensed to form a **nucleoid**. Prokaryotes have a thick cell wall made up of amino sugars (glycoproteins). This is for protection, to give the cell shape, and to keep the cell from bursting. Prokaryotes are the most numerous and widespread organisms on earth. Bacteria were most likely the first cells and date back in the fossil record to 3.5 billion years ago. Their ability to adapt to the environment allows them to thrive in a wide variety of habitats.

Eukaryotic cells are found in protists, fungi, plants, and animals. Most eukaryotic cells are larger than prokaryotic cells. They contain many organelles, which are membrane bound areas for specific functions. Their cytoplasm contains a cytoskeleton which provides a protein framework for the cell. The cytoplasm also supports the organelles and contains the ions and molecules necessary for cell function. The cytoplasm is contained by the plasma membrane. The plasma membrane allows molecules to pass in and out of the cell. The most significant differentiation between prokaryotes and eukaryotes is that eukaryotes have a **nucleus**. The nucleus is the brain of the cell that contains all of the cell's genetic information.

The following diagram is of a generalized animal cell.

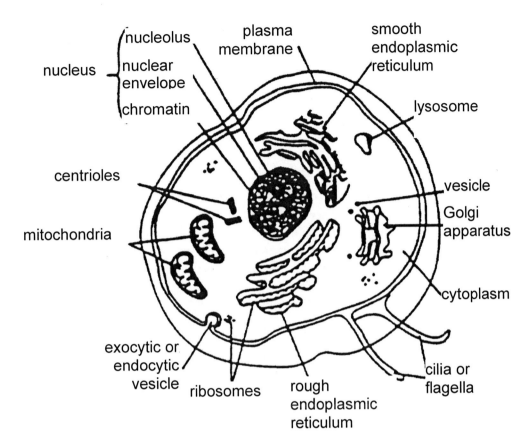

Archaea: There are three kinds of organisms with archaea cells: **methanogens** are obligate anaerobes that produce methane, **halobacteria** can live only in concentrated brine solutions, and **thermoacidophiles** can only live in acidic hot springs.

The Human Body

All of the major body systems work in a complementary way to promote well being. There is a continuation within the body, with each system being interconnected. The function of the cardiovascular system is to carry oxygenated blood and nutrients to all cells of the body and return carbon dioxide waste to be expelled from the lungs. Through breathing, the lungs function to bind oxygen to hemoglobin. Oxygen is then carried via the circulatory system and is delivered to muscles, which rely on oxygen to contract. The circulatory system also functions by removing carbon dioxide waste. The digestive and excretory systems are also linked. The function of the digestive system is to break food down into nutrients and absorb it into the blood stream where it can be delivered to all cells of the body for use in cellular respiration. Byproducts from digestion are excreted from the body, and excess water is filtered and reused by the body.

The human nervous system is responsible for relaying messages between the brain and body. It is comprised of two distinct parts, the CNS and PNS. The **central nervous system (CNS)** consists of the brain and spinal cord. The CNS is responsible for the body's response to environmental stimulation. The spinal cord is located inside the spine. It sends out motor commands for movement in response to stimuli. The brain is where responses to more complex stimuli occurs. The meninges are the connective tissues that protect the CNS. The CNS contains fluid filled spaces called ventricles. These ventricles are filled when cerebrospinal fluid which is formed in the brain. This fluid cushions the brain and circulates nutrients, white blood cells, and hormones. The CNS's response to stimuli is a reflex. The reflex is an unconscious, automatic response.

The **peripheral nervous system (PNS)** consists of the nerves that connect the CNS to the rest of the body. The sensory division brings information to the CNS from sensory receptors and the motor division sends signals from the CNS to effector cells. The motor division consists of somatic nervous system and the autonomic nervous system. The somatic nervous system is controlled consciously in response to external stimuli. The autonomic nervous system is unconsciously controlled by the hypothalamus of the brain to regulate the internal environment. This system is responsible for the movement of smooth and cardiac muscles as well as the muscles for other organ systems.

The molecular composition of the immediate environment outside of the organism is not the same as it is inside, and the temperature outside may not be optimal for metabolic activity within the organism. **Homeostasis** is the control of these differences between internal and external environments.

The muscular system's function is for movement. There are three types of muscle tissue. **Skeletal muscle** is voluntary. These muscles are attached to bones and are responsible for their movement. Skeletal muscle consists of long fibers and is striated due to the repeating patterns of the myofilaments (made of the proteins actin and myosin) that make up the fibers.

Cardiac muscle is found in the heart. Cardiac muscle is striated like skeletal muscle, but differs in that plasma membrane of the cardiac muscle causes the muscle to beat even when away from the heart. The action potentials of cardiac and skeletal muscles also differ.

Smooth muscle is involuntary. It is found in organs and enable functions such as digestion and respiration. Unlike skeletal and cardiac muscle, smooth muscle is not striated. Smooth muscle has less myosin and does not generate as much tension as the striated muscles.

The **skin** consists of two distinct layers. The epidermis is the thinner outer layer and the dermis is the thicker inner layer. Layers of tightly packed epithelial cells make up the epidermis. The tight packaging of the epithelial cells supports the skin's function as a protective barrier against infection.

The **immune system** is responsible for defending the body against foreign invaders. The first line of defense is the physical barriers of the body. These include the skin and mucous membranes. The skin prevents the penetration of bacteria and viruses as long as there are no abrasions on the skin. Mucous membranes form a protective barrier around the digestive, respiratory, and genitourinary tracts. Also, the pH of the skin and mucous membranes inhibit the growth of many microbes. Mucous secretions (tears and saliva) wash away many microbes and contain lysozymes that kill many microbes.

The second line of defense includes white blood cells and the inflammatory response. **Phagocytosis** is the ingestion of foreign particles. An alternate second line of defense is the inflammatory response. The blood supply to the injured area is increased, causing redness and heat. Swelling also typically occurs with inflammation.

The **specific** immune mechanism recognizes specific foreign material and responds by destroying the invader. These mechanisms are specific and diverse. They are able to recognize individual pathogens. An **antigen** is any foreign particle that elicits an immune response. An **antibody** is manufactured by the body and recognizes and latches onto antigens, hopefully destroying them. They also have recognition of foreign material versus the self. Memory of the invaders provides immunity upon further exposure.

Genetics

A chromosome is, in its basic state, a long strand of DNA located in the nucleus of every cell. DNA is wound tightly around proteins in order to conserve space. The DNA/protein combination makes up the chromosome. DNA controls the synthesis of proteins, thereby controlling the total cell activity. DNA is capable of making copies of itself. Chromosomes are the blueprint of their host organism. Each species has a defined number of chromosomes, with a haploid number in non-sex cells and a diploid number (or twice as many) in sex cells (gametes). The significance of haploid and diploid will be discussed elsewhere in this text.

Each chromosome contains a very large number of genes, with alleles, or two different versions, of the same gene. These variants of the same gene help to explain Mendel's observations of phenotype; when recombined the alternative genes introduce the different genotypes that are possible through reproduction.

Meiosis and fertilization are responsible for genetic diversity. There are several mechanisms that contribute to genetic variation in sexual reproductive organisms. Three of them are independent assortment of chromosomes, crossing over, and random fertilization.

Gregor Mendel is recognized as the father of genetics. His work in the late 1800s is the basis of our knowledge of genetics. Although unaware of the presence of DNA or genes, Mendel realized there were factors (now known as **genes**) that were transferred from parents to their offspring. Mendel worked with pea plants and fertilized the plants himself, keeping track of subsequent generations which led to the Mendelian laws of genetics. Mendel found that two "factors" governed each trait, one from each parent. Traits or characteristics came in several forms, known as **alleles**. For example, the trait of flower color had white alleles (*pp*) and purple alleles (*PP*). Mendel formed two laws: the law of segregation and the law of independent assortment.

The **law of segregation** states that only one of the two possible alleles from each parent is passed on to the offspring. If the two alleles differ, then one is fully expressed in the organism's appearance (the dominant allele) and the other has no noticeable effect on appearance (the recessive allele). The two alleles for each trait segregate into different gametes. A Punnet square can be used to show the law of segregation. In a Punnet square, one parent's genes are put at the top of the box and the other parent's on the side. Genes combine in the squares just like numbers are added in addition tables. This Punnet square shows the result of the cross of two F_1 hybrids.

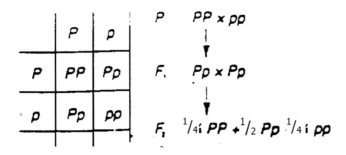

This cross results in a 1:2:1 ratio of F_2 offspring. Here, the *P* is the dominant allele and the *p* is the recessive allele. The F_1 cross produces three offspring with the dominant allele expressed (two *PP* and *Pp*) and one offspring with the recessive allele expressed (*pp*).

Ecology

Trophic levels are based on the feeding relationships that determine energy flow and chemical cycling.

Autotrophs are the primary producers of the ecosystem. **Producers** mainly consist of plants. **Primary consumers** are the next trophic level. The primary consumers are the herbivores that eat plants or algae. **Secondary consumers** are the carnivores that eat the primary consumers. **Tertiary consumers** eat the secondary consumer. These trophic levels may go higher depending on the ecosystem. **Decomposers** are consumers that feed off animal waste and dead organisms. This pathway of food transfer is known as the food chain.

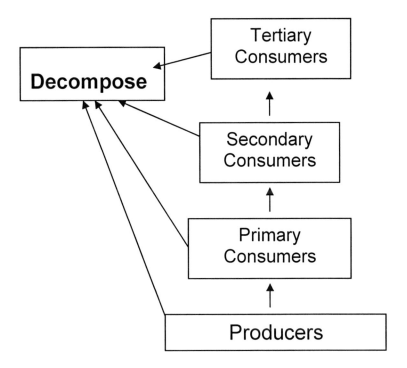

Skill 7.5 **Basic concepts and principles of the physical and Earth sciences (e.g., as related to matter and energy, the motion of objects, the forces that shape the Earth, the water cycle, the atmosphere and weather, the solar system)**

Everything in our world is made up of **matter**, whether it is a rock, a building, an animal, or a person. Matter is defined by its characteristics: It takes up space and it has mass.

Mass is a measure of the amount of matter in an object. Two objects of equal mass will balance each other on a simple balance scale no matter where the scale is located. For instance, two rocks with the same amount of mass that are in balance on earth will also be in balance on the moon. They will feel heavier on earth than on the moon because of the gravitational pull of the earth. So, although the two rocks have the same mass, they will have different **weight.**

Weight is the measure of the earth's pull of gravity on an object. It can also be defined as the pull of gravity between other bodies. The units of weight measurement commonly used are the pound (English measure) and the kilogram (metric measure).

In addition to mass, matter also has the property of volume. **Volume** is the amount of cubic space that an object occupies. Volume and mass together give a more exact description of the object. Two objects may have the same volume, but different mass, or the same mass but different volumes, etc. For instance, consider two cubes that are each one cubic centimeter, one made from plastic, one from lead. They have the same volume, but the lead cube has more mass. The measure that we use to describe the cubes takes into consideration both the mass and the volume. **Density** is the mass of a substance contained per unit of volume. If the density of an object is less than the density of a liquid, the object will float in the liquid. If the object is denser than the liquid, then the object will sink.

Physical properties and chemical properties of matter describe the appearance or behavior of a substance. A **physical property** can be observed without changing the identity of a substance. For instance, you can describe the color, mass, shape, and volume of a book. **Chemical properties** describe the ability of a substance to be changed into new substances. Baking powder goes through a chemical change as it changes into carbon dioxide gas during the baking process.

Matter constantly changes. A **physical change** is a change that does not produce a new substance. The freezing and melting of water is an example of physical change. A **chemical change** (or chemical reaction) is any change of a substance into one or more other substances. Burning materials turn into smoke; a seltzer tablet fizzes into gas bubbles.

The **phase of matter** (solid, liquid, or gas) is identified by its shape and volume. A **solid** has a definite shape and volume. A **liquid** has a definite volume, but no shape. A **gas** has no shape or volume because it will spread out to occupy the entire space of whatever container it is in.

Energy is the ability to cause change in matter. Applying heat to a frozen liquid changes it from solid back to liquid. Continue heating it and it will boil and give off steam, a gas. **Evaporation** is the change in phase from liquid to gas. **Condensation** is the change in phase from gas to liquid.

Magnetism

A **magnet** is a material or object that attracts certain metals, such as cobalt, nickel, and iron and can also repel or attract another magnet. All magnets have poles: a North-seeking (N) and a South-seeking (S). In a compass, the side marked N will point toward the Earth's North magnetic pole, which is different from the North Pole (they are actually several hundred miles apart). If you cut a magnet into parts, each part will have both North and South poles.

If you place magnets near each other, the opposite poles will attract and the like poles will repel each other. Therefore, a North pole will repel a North pole and attract a South pole.

The first true application of a magnet was the compass, which not only helps in navigation but also can help in detecting small magnetic fields. Magnets are also found in loudspeakers, electrical generators, and electrical motors. A very common use of magnets is to stick things to the refrigerator.

A **magnetic field** is made up of imaginary lines of flux resulting from moving or spinning electrically charged particles. These lines of magnetic flux move from one end of a magnetic object to the other, or rather, from the North-seeking pole to the South-seeking pole.

Heat

Heat and temperature are different physical quantities. **Heat** is a measure of energy. **Temperature** is the measure of how hot (or cold) a body is with respect to a standard object.

We can not rely on our sense of touch to determine temperature because the heat from a hand may be conducted more efficiently by certain objects, making them feel colder. **Thermometers** are used to measure temperature. A small amount of mercury in a capillary tube will expand when heated. The thermometer and the object whose temperature it is measuring are put in contact long enough for them to reach thermal equilibrium. Then the temperature can be read from the thermometer scale. Three temperature scales are used. These are Celsius, Fahrenheit, and Kelvin.

Dynamics is the study of the relationship between motion and the forces affecting motion. **Force** causes motion.

Speed is a scalar quantity that refers to how fast an object is moving (ex. the car was traveling 60 mi/hr). **Velocity** is a vector quantity that refers to the rate at which an object changes its position. In other words, velocity is speed with direction (ex. the car was traveling 60 mi./hr east).

Push and pull –Pushing a volleyball or pulling a bowstring applies muscular force when the muscles expand and contract. Elastic force is when any object returns to its original shape (for example, when a bow is released).

Rubbing – Friction opposes the motion of one surface past another. Friction is common when slowing down a car or sledding down a hill.

Pull of gravity – is a force of attraction between two objects. Gravity questions can be raised not only on earth but also between planets and even black hole discussions.

Forces on objects at rest – The formula **F= m/a** is shorthand for force equals mass over acceleration. An object will not move unless the force is strong enough to move the mass. Also, there can be opposing forces holding the object in place. For instance, a boat may want to be forced by the currents to drift away but an equal and opposite force is a rope holding it to a dock.

Forces on a moving object - Overcoming inertia is the tendency of any object to oppose a change in motion. An object at rest tends to stay at rest. An object that is moving tends to keep moving.

Inertia and circular motion – The centripetal force is provided by the high banking of the curved road and by friction between the wheels and the road. This inward force that keeps an object moving in a circle is called centripetal force.

Vibrations

Sound waves are produced by a vibrating body. The vibrating object moves forward and compresses the air in front of it, then reverses direction so that pressure on the air is lessened and expansion of the air molecules occurs. The vibrating air molecules move back and forth parallel to the direction of motion of the wave as they pass the energy from adjacent air molecules closer to the source to air molecules farther away from the source.

Space Satellites

An artificial satellite is any object placed into orbit by human endeavor. A satellite revolves around a planet in a circular or elliptical path. Most man-made satellites are useful objects placed in orbit purposely to perform some specific mission or task. Such satellites may include weather satellites, communication satellites, navigational satellites, reconnaissance satellites and scientific study satellites. Satellites are placed into orbit by first riding on a rocket or in the cargo bay of a space shuttle that is launched into space. Once the vessel has reached the satellite's destination, the satellite is released into space and remains in orbit due to the Earth's gravitational pull. The largest artificial satellite currently orbiting the Earth is the International Space Station. Currently, there are approximately 23,000 items of space junk - objects large enough to track with radar that were inadvertently placed in orbit or have outlived their usefulness - floating above Earth.

Airplanes

Airplanes or fixed-wing aircraft are heavier than aircraft that utilize the laws of physics to achieve flight. Airplanes achieve flight using the concepts of lift, weight, thrust and drag. Lift pushes the plane upward, and is created by the design of aircraft wings, which have flat bottoms and slightly rounded tops. As the aircraft is propelled forward by thrust from the engines, air moves faster over the top of the wings, and slower under the bottom. The slower airflow beneath the wing generates more pressure, while the faster airflow above generates less. This difference in pressure results in upward lift. Weight is Earth's gravity pulling down on a plane. Planes are designed to remain level, with equal weight in the front and back of the plane. Drag is the opposite force that slows a plane. Planes minimize drag with aerodynamic design.

Humankind's interest in flight is documented as far back as Greek mythology. The first real study of flight, however, is attributed to Leonardo da Vinci, who designed a craft called the orthinopter, on which the modern day helicopter is based. The first successful flight was achieved by the Wright Brothers off the outer banks of North Carolina. Their craft was developed by first studying many early attempts at flight, and then testing their own theories using balloons and kites. The brothers designed gliders to understand craft control and wind effects. Using a wind tunnel, the Wright Brothers tested many different wing and tail shapes. After determining a glider shape that consistently passed flight tests, they began to develop a propulsion system capable of creating lift. Eventually, the brothers constructed an engine capable of generating almost 12 horsepower. On December 17, 1903, the Wright Brother's craft known as the "Flyer" lifted from ground level piloted by brother Orville, and traveled one hundred and twenty feet.

Natural Objects in the Sky

There are eight established planets in our solar system. These are Mercury, Venus, Earth, Mars, Jupiter, Saturn, Uranus, and Neptune. Pluto was known as an established planet in our solar system, but as of Summer 2006, its status is being reconsidered. The planets are divided into two groups based on their distance from the Sun. The inner planets include: Mercury, Venus, Earth, and Mars. The outer planets include: Jupiter, Saturn, Uranus, and Neptune.

Mercury - the closest planet to the Sun. Its surface has craters and rocks. The atmosphere is composed of hydrogen, helium and sodium. Mercury was named after the Roman messenger god.

Venus - has a slow rotation when compared to Earth. Venus and Uranus rotate in opposite directions from the other planets. This opposite rotation is called retrograde rotation. The surface of Venus is not visible due to the extensive cloud cover. The atmosphere is composed mostly of carbon dioxide. Sulfuric acid droplets in the dense cloud cover give Venus a yellow appearance. Venus has a greater greenhouse effect than observed on Earth. The dense clouds combined with carbon dioxide trap heat. Venus was named after the Roman goddess of love.

Earth - considered a water planet with 70% of its surface covered by water. Gravity holds the masses of water in place. The different temperatures observed on earth allow for the different states (solid, liquid, gas) of water to exist. The atmosphere is composed mainly of oxygen and nitrogen. Earth is the only planet that is known to support life.

Mars - surface contains numerous craters, active and extinct volcanoes, ridges, and valleys with extremely deep fractures. Iron oxide found in the dusty soil makes the surface seem rust colored and the skies seem pink in color. The atmosphere is composed of carbon dioxide, nitrogen, argon, oxygen and water vapor. Mars has polar regions with ice caps composed of water. Mars has two satellites and was named after the Roman war god.

Jupiter - largest planet in the solar system. Jupiter has 16 moons. The atmosphere is composed of hydrogen, helium, methane and ammonia. There are white colored bands of clouds indicating rising gas and dark colored bands of clouds indicating descending gases. The gas movement is caused by heat resulting from the energy of Jupiter's core. Jupiter has a Great Red Spot that is thought to be a hurricane type cloud. Jupiter has a strong magnetic field.

Saturn - the second largest planet in the solar system. Saturn has rings of ice, rock, and dust particles circling it. Saturn's atmosphere is composed of hydrogen, helium, methane, and ammonia. Saturn has 20 plus satellites and was named for the Roman god of agriculture.

Uranus - the second largest planet in the solar system with retrograde revolution. Uranus is a gaseous planet. It has 10 dark rings and 15 satellites. Its atmosphere is composed of hydrogen, helium, and methane. Uranus was named after the Greek god of the heavens.

Neptune - another gaseous planet with an atmosphere consisting of hydrogen, helium, and methane. Neptune has 3 rings and 2 satellites. Neptune was named after the Roman sea god because its atmosphere is the same color as the seas.

Pluto - once considered the smallest planet in the solar system; its status as a planet is being reconsidered. Pluto's atmosphere probably contains methane, ammonia, and frozen water. Pluto has 1 satellite. Pluto revolves around the Sun every 250 years. Pluto was named after the Roman god of the underworld.

Astronomers believe that rocky fragments may have been the remains of the birth of the solar system that never formed into a planet. **Asteroids** are found in the region between Mars and Jupiter.

Comets are masses of frozen gases, cosmic dust, and small rocky particles. Astronomers think that most comets originate in a dense comet cloud beyond Pluto. Comet consists of a nucleus, a coma, and a tail. A comet's tail always points away from the sun. The most famous comet, **Halley's Comet,** is named after the person whom first discovered it in 240 B.C. It returns to the skies near earth every 75 to 76 years.

Meteoroids are composed of particles of rock and metal of various sizes. When a meteoroid travels through the earth's atmosphere, friction causes its surface to heat up and it begins to burn. The burning meteoroid falling through the earth's atmosphere is called a **meteor** (also known as a "shooting star").

Meteorites are meteors that strike the earth's surface. A physical example of a meteorite's impact on the earth's surface can be seen in Arizona. The Barringer Crater is a huge meteor crater. There are many other meteor craters throughout the world.

Astronomers use groups or patterns of stars called **constellations** as reference points to locate other stars in the sky. Familiar constellations include Ursa Major (also known as the big bear) and Ursa Minor (known as the little bear). Within the Ursa Major, the smaller constellation, The Big Dipper is found. Within the Ursa Minor, the smaller constellation, The Little Dipper is found.

Different constellations appear as the earth continues its revolution around the sun with the seasonal changes. Magnitude stars are 21 of the brightest stars that can be seen from earth. These are the first stars noticed at night. There are 15 commonly observed first magnitude stars in the Northern Hemisphere.

A vast collection of stars is defined as a **galaxy**. Galaxies are classified as irregular, elliptical, and spiral. An irregular galaxy has no real structured appearance; most are in their early stages of life. An elliptical galaxy consists of smooth ellipses, containing little dust and gas, but composed of millions or trillion stars. Spiral galaxies are disk-shaped and have extending arms that rotate around its dense center. Earth's galaxy is found in the Milky Way and it is a spiral galaxy.

Origin of the Solar System

Two main hypotheses of the origin of the solar system are the tidal hypothesis and theory and the condensation hypothesis theory.

The tidal hypothesis proposes that the solar system began with a near collision of the sun and a large star. Some astronomers believe that as these two stars passed each other, the great gravitational pull of the large star extracted hot gases out of the sun. The mass from the hot gases started to orbit the sun, which began to cool then condensing into the nine planets. (Few astronomers support this example).

The condensation hypothesis proposes that the solar system began with rotating clouds of dust and gas. Condensation occurred in the center forming the sun and the smaller parts of the cloud formed the nine planets. (This example is widely accepted by many astronomers).

Two main theories to explain the origins of the universe include the **Big Bang Theory** and the **Steady-State Theory.**

The Big Bang Theory has been widely accepted by many astronomers. It states that the universe originated from a magnificent explosion spreading mass, matter and energy into space. The galaxies formed from this material as it cooled during the next half-billion years.

The Steady-State Theory is the least accepted theory. It states that the universe is a continuously being renewed. Galaxies move outward and new galaxies replace the older galaxies. Astronomers have not found any evidence to prove this theory.

The future of the universe is hypothesized with the **Oscillating Universe Hypothesis**. It states that the universe will oscillate or expand and contract. Galaxies will move away from one another and will in time slow down and stop. Then a gradual moving toward each other will again activate the explosion or The Big Bang theory.

The stages of life of a star begin with a mass of gas and dust that becomes a nebula, then a main sequence star. Next it becomes a red giant, then a nova and then in its final stages, a white dwarf (the dying core of a giant star), a neutron star or a black hole.

When hydrogen becomes exhausted in a small, or even an average star, its core will collapse and cause its temperature to rise. This released heat causes nearby gases to heat, contract, carry out fusion, and produce helium. Stars at this stage are nearing the end of their life. These stars are called red giants; also called supergiants. A white dwarf is the dying core of a giant star. A nova is an ordinary star that experiences a sudden increase in brightness and then fades back to its original brightness. A supernova radiates even greater light energy. A neutron star is the result of mass left behind after a supernova. A black hole is a star with condensed matter and gravity so intense that light can not escape.

Weather and Seasons

Seasonal change on Earth is caused by the orbit and axial tilt of the planet in relation to the Sun's Ecliptic: the rotational path of the Sun. These factors combine to vary the degree of insolation (distribution of solar energy) at a particular location and thereby change the seasons.

World weather patterns are greatly influenced by ocean surface currents in the upper layer of the ocean. These current continuously move along the ocean surface in specific directions. Surface currents are caused by winds and classified by temperature. Cold currents originate in the Polar regions and flow through surrounding water that is measurably warmer. Those currents with a higher temperature than the surrounding water are called warm currents and can be found near the **equator**. These currents follow swirling routes around the ocean basins and the equator. The Gulf Stream and the California Current are the two main surface currents that flow along the coastlines of the United States. The California Current is a cold current that originates in the Arctic regions and flows southward along the western coast of the United States.

The wind belts in each hemisphere consist of convection cells that encircle Earth like belts. There are three major wind belts on Earth: (1) trade winds (2) prevailing westerlies, and (3) polar easterlies.

Winds caused by local temperature changes include sea breezes and land breezes. **Sea breezes** are caused by the unequal heating of the land and an adjacent, large body of water. Land heats up faster than water. The movement of cool ocean air toward the land is called a sea breeze. Sea breezes usually begin blowing about mid-morning; ending about sunset. A breeze that blows from the land to the ocean or a large lake is called a **land breeze.**

Monsoons are huge wind systems that cover large geographic areas and that reverse direction seasonally. The monsoons of India and Asia are examples of these seasonal winds. They alternate wet and dry seasons. As denser cooler air over the ocean moves inland, a steady seasonal wind called a summer or wet monsoon is produced.

A **thunderstorm** is a brief, local storm produced by the rapid upward movement of warm, moist air within a cumulonimbus cloud. Thunderstorms always produce lightning and thunder, and are accompanied by strong wind gusts and heavy rain or hail.

A severe storm with swirling winds that may reach speeds of hundreds of km per hour is called a **tornado**. Such a storm is also referred to as a "twister". The sky is covered by large cumulonimbus clouds and violent thunderstorms; a funnel-shaped swirling cloud may extend downward from a cumulonimbus cloud and reach the ground. Tornadoes are storms that leave a narrow path of destruction on the ground.

A swirling, funnel-shaped cloud that **extends** downward and touches a body of water is called a **waterspout.**

Hurricanes are storms that develop when warm, moist air carried by trade winds rotates around a low-pressure "eye". A large, rotating, low-pressure system accompanied by heavy precipitation and strong winds is called a tropical cyclone (better known as a hurricane). In the Pacific region, a hurricane is called a typhoon.

Storms that occur only in the winter are known as blizzards or ice storms. A **blizzard** is a storm with strong winds, blowing snow and frigid temperatures. An **ice storm** consists of falling rain that freezes when it strikes the ground, covering everything with a layer of ice.

Erosion

Erosion is the inclusion and transportation of surface materials by another moveable material, usually water, wind, or ice. The most important cause of erosion is running water. Streams, rivers, and tides are constantly at work removing weathered fragments of bedrock and carrying them away from their original location.

A stream erodes bedrock by the grinding action of the sand, pebbles and other rock fragments. This grinding against each other is called abrasion. Streams also erode rocks by dissolving or absorbing their minerals. Limestone and marble are readily dissolved by streams.

The breaking down of rocks at or near to the Earth's surface is known as **weathering**. Weathering breaks down these rocks into smaller and smaller pieces. There are two types of weathering: physical weathering and chemical weathering.

Physical weathering is the process by which rocks are broken down into smaller fragments without undergoing any change in chemical composition. Physical weathering is mainly caused by the freezing of water, the expansion of rock, and the activities of plants and animals.

Frost wedging is the cycle of daytime thawing and refreezing at night. This cycle causes large rock masses, especially the rocks exposed on mountain tops, to be broken into smaller pieces.

Chemical weathering is the breaking down of rocks through changes in their chemical composition. An example would be the change of feldspar in granite to clay. Water, oxygen, and carbon dioxide are the main agents of chemical weathering. When water and carbon dioxide combine chemically, they produce a weak acid that breaks down rocks.

Deposition, also known as sedimentation, is the term for the process by which material from one area is slowly deposited into another area. This is usually due to the movement of wind, water, or ice containing particles of matter. When the rate of movement slows down, particles filter out and remain behind, causing a build up of matter. Note that this is a result of matter being eroded and removed from another site.

Plate Tectonics

Plate Tectonic Theory proposes that the Earth's surface is composed of lithospheric plates that "float" atop the Asthenosphere and are in constant motion. **Plate Tectonics** is the study of the movement of the lithospheric plates and the consequences of that movement. According to the theory, the Earth is composed of three layers. The Lithosphere is comprised of both the continental and oceanic crust and uppermost part of the mantle. It consists of cool, rigid and brittle materials. The asthenosphere layer is the semi-plastic molten rock material located directly below the lithosphere. At the base of the asthenosphere, the mantle again becomes more rigid and less plastic, and it remains in that rigid state all the way to the core. The Earth constantly recycles its materials through a process of upwelling from the center and subducting in the lithosphere, which subsequently causes the movement of Earth's tectonic plates.

Water Cycle

Hydrologic Cycle: the Earth's water balance. All the water on our planet is all that there is available. It changes location and form, but new water is not produced. It simply recycles itself. The hydrologic cycle of water movement is driven by solar radiation from the Sun. The cycle of water evaporating from the oceans, precipitation, and flow over land in its return to the ocean is the methodology employed by nature to maintain the water balance at any given location.

Skill 7.6   The role of science and technology in addressing ecological issues and problems

Science and technology have increasing effects on our daily lives. We can use the scientific method and experiments to more fully understand many of the phenomena around us. Scientists use technology to enhance the study of nature and solve problems that nature presents. There are two broad happenings in environmental science and technology. First, there are many studies being conducted to determine the effects of changing environmental conditions and pollutants. New instruments and monitoring systems have increased the accuracy of these results. Second, advances are being made to mitigate the effects of pollution, develop sustainable methods of agriculture and energy production, and improve waste management.

Development of new technology in agriculture is particularly important as we strive to feed more people with less arable land. We see the importance of genetic technology in developing hybrids that have desirable characteristics. New strains of plants and farming techniques may allow the production of more nutrient rich food and/or allow crops to be grown successfully in harsh conditions. However, it is also important to consider the environmental impact of transgenic species and the use of pesticides and fertilizers. Scientific reasoning and experimentation can assist us in ascertaining the real effect of modern agricultural practices and ways to minimize their impact.

Technological design is the identification of a problem and the application of scientific knowledge to solve the problem. While technology and technological design can provide solutions to problems faced by humans, technology must exist within nature and cannot contradict physical or biological principles. In addition, technological solutions are temporary and new technologies typically provide better solutions in the future. Monetary costs, available materials, time, and available tools also limit the scope of technological design and solutions. Finally, technological solutions have intended benefits and unexpected consequences. Scientists must attempt to predict the unintended consequences and minimize any negative impact on nature or society.

The problems and needs, ranging from very simple to highly complex, that technological design can solve are nearly limitless. Disposal of toxic waste, routing of rainwater, crop irrigation, and energy creation are but a few examples of real-world problems that scientists address or attempt to address with technology. The technological design process has five basic steps:

1. Identify a problem
2. Propose designs and choose between alternative solutions
3. Implement the proposed solution
4. Evaluate the solution and its consequences
5. Report results

After the identification of a problem, the scientist must propose several designs and choose between the alternatives. Scientists often utilize simulations and models in evaluating possible solutions. Implementation of the chosen solution involves the use of various tools depending on the problem, solution, and technology. Scientists may use both physical tools and objects and computer software. After implementation of the solution, scientists evaluate the success or failure of the solution against pre-determined criteria. In evaluating the solution, scientists must consider the negative consequences as well as the planned benefits. Finally, scientists must communicate results in different ways – both orally and written, with models, diagrams, and demonstrations.

Example:

Problem – toxic waste disposal
Chosen solution – genetically engineered microorganisms to digest waste
Implementation – use genetic engineering technology to create organism capable of converting waste to environmentally safe product
Evaluate – introduce organisms to waste site and measure formation of products and decrease in waste; also evaluate any unintended effects
Report – prepare a written report of results complete with diagrams and figures

Skill 7.7   Principles and procedures of scientific inquiry and experimentation

Only certain types of questions can truly be answered by science because the scientific method relies on observable phenomenon. That is, only hypotheses that can be tested are valid. Often this means that we can control the variables in a system to an extent that allows us to truly determine their effects. If we don't have full control over the variables, for instance, in environmental biology, we can study several different naturally occurring systems in which the desired variable is different.

The scientific method is particularly useful for determining 'cause and effect' type relationships. Thus, appropriate hypotheses are often of this nature. The hypothesis is simply a prediction about a certain behavior that occurs in a system. Variables are changed to determine whether the hypothesis is correct. For instance, let's consider several identical potted African violets and suppose we have lights of different color, fertilizer, water and a variety of common household items. Below are some possible questions, phrased as hypotheses, and a bit about why they are or are not valid.

1. African violets will grow taller in blue light than they will in red light. This hypothesis is valid because it could easily be tested by growing one violet in blue light and another in red. The results are easily observed by measuring the height of the violets.

2. Invisible microbes cause the leaves of African violets to turn yellow. This hypothesis is not valid because we cannot know whether a given violet is infected with the microbe. This hypothesis could be tested if we had appropriate technology to detect the presence of the microbe..

3. Lack of water will stop the growth of African violets. This hypothesis is also valid because it could be tested by denying water to one violet while continuing to water another. The hypothesis may need to be refined to more specifically define how growth will be measured, but presumably this could be easily done.

4. African violets will not grow well in swamps. This hypothesis is not valid in our specific situation because we have only potted plants. It could be tested by actually attempting to grow African violets in a swamp, but that is not within this scenario.

The scientific method involves several steps beginning with hypothesis formulation and working through to the conclusion.

Pose a question
Although many discoveries happen by chance, the standard thought process of a scientist begins with forming a question to research. The more limited the question, the easier it is to set up an experiment to answer it.

Form a hypothesis
Once the question is formulated take an educated guess about the answer to the problem or question. This 'best guess' is your hypothesis.

Conduct a test
To make a test fair, data from an experiment must have a **variable** or any condition that can be changed such as temperature or mass. A good test will try to manipulate as few variables as possible to see which variable is responsible for the result. This requires a second example called a **control**. A control is an extra setup in which all the conditions are the same except for the variable being tested.

Observe and record the data
Reporting of the data should state specifics of how the measurements were calculated. A graduated cylinder needs to be read with proper procedures. As beginning students, technique must be part of the instructional process so as to give validity to the data.

Drawing a conclusion
After recording data, you compare your data with that of other groups. A conclusion is the judgment derived from the data results and should explain why the experiment either proved or disproved the hypothesis.

Graphing data

Graphing utilizes numbers to demonstrate patterns. The patterns offer a visual representation, making it easier to draw conclusions. The type of graphic representation used to display observations depends on the data that is collected. Line graphs are used to compare different sets of related data or to predict data that has not yet be measured. An example of a line graph would be comparing the rate of activity of different enzymes at varying temperatures. A bar graph or histogram is used to compare different items and make comparisons based on this data. An example of a bar graph would be comparing the ages of children in a classroom. A pie chart is useful when organizing data as part of a whole. A good use for a pie chart would be displaying the percent of time students spend on various after school activities.

Communication

After the conclusion is drawn, the final step is communication. The conclusions must be communicated by clearly describing the information using accurate data, visual presentation like bar/line/pie graphs, tables/charts, diagrams, artwork, and other appropriate media such as a power point presentation. The method of communication must be suitable to the audience. Written communication is as important as oral communication.

A scientific theory is an explanation of a set of related observations based on a proven hypothesis. A scientific law usually lasts longer than a scientific theory and has more experimental data to support it.

SUBAREA IV. INTEGRATION OF KNOWLEDGE AND UNDERSTANDING

Competency 008 **Prepare an organized, developed analysis that relates child development to two or more of the following Language arts, mathematics, history and social science, and science**

This skill level requires the preparation of a written analysis which relates to child development skill areas. Analysis can include a variety of topics such:

- Children's literature
- Mathematical concepts, reasoning, and problem solving
- Major developments in U.S. and world history
- Government and citizenship in the United States
- Basic principles of economics
- Geographic concepts, phenomena, and processes
- Basic concepts of science and technology
- Principles and procedures of scientific inquiry and experimentation
- Child development during the early childhood years

The samples provided on the next page can serve as guidance for this skill area.

Sample 1: Use the information below to complete the exercise that follows.

For young students, understanding fractions can often be difficult at first. However, a "hands-on" activity can allow students to understand fractions more easily.

Using your knowledge of mathematics and child development, prepare a response in which you:

- summarize a "hands-on" activity that would help prekindergarten children learn about fractions;

- explain how this experience would help prekindergarten children learn about fractions.

Sample Response

While fractions are difficult to learn, students will quickly understand the concept of fractions if using manipulatives and hands-on activities.

First, I would draw a picture of a pie on the overhead. I would then start to draw lines to divide the pie into different sections. One piece would be very large, a few pieces would be quite small, and the last few would be regular pieces of pie. Students would recognize that the pieces are a variety of different sizes. I would then ask them to help me cut the pie so that my five guests would have a similar-sized slice.

The next step would be to get the students into small groups. I would give them cut-outs of a pizza, and I would ask them to determine how many slices they would need to make sure everyone got one similarly-sized slice, and then cut the pizza.

The final step of this "hands-on" lesson would be to have the groups show me what one-half a pizza would be. On each pizza, they would count up their slices. This would go on and on until they understand that one-half or one-quarter could constitute a variety of numbers of slices depending how many slices were cut for each pizza.

This activity would help students learn the concept of fractions by giving them a practical, simple method of seeing fractions. They would understand that one pizza could have many different combinations of slices. Overall, this is a fun, practical, and useful way to teach the very difficult concept of fractions.

Sample 2: Use the information below to complete the exercise that follows.

Differentiated instruction is a way that teachers can address and accommodate individual students' strengths and challenges.

Using your knowledge of differentiated instruction and child development, prepare a response in which you:

- summarize the benefits of differentiated instruction for students; and

- summarize how you would incorporate differentiated instruction into learning activities.

Sample Response

A class contains a diverse range of students with different strengths, weaknesses, and needs. The main benefit of differentiated instruction is that it allows each student to learn in a way that is suited to them. For example, a gifted student would have the opportunity to complete a challenging project and use their strengths. At the same time, a student with a learning difficulty could learn in a more guided way that suits their needs.

The first thing I would do to incorporate differentiated instruction into learning activities would be to understand the strengths, weaknesses, and needs of students. Once I knew this, I would then be able to design activities that meet the requirements of my diverse students.

When designing activities, I would consider content, process, and product. When considering content, I might identify that some students lack knowledge of the material, while others already have the knowledge. I could then have some students focusing on learning the knowledge, while others focus on applying it. When considering process, I might identify that some students prefer to work independently, while others prefer to work in pairs or small groups. I would design activities to meet each of these needs. I would also consider product, which is how students will demonstrate their understanding. For example, if I had a student with dyslexia in my class, I would recognize that a written assignment may be challenging to the student, while the opportunity to give an oral talk on what they learned may be more suitable. As another example, I could have advanced students engage in a debate with each other to show their understanding, or a student who is artistically gifted design a poster summarizing the subject being studied.

Open Response Scoring Scale

The scoring scale below, which is related to the performance characteristics for the tests, is used by scorers in assigning scores to responses to the open-response items.

Score Point Score Point Description

4 - The "4" response reflects a thorough knowledge and understanding of the subject matter.
• The purpose of the assignment is fully achieved.
• There is substantial, accurate, and appropriate application of subject matter knowledge.
• The supporting evidence is sound; there are high-quality, relevant examples.
• The response reflects an ably reasoned, comprehensive understanding of the topic.

3 - The "3" response reflects an adequate knowledge and understanding of the subject matter.
• The purpose of the assignment is largely achieved.
• There is a generally accurate and appropriate application of subject matter knowledge.
• The supporting evidence is adequate; there are some acceptable, relevant examples.
• The response reflects an adequately reasoned understanding of the topic.

2 - The "2" response reflects a limited knowledge and understanding of the subject matter.
• The purpose of the assignment is partially achieved.
• There is a limited, possibly inaccurate or inappropriate application of subject matter knowledge.
• The supporting evidence is limited; there are few relevant examples.
• The response reflects a limited, poorly reasoned understanding of the topic.

1 - The "1" response reflects a weak knowledge and understanding of the subject matter.
• The purpose of the assignment is not achieved.
• There is little or no appropriate or accurate application of subject matter knowledge.
• The supporting evidence, if present, is weak; there are few or no relevant examples.
• The response reflects little or no reasoning about or understanding of the topic.
A response to an open-response item is designated "unscorable" if it is unrelated to the assigned topic, illegible, not in the appropriate language, of insufficient length to score, or merely a repetition of the assignment. If there is no response to an open-response item, it is designated "blank."

Pre Test

Subarea I. Knowledge of Child Development

1. How many stages of intellectual development does Piaget define? (Skill 1.1; Easy)

    A. Two

    B. Four

    C. Six

    D. Eight

2. Which level of Bloom's taxonomy involves having students categorize, compare, and distinguish? (Skill 1.1; Average rigor)

    A. Application

    B. Analysis

    C. Synthesis

    D. Evaluation

3. According to Piaget, during what stage do children learn to manipulate symbols and objects? (Skill 1.1; Average rigor)

    A. Concrete operations

    B. Pre-operational

    C. Formal operations

    D. Conservative operational

4. What does the Multiple Intelligence Theory developed by Howard Gardner explain? (Skill 1.1; Average rigor)

    A. How the intelligence of students depends on the environment

    B. How the intelligence of students constantly change

    C. How students have different levels of overall intelligence

    D. How students learn in at least seven different ways

5. According to Kohlberg, what is the first level of moral development in which judgments are made on the basis of physical consequences and personal needs? (Skill 1.1; Easy)

    A. Anxiety level

    B. Pre-conventional level

    C. Post-conventional level

    D. Symbolic level

6. **Why is Kohlberg's theory important to classroom teachers? (Skill 1.1; Rigorous)**

   A. It is a theory that explains how language is acquired.

   B. It is a theory that explains how complex and logical thought is developed.

   C. It is a theory that explains the stages of moral development in a child.

   D. It is a theory that explains how higher mental functions develop in a child.

7. **Which of the following is an example of a synthesis task according to Bloom's taxonomy? (Skill 1.1; Rigorous)**

   A. Write a definition of nuclear fission.

   B. Compare nuclear power to electrical power.

   C. Classify the outcomes of using nuclear power as negative or positive.

   D. Propose an alternative to nuclear power and explain why it is superior to nuclear power.

8. **According to Erikson's theory of psychosocial development, what is the cause of temper tantrums in children aged 1 to 3? (Skill 1.1; Rigorous)**

   A. A desire to be independent

   B. A lack of empathy

   C. A sense of general confusion

   D. An increase in feelings of guilt

9. **Why is it most important for teachers to ensure that students from different economic backgrounds have access to the resources they need to acquire the academic skills being taught? (Skill 1.2; Rigorous)**

   A. All students must work together on set tasks.

   B. All students must achieve the same results in performance tasks.

   C. All students must have equal opportunity for academic success.

   D. All students must be fully included in classroom activities.

10. Family members with high levels of education often have high expectations for student success. This shows how students are influenced by their family's: (Skill 1.2; Easy)

    A.   Attitude

    B.   Resources

    C.   Income

    D.   Culture

11. Which of the following is a sign of emotional neglect? (Skill 1.3; Average rigor)

    A.   Jealousy of other children

    B.   Aggression

    C.   Lack of attention to schoolwork

    D.   All of the above

12. A teacher is planning to get all of her students involved in sports for the purpose of helping develop hand-eye coordination and teamwork skills. What would be the most appropriate approach when planning the sports activities? (Skill 1.4; Rigorous)

    A.   Encourage competition among students so they become used to the pressure of competing.

    B.   Ensure that students who dislike sports continue until they enjoy sports.

    C.   Choose activities that are beyond the student's current abilities so students are prompted to improve.

    D.   Maintain a relaxed atmosphere and remind students that the sport is designed to be fun.

13. Which of the following is a true statement? (Skill 1.4; Rigorous)

   A. Recess is not important to a child's development.

   B. Playtime is only provided in schools to help children release energy.

   C. Play has an important and positive role in child development.

   D. Solitary play is always an indication that a child has development issues.

14. A student has developed and improved their vocabulary. However, the student is not confident enough to use their improved vocabulary, and the teacher is not aware of the improvement. What is this an example of? (Skill 1.5; Rigorous)

   A. Latent development

   B. Dormant development

   C. Random development

   D. Delayed development

15. Which of the following best describes how different areas of development impact each other? (Skill 1.5; Average rigor)

   A. Development in other areas cannot occur until cognitive development is complete.

   B. Areas of development are inter-related and impact each other.

   C. Development in each area is independent of development in other areas.

   D. Development in one area leads to a decline in other areas.

16. A child exhibits the following symptoms: inability to appreciate humor, indifference to physical contact, abnormal social play, and abnormal speech. What is the likely diagnosis for this child? (Skill 2.1; Average rigor)

   A. Separation anxiety

   B. Mental retardation

   C. Autism

   D. Hypochondria

17. **What type of disability does a student who talks incessantly using bizarre words most likely have? (Skill 2.1; Easy)**

    A. Attention deficit hyperactivity disorder

    B. Severe emotional stress

    C. Schizophrenia

    D. Dyslexia

18. **A child with a disability is one who has: (Skill 2.1; Easy)**

    A. Sensory impairments

    B. Emotional disturbances

    C. Mental retardation

    D. Any of the above

19. **Which of the following is the most likely cause of a child becoming easily agitated in class? (Skill 2.2; Average rigor)**

    A. Lack of sleep

    B. Lack of training in manners

    C. Being raised in a single parent home

    D. Watching too much television

20. **Who should you talk to if you suspect child abuse? (Skill 2.2; Easy)**

    A. The child

    B. The child's parent

    C. Your supervisor

    D. Another teacher

21. **What is the most important factor in improving the developmental and educational gains for students with language delays? (Skill 2.3; Average rigor)**

    A. Varied teaching procedures

    B. The social environment

    C. Early intervention

    D. Encouraging independence

22. **What is the most significant development emerging in children at age two? (Skill 2.3; Rigorous)**

    A. Immune system development

    B. Language development

    C. Socialization development

    D. Perception development

23. **What actions are observed in aggressive children? (Skill 2.4; Easy)**

   A.   Vandalism

   B.   Destruction of property

   C.   Verbal abuse

   D.   All of the above

24. **What area of differentiated instruction is a teacher focusing on when planning how to teach the material? (Skill 2.5; Average rigor)**

   A.   Content

   B.   Process

   C.   Product

   D.   Assessment

25. **What criteria are used to assess whether a child qualifies for services under IDEA? (Skill 2.5; Rigorous)**

   A.   Having a disability only

   B.   Having a disability and demonstrating educational need only

   C.   Demonstrating educational need only

   D.   Having a disability, demonstrating educational need, and having financial support

26. **According to IDEA, who must be involved in developing a child's IEP? (Skill 2.6; Average rigor)**

   A.   A medical doctor

   B.   The school psychologist

   C.   The parents or guardians

   D.   The principal

27. **What would be put into place for a student with a physical disability in order to make accommodations in the classroom? (Skill 2.7; Average rigor)**

   A.   504

   B.   IEP

   C.   IFSP

   D.   All of the above

28. **Because teachers today will deal with an increasingly diverse group of cultures in their classrooms, they must: (Skill 2.8; Average rigor)**

   A.   Ignore the cultures represented

   B.   Show respect to all parents and families

   C.   Provide a celebration for each culture represented

   D.   Focusing on teaching the majority

29. **What should a teacher begin a parent-teacher conference with? (Skill 2.8; Average rigor)**

    A. Student weaknesses

    B. Positive comments

    C. Entertaining anecdotes

    D. Issues of concern

30. **The commitment that a community shows to its educational communities is: (Skill 2.9; Average rigor)**

    A. Judged by how much money is contributed

    B. Something that doesn't matter much to the school

    C. A valuable investment in the future

    D. Something that will cause immediate gains

Subarea II. Knowledge of Children's Literature and the Writing Process

31. **Which of the following is NOT a characteristic of a fable? (Skill 3.1; Easy)**

    A. Have animal characters that act like humans

    B. Considered to be true

    C. Teaches a moral

    D. Reveals human foibles

32. **Ms. Smith considers the use of quality children's literature to be one of the most important qualities of an early childhood teacher. She is asked to justify her reasons behind this consideration to her principal. Which of the following is an appropriate justification? (Skill 3.1; Rigorous)**

    A. There are many different types of children's literature, so there will be something to which every child can relate.

    B. Children's literature in early childhood classrooms provides the students with the opportunity to learn to read and process language.

    C. Children are like adults in many ways and need to be exposed to a variety of types of literature.

    D. Children's literature helps children improve their mental, social, and psychological skills and aids in the development in all of these areas.

33. In her kindergarten class, Mrs. Thomas has been watching the students in the drama center. She has watched the children pretend to complete a variety of magic tricks. Mrs. Thomas decides to use stories about magic to share with her class. Her decision to incorporate their interests into the reading shows that Mrs. Thomas understands that: (Skill 3.2; Rigorous)

A. Including student interests is important at all times

B. Teaching by themes is crucial for young children

C. Young children respond to literature that reflects their lives

D. Science fiction and fantasy are the most popular genres

34. Which of the following literary devices is most commonly found in kindergarten classrooms? (Skill 3.3; Easy)

A. Metaphor

B. Repetition

C. Simile

D. Analogy

35. George has read his second graders three formats of the story "The Three Little Pigs." One is the traditional version, one is written from the wolf's point of view, and the third is written from the first pig's point of view. As George leads a discussion on the three texts with his students, he is trying to help his students develop their ability to: (Skill 3.4; Rigorous)

A. Compare and contrast texts

B. Understand point of view

C. Recognize metaphors

D. Rewrite fictional stories

36. What question would it be most important for a teacher to ask when deciding if a book will be appropriate for classroom use? (Skill 3.5; Average rigor)

A. Do the characters provide positive role models for children?

B. Is the setting of the book modern?

C. Will every student in the class be interested in the subject of the book?

D. Is the book short enough for students to read in one sitting?

37. **The attitude an author takes toward his or her subject is the: (Skill 3.6; Easy)**

   A.   Style

   B.   Tone

   C.   Point of view

   D.   Theme

38. **A book on the history of Massachusetts uses long sentences and advanced vocabulary. A children's novel set in Massachusetts 100 years ago has short sentences and simple vocabulary. What is different about the two books? (Skill 3.6; Average rigor)**

   A.   Style

   B.   Tone

   C.   Point of view

   D.   Theme

39. **Mr. Adams uses a short story about early train travel as part of a history lesson. This shows that literature: (Skill 3.7; Average rigor)**

   A.   Can be used to expand students' vocabulary

   B.   Can be used to build students' communication skills

   C.   Can be used to help students empathize

   D.   Can be used to enhance other areas of the curriculum

40. **What is the first step in developing writing skills? (Skill 4.1; Easy)**

   A.   Early writing

   B.   Experimental writing

   C.   Role play writing

   D.   Conventional writing

41. **Which prewriting strategy involves making a list of all the ideas connected with a topic? (Skill 4.2; Average rigor)**

   A.   Brainstorming

   B.   Visual mapping

   C.   Observing

   D.   Visualizing

42. A second grader is writing his first book review. He is identifying the purpose of his book report, deciding his main point, and determining the supporting details he will used to make his point. What stage of the writing process is the student at? (Skill 4.3; Rigorous)

A. Discovery stage

B. Organization stage

C. First draft stage

D. Analysis stage

43. The students in Tina's classroom are working together in pairs. Each student is reading another student's paper and asking who, what, when, where, why, and who questions. What is this activity helping the students to do? (Skill 4.4; Rigorous)

A. Draft their writing

B. Paraphrase their writing

C. Revise their writing

D. Outline their writing

44. Ms. Michaels is teaching her students about revising. What would Ms. Michaels be best to tell her students about revising? (Skill 4.4; Average rigor)

A. Revising is an important part of the writing process and all writing should be revised.

B. You will only have to revise until you become a good enough writer to get it perfect the first time.

C. Revising can be skipped sometimes if you think it might ruin your writing.

D. You will only need to revise work you complete that is to be handed in for assessment.

45. Which sentence has correct subject-verb agreement? (Skill 4.5; Rigorous)

A. A workers and his bosses were having a long meeting.

B. A workers and his bosses was having a long meeting.

C. A worker and his boss was having a long meeting.

D. A worker and his boss were having a long meeting.

46. An adolescent has not yet mastered spelling. What would be the best way for a teacher to address this? (Skill 4.5; Rigorous)

   A. Provide the student with extra instruction on spelling rules

   B. Ensure that the student fully understands all the exceptions to rules

   C. Encourage the student to master the use of a dictionary and thesaurus

   D. Focus on teaching spelling and grammar in isolation

47. A classroom activity involves students writing letters to a mayor to ask for more bike paths to be built. What type of discourse are the students engaged in? (Skill 4.6; Easy)

   A. Exposition

   B. Persuasion

   C. Narration

   D. Description

48. Which of the following approaches to student writing assignments is most likely to lead to students becoming disinterested? (Skill 4.6; Average rigor)

   A. Designing assignments where students write for a variety of audiences.

   B. Designing assignments where the teacher is the audience.

   C. Designing assignments where students write to friends and family.

   D. Designing assignments where students write to real people such as mayors, the principle, or companies.

49. A teacher is using the sentence "Beautiful Beth is the best girl in the Bradley Bay area" in a writing lesson. What are the students learning about? (Skill 4.7; Easy)

   A. Assonance

   B. Alliteration

   C. Onomatopoeia

   D. Metaphor

50. A student writes in a book report that a book they read has a writing style like no other book they have ever read before. When the student revises their report, they write that the book has a unique writing style. What improvement has been made? (Skill 4.8; Rigorous)

   A.   The tone is less formal.

   B.   The sentence structure is more complex.

   C.   Figurative language is removed.

   D.   The vocabulary is precise.

Subarea III. Core Knowledge in the Content Areas

51. What math principle is reinforced by matching numerals with number words? (Skill 5.1; Rigorous)

   A.   Sequencing

   B.   Greater than and less than

   C.   Number representations

   D.   Rote counting

52. How is the following read? (Skill 5.1; Easy)

$$3 < 5$$

   A.   Three is less than five

   B.   Five is greater than three

   C.   Three is greater than five

   D.   Five is less than three

53. Which words in a test problem would indicate that an addition operation is needed? (Skill 5.1; Average rigor)

   A.   Each

   B.   How many

   C.   In each group

   D.   How many more than

54. Kindergarten students are participating in a calendar time activity. One student adds a straw to the "ones can" to represent that day of school. What math principle is being reinforced? (Skill 5.4; Rigorous)

   A.   Properties of a base ten number system

   B.   Sorting

   C.   Counting by twos

   D.   Even and odd numbers

55. First grade students are arranging four small squares of identical size to form a larger square. Each small square represents what part of the larger square? (Skill 5.5; Average rigor)

   A. One half

   B. One whole

   C. One fourth

   D. One fifth

56. Third grade students are looking at a circle graph. Most of the graph is yellow. A small wedge of the graph is blue. Each colored section also has a number followed by a symbol. What are the students most likely learning about? (Skill 5.5; Rigorous)

   A. Addition

   B. Venn diagrams

   C. Percent

   D. Pictographs

57. A teacher is introducing the concept of multiplication to her third grade students. What is another way she might write 4 x 5? (Skill 5.6; Average rigor)

   A. 4 + 5

   B. 5 + 4

   C. 4 + 4 + 4 + 4 + 4

   D. 5 + 5 + 5 + 5 + 5

58. What is the answer to this problem? (Skill 5.7; Easy)

   25 ÷ 5 =

   A. 5

   B. 30

   C. 125

   D. 20

59. Which other equation is a part of this fact family? (Skill 5.7; Rigorous)

   2 + 6 = 8
   8 − 2 = 6
   6 + 2 = 8

   A. 6 − 2 = 4

   B. 8 + 6 = 14

   C. 8 − 6 = 2

   D. 8 + 2 = 10

60. What is the main purpose of having kindergarten students count by twos? (Skill 5.8; Rigorous)

    A.   To hear a rhythm

    B.   To recognize patterns in numbers

    C.   To practice addition

    D.   To become familiar with equations

61. A teacher plans an activity that involves students calculating how many chair legs are in the classroom, given that there are 30 chairs and each chair has 4 legs. This activity is introducing the ideas of: (Skill 5.8; Average rigor)

    A.   Probability

    B.   Statistics

    C.   Geometry

    D.   Algebra

62. Square is to cube as triangle is to: (Skill 5.9; Rigorous)

    A.   Sphere

    B.   Rectangle

    C.   Cone

    D.   Tetrahedron

63. Kindergarten students are doing a butterfly art project. They fold paper in half. On one half, they paint a design. Then they fold the paper closed and reopen. The resulting picture is a butterfly with matching sides. What math principle does this demonstrate? (Skill 5.10; Rigorous)

    A.   Slide

    B.   Rotate

    C.   Symmetry

    D.   Transformation

64. Students completing an activity with tangrams are learning what math principle? (Skill 5.10; Average rigor)

    A.   Basic geometric concepts

    B.   Repeating patterns

    C.   Counting

    D.   Identity property

65. When a student completes the following number sentence, which math concept is being learned? (Skill 5.11; Rigorous)

$$15 - \clubsuit = 6$$

A. Addition/subtraction and basic algebraic concepts

B. Counting and addition/subtraction

C. Counting and basic algebraic concepts

D. Counting and pattern recognition

66. Students are working with a set of rulers and various small objects from the classroom. Which concept are these students exploring? (Skill 5.12; Average rigor)

A. Volume

B. Weight

C. Length

D. Temperature

67. The term "cubic feet" indicates which kind of measurement? (Skill 5.12; Average rigor)

A. Volume

B. Mass

C. Length

D. Distance

68. Which of the following types of graphs would be best to use to record the eye color of the students in the class? (Skill 5.13; Average rigor)

A. Bar graph or circle graph

B. Pictograph or bar graph

C. Line graph or pictograph

D. Line graph or bar graph

69. Which type of graph uses symbols to represent quantities? (Skill 5.13; Average rigor)

A. Bar graph

B. Line graph

C. Pictograph

D. Circle graph

70. Jason has five baseball cards. His friend Marcus gives him six more baseball cards. How many baseball cards does Jason have in all? (Skill 5.14; Easy)

    A.   5

    B.   11

    C.   30

    D.   1

71. Mr. Lacey is using problem solving to help students develop their math skills. He gives the class a box of pencils. He says that the pencils have to be divided so that each student has the same number of pencils. What step should come first in problem solving? (Skill 5.14; Rigorous)

    A.   Find a strategy to solve the problem

    B.   Identify the problem

    C.   Count the number of pencils

    D.   Make basic calculations

72. Which of the following should NOT be associated with the early history of Massachusetts? (Skill 6.1; Average rigor)

    A.   Plymouth Colony

    B.   Jamestown

    C.   Witchcraft

    D.   Pilgrims

73. Which of the following ancient civilizations is considered the cradle of democracy? (Skill 6.2; Rigorous)

    A.   Israel

    B.   Mesopotamia

    C.   Greece

    D.   Macedonia

74. Which ancient people practiced what is believed to be the earliest form of monotheism? (Skill 6.2; Rigorous)

    A.   Chaldeans

    B.   Persians

    C.   Mycenaeans

    D.   Israelites

75. Which of the following contributed the most to the growth of densely populated cities? (Skill 6.3; Average rigor)

    A. Scientific Revolution

    B. Agricultural Revolution

    C. Industrial Revolution

    D. Information Revolution

76. What does geography include the study of? (Skill 6.4; Easy)

    A. Location

    B. Distribution of living things

    C. Distribution of the earth's features

    D. All of the above

77. Which of the following is NOT one of the basic themes of geography? (Skill 6.4; Rigorous)

    A. Spatial organization

    B. Polarity

    C. Location

    D. Movement

78. Economics is the study of how a society allocates its scarce resources to satisfy: (Skill 6.5; Average rigor)

    A. Unlimited and competing wants

    B. Limited and competing wants

    C. Unlimited and cooperative wants

    D. Limited and cooperative wants

79. The two elements of a market economy are: (Skill 6.5; Rigorous)

    A. Inflation and deflation

    B. Supply and demand

    C. Cost and price

    D. Wants and needs

80. Which of the following is NOT one of the branches of government established by the U.S. Constitution? (Skill 6.6; Average rigor)

    A. Executive

    B. Legislative

    C. Federal

    D. Judicial

81. Which of the following powers are reserved to the states by the U.S. Constitution? (Skill 6.6; Rigorous)

   A. Regulate intrastate trade

   B. Raise and support the armed forces

   C. Govern territories

   D. Establish courts

82. Who has the power to veto a bill that has passed the House of Representatives and the Senate? (Skill 6.7; Rigorous)

   A. The President

   B. The Vice President

   C. The Speaker of the House

   D. Any member of Congress

83. What is the basic unit of local government and its governing body in Massachusetts? (Skill 6.8; Average rigor)

   A. City; city council

   B. County; county board

   C. Town; town meeting

   D. Commonwealth of Massachusetts; Congress of Massachusetts

84. Which of the following is NOT one of the first ten amendments to the U.S. Constitution, also known as the Bill of Rights? (Skill 6.8; Rigorous)

   A. Right to trial by jury, right to legal council

   B. Right against unreasonable search and seizures

   C. Right to immediate trial

   D. Right to jury trial for civil actions

85. The rights of U.S. citizens also imply certain responsibilities to be exercised. What are the most important responsibilities of citizens? (Skill 6.9; Rigorous)

   A. Jury duty, voting, freedom of religion, right to due process

   B. Voting, respecting the rights of others, right to due process

   C. Obeying rules and laws, paying taxes, justice, due process

   D. Voting, obeying rules and laws, paying taxes, respecting the rights of others, jury duty

86. **Scientific inquiry begins with: (Skill 7.1; Easy)**

    A.   A hypothesis

    B.   An observation

    C.   A conclusion

    D.   An experiment

87. **Which of the following is true about the human genome project? (Skill 7.2; Average rigor)**

    A.   Its purpose was to map and sequence the human genome.

    B.   It was a United States private project.

    C.   It began in 1950.

    D.   It led to the development of cloning technology.

88. **Science and technology are best described as: (Skill 7.3; Average rigor)**

    A.   Different names for the same thing

    B.   Competing against each other

    C.   Closely related and intertwined

    D.   Independent of each other

89. **Which term correctly describes skeletal muscle? (Skill 7.4; Rigorous)**

    A.   Voluntary

    B.   Involuntary

    C.   Active

    D.   Inactive

90. **Who is known as the father of genetics? (Skill 7.4; Average rigor)**

    A.   Charles Darwin

    B.   Carl von Linnaeus

    C.   Gregor Mendel

    D.   Louis Pasteur

91. **Phase of matter is identified by: (Skill 7.5; Rigorous)**

    A.   Shape and mass

    B.   Shape and volume

    C.   Volume and mass

    D.   Shape, mass, and volume

92. On the moon, an object's _____ will differ from its calculated amount on Earth because of the Moon's lack of gravity. (Skill 7.5; Easy)

    A.   Weight

    B.   Mass

    C.   Volume

    D.   Density

93. Which of the following units is a measure of temperature? (Skill 7.5; Average rigor)

    A.   Watts

    B.   Joules

    C.   Kelvin

    D.   Ounces

94. Which of the following causes the Earth to have seasons? (Skill 7.5; Rigorous)

    A.   The Earth's magnetic field

    B.   The Earth's tilt on its axis

    C.   The Earth's moon

    D.   The Earth's tectonic plates

95. Which of the following is a vector quantity that refers to the rate at which an object changes its position? (Skill 7.5; Rigorous)

    A.   Speed

    B.   Momentum

    C.   Velocity

    D.   Motion

96. What groups or patterns of stars do astronomers use as reference points in the sky? (Skill 7.5; Average rigor)

    A.   Galaxies

    B.   Nebula

    C.   Constellations

    D.   All of the above

97. Plate Tectonic Theory proposes that the Earth's surface is composed of: (Skill 7.5; Rigorous)

    A.   Lithospheric plates

    B.   Atmospheric plates

    C.   Hydrospheric plates

    D.   Biospheric plates

98. **What should an experiment have a minimum number of to produce accurate and easily correlated results? (Skill 7.7; Easy)**

    A.   Controls

    B.   Variables

    C.   Samples

    D.   Participants

99. **Which hypothesis is valid? (Skill 7.7; Rigorous)**

    A.   An unknown factor causes tomato plants to produce no fruit sometimes.

    B.   A tomato plant will produce tasty fruit if it is watered.

    C.   A tomato plant will grow faster in full sunlight than partial sunlight.

    D.   A tomato plant given this fertilizer will produce better fruit than all others.

100. **What is the last step in the scientific method? (Skill 7.7; Average rigor)**

    A.   Pose a question

    B.   Draw a conclusion

    C.   Conduct a test

    D.   Record data

Pre Test Answer Key

1.	B	35.	A	69.	C
2.	B	36.	A	70.	B
3.	A	37.	B	71.	B
4.	D	38.	A	72.	B
5.	B	39.	D	73.	C
6.	C	40.	C	74.	D
7.	D	41.	A	75.	C
8.	A	42.	A	76.	D
9.	C	43.	C	77.	B
10.	A	44.	A	78.	A
11.	D	45.	D	79.	B
12.	D	46.	C	80.	C
13.	C	47.	B	81.	A
14.	A	48.	A	82.	A
15.	B	49.	B	83.	C
16.	C	50.	D	84.	C
17.	C	51.	C	85.	D
18.	D	52.	A	86.	B
19.	A	53.	B	87.	A
20.	C	54.	A	88.	C
21.	C	55.	C	89.	A
22.	B	56.	C	90.	C
23.	D	57.	C	91.	B
24.	B	58.	A	92.	A
25.	B	59.	C	93.	C
26.	C	60.	B	94.	B
27.	A	61.	D	95.	C
28.	B	62.	D	96.	C
29.	B	63.	C	97.	A
30.	C	64.	A	98.	B
31.	B	65.	A	99.	C
32.	D	66.	C	100.	B
33.	C	67.	A		
34.	B	68.	B		

Pre Test Rigor Table

	Easy %20	Average Rigor %40	Rigorous %40
Question #	1, 5, 10, 17, 18, 20, 23, 31, 34, 37, 40, 47, 49, 52, 58, 70, 76, 86, 92, 98	2, 3, 4, 11, 15, 16, 19, 21, 24, 26, 27, 28, 29, 30, 36, 38, 39, 41, 44, 48, 53, 55, 57, 61, 64, 66, 67, 68, 69, 72, 75, 78, 80, 83, 87, 88, 90, 93, 96, 100	6, 7, 8, 9, 12, 13, 14, 22, 25, 32, 33, 35, 42, 43, 45, 46, 50, 51, 54, 56, 59, 60, 62, 63, 65, 71, 73, 74, 77, 79, 81, 82, 84, 85, 89, 91, 94, 95, 97, 99

Pre Test Answer Key Rationale

Subarea I. Knowledge of Child Development

1. **How many stages of intellectual development does Piaget define? (Skill 1.1; Easy)**

    A. Two
    B. Four
    C. Six
    D. Eight

Answer B: Four

Jean Piaget's theory describes how human minds develop through four stages. The first stage is the sensory-motor stage. This occurs up to age 2 and involves understanding the world via the senses. The second stage is the pre-operational stage. It occurs from ages 2 to 7 and involves understanding symbols. The concrete operations stage occurs from ages 7 to 11 and is where children begin to develop reason. The final stage is the formal operations stage. It involves the development of logical and abstract thinking.

2. **Which level of Bloom's taxonomy involves having students categorize, compare, and distinguish? (Skill 1.1; Average rigor)**

    A. Application
    B. Analysis
    C. Synthesis
    D. Evaluation

Answer B: Analysis

Bloom's taxonomy classifies critical thinking and learning skills/objectives into six tiered levels. The six levels are: knowledge, understanding/comprehension, application, analysis, synthesis, and evaluation. Tasks at the analysis stage tasks ask students to calculate, categorize, compare, contrast, criticize, distinguish, examine, and experiment.

3. **According to Piaget, during what stage do children learn to manipulate symbols and objects? (Skill 1.1; Average rigor)**

    A. Concrete operations
    B. Pre-operational
    C. Formal operations
    D. Conservative operational

Answer A: Concrete operations

In the pre-operational stage, children begin to understand symbols. In the concrete operations stage, children go one step beyond this and begin to learn to manipulate symbols, objects and other elements.

4. **What does the Multiple Intelligence Theory developed by Howard Gardner explain? (Skill 1.1; Average rigor)**

    A. How the intelligence of students depends on the environment
    B. How the intelligence of students constantly change
    C. How students have different levels of overall intelligence
    D. How students learn in at least seven different ways

Answer D: How students learn in at least seven different ways

Gardner's Multiple Intelligence Theory suggests that students learn in (at least) seven different ways. These include visually/spatially, musically, verbally, logically/mathematically, interpersonally, intrapersonally, and bodily/kinesthetically.

5. **According to Kohlberg, what is the first level of moral development in which judgments are made on the basis of physical consequences and personal needs?** (Skill 1.1; Easy)

    A.   Anxiety level
    B.   Pre-conventional level
    C.   Post-conventional level
    D.   Symbolic level

Answer B: Pre-conventional level

Kohlberg's stages of moral development theory has six stages grouped into three levels: pre-conventional, conventional, and post-conventional. The pre-conventional stage includes the punishment/obedience level, where morality is based on following rules and avoiding negative consequences. The pre-conventional stage also includes the instrumental purpose stage, where whatever satisfies the child's needs is considered moral by that child.

6. **Why is Kohlberg's theory important to classroom teachers?** (Skill 1.1; Rigorous)

    A.   It is a theory that explains how language is acquired.
    B.   It is a theory that explains how complex and logical thought is developed.
    C.   It is a theory that explains the stages of moral development in a child.
    D.   It is a theory that explains how higher mental functions develop in a child.

Answer C: It is a theory that explains the stages of moral development in a child.

Kohlberg's theory explains how stages progress through stages of moral development. In the pre-conventional level, morality is based on obeying rules and avoiding punishment, and satisfying one's own needs. This occurs up to age 9. From 9 to adolescence is the conventional level. In this level, morality is based on acting based on the expectation of others and fulfilling obligations. The post-conventional level occurs in adulthood. In this level, morality is based on a social contract and on reasoning based on universal ethical principles such as fairness.

7. **Which of the following is an example of a synthesis task according to Bloom's taxonomy? (Skill 1.1; Rigorous)**

   A. Write a definition of nuclear fission.
   B. Compare nuclear power to electrical power.
   C. Classify the outcomes of using nuclear power as negative or positive.
   D. Propose an alternative to nuclear power and explain why it is superior to nuclear power.

Answer D: Propose an alternative to nuclear power and explain why it is superior to nuclear power.

Bloom's taxonomy classifies critical thinking and learning skills/objectives into six tiered levels. The six levels are: knowledge, understanding/comprehension, application, analysis, synthesis, and evaluation. Tasks at the evaluation stage ask students to assess, appraise, predict, rate, support, evaluate, judge, and argue.

8. **According to Erikson's theory of psychosocial development, what is the cause of temper tantrums in children aged 1 to 3? (Skill 1.1; Rigorous)**

   A. A desire to be independent
   B. A lack of empathy
   C. A sense of general confusion
   D. An increase in feelings of guilt

Answer A: A desire to be independent

Erikson's theory of psychosocial development describes how humans go through eights stages of development as they go from infancy to adulthood. The Young Childhood stage occurs from ages 1 to 3. During this stage, children want to be independent. If children are unable to be independent, they can use temper tantrums as a way to test the adults in charge.

9. **Why is it most important for teachers to ensure that students from different economic backgrounds have access to the resources they need to acquire the academic skills being taught? (Skill 1.2; Rigorous)**

    A. All students must work together on set tasks.
    B. All students must achieve the same results in performance tasks.
    C. All students must have equal opportunity for academic success.
    D. All students must be fully included in classroom activities.

Answer C: All students must have equal opportunity for academic success.

The economic backgrounds of students can impact the resources they have. Regardless of the positive or negative impacts on the students' education from outside sources, it is the teacher's responsibility to ensure that all students in the classroom have an equal opportunity for academic success. This includes ensuring that all students have equal access to the resources needed to acquire the skills being taught.

10. **Family members with high levels of education often have high expectations for student success. This shows how students are influenced by their family's: (Skill 1.2; Easy)**

    A. Attitude
    B. Resources
    C. Income
    D. Culture

Answer A: Attitude

Parental/family influences on students include the influence of attitude. Family members with high levels of education often have high expectations for student success and this can have a positive impact on the student. The opposite can occur for some students from families with low levels of education. However, some families have high expectations for student success based on aspirations for their children regardless of their own status.

11. **Which of the following is a sign of emotional neglect? (Skill 1.3; Average rigor)**

    A. Jealousy of other children
    B. Aggression
    C. Lack of attention to schoolwork
    D. All of the above

Answer D: All of the above

Signs of emotional neglect include jealousy of other children, aggression, lack of attention to schoolwork, and feelings of anger toward others. These can also be signs that a student has recently endured a family upset.

12. **A teacher is planning to get all of her students involved in sports for the purpose of helping develop hand-eye coordination and teamwork skills. What would be the most appropriate approach when planning the sports activities? (Skill 1.4; Rigorous)**

    A. Encourage competition among students so they become used to the pressure of competing.
    B. Ensure that students who dislike sports continue until they enjoy sports.
    C. Choose activities that are beyond the student's current abilities so students are prompted to improve.
    D. Maintain a relaxed atmosphere and remind students that the sport is designed to be fun.

Answer D: Maintain a relaxed atmosphere and remind students that the sport is designed to be fun.

Sports can be valuable in child development. They can develop motor skills, social skills, and help students develop personal interests. It is important that sporting activities for young children focus on the positive benefits such as the development of motor skills and personal interests, rather than focusing on competition.

13. **Which of the following is a true statement? (Skill 1.4; Rigorous)**

   A.   Recess is not important to a child's development.
   B.   Playtime is only provided in schools to help children release energy.
   C.   Play has an important and positive role in child development.
   D.   Solitary play is always an indication that a child has development issues.

Answer C: Play has an important and positive role in child development.

Too often, recess and play is considered peripheral or unimportant to a child's development. It's sometimes seen as a way to allow kids to just get physical energy out or a "tradition" of childhood. The truth is, though, that play is very important to human development. Play is an activity that helps teach basic values such as sharing and cooperation. It also teaches that taking care of oneself (as opposed to constantly working) is good for human beings and further creates a more enjoyable society.

14. **A student has developed and improved their vocabulary. However, the student is not confident enough to use their improved vocabulary, and the teacher is not aware of the improvement. What is this an example of? (Skill 1.5; Rigorous)**

   A.   Latent development
   B.   Dormant development
   C.   Random development
   D.   Delayed development

Answer A: Latent development

Latent development refers to the way that development in students may not always be observable. A student that has developed and improved their vocabulary, but lacks the confidence to use the vocabulary would not show any outward signs of the development, and so the change may remain hidden. Teachers should be aware of this in order to identify a child's future or near-future capabilities.

15. **Which of the following best describes how different areas of development impact each other? (Skill 1.5; Average rigor)**

   A. Development in other areas cannot occur until cognitive development is complete.
   B. Areas of development are inter-related and impact each other.
   C. Development in each area is independent of development in other areas.
   D. Development in one area leads to a decline in other areas.

Answer B: Areas of development are inter-related and impact each other.

Child development does not occur in a vacuum. Each element of development impacts other elements of development. For example, as cognitive development progresses, social development often follows. The reason for this is that all areas of development are fairly inter-related.

16. **A child exhibits the following symptoms: inability to appreciate humor, indifference to physical contact, abnormal social play, and abnormal speech. What is the likely diagnosis for this child? (Skill 2.1; Average rigor)**

   A. Separation anxiety
   B. Mental retardation
   C. Autism
   D. Hypochondria

Answer C: Autism

According to many psychologists who have been involved with treating autistic children, it seems that these children have built a wall between themselves and everyone else, including their families and even their parents. They are often indifferent to physical contact, engage in abnormal social play, display abnormal speech, are unable to appreciate humor, and cannot empathize with others.

17. **What type of disability does a student who talks incessantly using bizarre words most likely have? (Skill 2.1; Easy)**

   A.   Attention deficit hyperactivity disorder
   B.   Severe emotional stress
   C.   Schizophrenia
   D.   Dyslexia

Answer C: Schizophrenia

The most common psychosis of childhood is schizophrenia, which is a deliberate escape from reality and a withdrawal from relationships with others. One of the major signs of this disorder is a habitually flat or habitually agitated facial expression. Children suffering from schizophrenia are occasionally mute, but at times they talk incessantly using bizarre words in ways that make no sense.

18. **A child with a disability is one who has: (Skill 2.1; Easy)**

   A.   Sensory impairments
   B.   Emotional disturbance
   C.   Mental retardation
   D.   Any of the above

Answer D: Any of the above

Special education teachers should be aware that although students across disabilities may demonstrate difficulty in similar ways, the causes may be very different. For example, some disabilities are due to specific sensory impairments (hearing or vision), some due to cognitive ability (mental retardation), and some due to neurological impairment (autism or some learning disabilities). The reason for the difficulty should be a consideration when planning the program of special education intervention.

19. **Which of the following is the most likely cause of a child becoming easily agitated in class? (Skill 2.2; Average rigor)**

   A. Lack of sleep
   B. Lack of training in manners
   C. Being raised in a single parent home
   D. Watching too much television

Answer A: Lack of sleep

Symptoms of a lack of nutrition and sleep most notably include a lack of concentration, particularly in the classroom. Furthermore, children who lack sufficient sleep or nutrition may become agitated more easily than other children.

20. **Who should you talk to if you suspect child abuse? (Skill 2.2; Easy)**

   A. The child
   B. The child's parent
   C. Your supervisor
   D. Another teacher

Answer C: Your supervisor

The best action to take when children abuse is suspected is immediately contact a superior at the school, such as your supervisor. The child who is undergoing the abuse is the one whose needs must be served first. A suspected case gone unreported may destroy a child's life, and their subsequent life as a functional adult. It is the duty of any citizen who suspects abuse and neglect to make a report, and it is especially important and required for State licensed and certified persons to make a report.

21. **What is the most important factor in improving the developmental and educational gains for students with language delays? (Skill 2.3; Average rigor)**

   A. Varied teaching procedures
   B. The social environment
   C. Early intervention
   D. Encouraging independence

Answer C: Early intervention

Teachers and parents who have concerns about a child's language development should be proactive in addressing language delays. Early intervention is the key to addressing children's language delays or differences.

22. **What is the most significant development emerging in children at age two? (Skill 2.3; Rigorous)**

    A. Immune system development
    B. Language development
    C. Socialization development
    D. Perception development

Answer B: Language development

The most significant development emerging in children at age two is language development. General researchers have shown that children at 2 years old should have speech patterns that are about 70% intelligible.

23. **What actions are observed in aggressive children? (Skill 2.4; Easy)**

    A. Vandalism
    B. Destruction of property
    C. Verbal abuse
    D. All of the above

Answer D: All of the above

Aggressive children often fight or instigate their peers to strike back at them. Aggressiveness may also take the form of vandalism or destruction of property. Aggressive children also engage in verbal abuse.

24. **What area of differentiated instruction is a teacher focusing on when planning how to teach the material? (Skill 2.5; Average rigor)**

    A. Content
    B. Process
    C. Product
    D. Assessment

Answer B: Process

The effective teacher will seek to connect all students to the subject matter through multiple techniques, with the goal that each student, through their own abilities, will relate to one or more techniques and excel in the learning process. This is known as differentiated instruction, and focuses on content (what is being taught), process (how the material will be taught), and product (the expectations placed on students to demonstrate their knowledge or understanding).

25. **What criteria are used to assess whether a child qualifies for services under IDEA? (Skill 2.5; Rigorous)**

    A. Having a disability only
    B. Having a disability and demonstrating educational need only
    C. Demonstrating educational need only
    D. Having a disability, demonstrating educational need, and having financial support

Answer B: Having a disability and demonstrating educational need only

Based on IDEA, eligibility for special education services is based on a student having one of a listed set of disabilities (or a combination thereof) and demonstration of educational need through professional evaluation.

26. **According to IDEA, who must be involved in developing a child's IEP? (Skill 2.6; Average rigor)**

    A. A medical doctor
    B. The school psychologist
    C. The parents or guardians
    D. The principal

Answer C: The parents or guardians

Under the IDEA, parent/guardian involvement in the development of the student's IEP is required and absolutely essential for the advocacy of the disabled student's educational needs. IEPs must be tailored to meet the student's needs, and no one knows those needs better than the parent/guardian and other significant family members.

27. **What would be put into place for a student with a physical disability in order to make accommodations in the classroom? (Skill 2.7; Average rigor)**

    A. 504
    B. IEP
    C. IFSP
    D. All of the above

Answer A: 504

For students diagnosed with a physical or emotional disability, the plan of action is called a 504. It is not an IEP, but it is similar in some respects in that it lists accommodations that are to be made for the student within the regular classroom setting.

28. **Because teachers today will deal with an increasingly diverse group of cultures in their classrooms, they must: (Skill 2.8; Average rigor)**

    A. Ignore the cultures represented
    B. Show respect to all parents and families
    C. Provide a celebration for each culture represented
    D. Focusing on teaching the majority

Answer B: Show respect to all parents and families

To deal with a diverse group of cultures in their classrooms, teachers must show respect to all parents and families. They need to set the tone that suggests that their mission is to develop students into the best people they can be. They also need to realize that various cultures have different views of how children should be educated.

29. **What should a teacher begin a parent-teacher conference with? (Skill 2.8; Average rigor)**

    A. Student weaknesses
    B. Positive comments
    C. Entertaining anecdotes
    D. Issues of concern

Answer B: Positive comments

A parent-teacher conference should begin with positive comments about the students. However, these should be accurate statements and not exaggerate the student's good points.

30. **The commitment that a community shows to its educational communities is: (Skill 2.9; Average rigor)**

    A. Judged by how much money is contributed
    B. Something that doesn't matter much to the school
    C. A valuable investment in the future
    D. Something that will cause immediate gains

Answer C: A valuable investment in the future

The commitment that a community shows to its educational communities is a valuable investment in the future. While monetary gifts are valued, there are many ways for the community to invest in the school. Having an involved community will create a better school for all children and will eventually lead to improved academic results.

Subarea II. Knowledge of Children's Literature and the Writing Process

31. Which of the following is NOT a characteristic of a fable? (Skill 3.1; Easy)

    A. Have animal characters that act like humans
    B. Considered to be true
    C. Teaches a moral
    D. Reveals human foibles

Answer B: Considered to be true

The common characteristics of fables are animals that act like humans, a focus on revealing human foibles, and teaching a moral or lesson. Fables are not considered to be true.

32. Ms. Smith considers the use of quality children's literature to be one of the most important qualities of an early childhood teacher. She is asked to justify her reasons behind this consideration to her principal. Which of the following is an appropriate justification? (Skill 3.1; Rigorous)

    A. There are many different types of children's literature, so there will be something to which every child can relate.
    B. Children's literature in early childhood classrooms provides the students with the opportunity to learn to read and process language.
    C. Children are like adults in many ways and need to be exposed to a variety of types of literature.
    D. Children's literature helps children improve their mental, social, and psychological skills and aids in the development in all of these areas.

Answer D: Children's literature helps children improve their mental, social, and psychological skills and aids in the development in all of these areas.

Modern educators acknowledge that introducing elementary students to a wide range of reading experiences plays an important role in their mental, social, and psychological development.

33. **In her kindergarten classroom, Mrs. Thomas has been watching the students in the drama center. She has watched the children pretend to complete a variety of magic tricks. Mrs. Thomas decides to use stories about magic to share with her class. Her decision to incorporate their interests into the reading shows that Mrs. Thomas understands that: (Skill 3.2; Rigorous)**

   A. Including student interests is important at all times
   B. Teaching by themes is crucial for young children
   C. Young children respond to literature that reflects their lives
   D. Science fiction and fantasy are the most popular genres

Answer C: Young children respond to literature that reflects their lives

Children's literature is intended to instruct students through entertaining stories, while also promoting an interest in the very act of reading, itself. Young readers respond best to themes that reflect their lives.

34. **Which of the following literary devices is most commonly found in kindergarten classrooms? (Skill 3.3; Easy)**

   A. Metaphor
   B. Repetition
   C. Simile
   D. Analogy

Answer B: Repetition

Young children often have difficulties with the more complex literary devices (metaphors, symbolism, similes and analogies). Often you will find text repetition used in big books or other forms of literature for young children.

35. **George has read his second graders three formats of the story "The Three Little Pigs." One is the traditional version, one is written from the wolf's point of view, and the third is written from the first pig's point of view. As George leads a discussion on the three texts with his students, he is trying to help his students develop their ability to: (Skill 3.4; Rigorous)**

    A. Compare and contrast texts
    B. Understand point of view
    C. Recognize metaphors
    D. Rewrite fictional stories

Answer A: Compare and contrast texts

George understands the importance of developing critical thinking skills in young children. He has read three different formats of the same story in order to help his students develop their ability to compare texts.

36. **What question would it be most important for a teacher to ask when deciding if a book will be appropriate for classroom use? (Skill 3.5; Average rigor)**

    A. Do the characters provide positive role models for children?
    B. Is the setting of the book modern?
    C. Will every student in the class be interested in the subject of the book?
    D. Is the book short enough for students to read in one sitting?

Answer A: Do the characters provide positive role models for children?

Children love to identify with the characters in books, so it is important to select books with characters that provide positive role models for children.

37. **The attitude an author takes toward his or her subject is the: (Skill 3.6; Easy)**

    A. Style
    B. Tone
    C. Point of view
    D. Theme

Answer B: Tone

Tone is the attitude an author takes toward his or her subject. That tone is exemplified in the language of the text.

38. **A book on the history of Massachusetts uses long sentences and advanced vocabulary. A children's novel set in Massachusetts 100 years ago has short sentences and simple vocabulary. What is different about the two books? (Skill 3.6; Average rigor)**

    A.   Style
    B.   Tone
    C.   Point of view
    D.   Theme

Answer A: Style

Style is the artful adaptation of language to meet various purposes. In an academic style such as the book on history, the author would use long, complex sentences, advanced vocabulary, and very structured paragraphing. However, in an informal style such as the children's novel, the author may use a conversational tone where simple words and simple sentence structures are utilized.

39. **Mr. Adams uses a short story about early train travel as part of a history lesson. This shows that literature: (Skill 3.7; Average rigor)**

    A.   Can be used to expand students' vocabulary
    B.   Can be used to build students' communication skills
    C.   Can be used to help students empathize
    D.   Can be used to enhance other areas of the curriculum

Answer D: Can be used to enhance other areas of the curriculum

"Learning across the curriculum" can be enhanced by using literature as another means to convey essential information. Using a short story with a subject related to history could be used to enhance the learning of history.

40. What is the first step in developing writing skills? (Skill 4.1; Easy)

A.   Early writing
B.   Experimental writing
C.   Role play writing
D.   Conventional writing

Answer C: Role play writing

Children develop writing skills through a series of steps. These steps are: role play writing, experimental writing, early writing, and then conventional writing. In the role play writing stage, the child writes in scribbles and assigns a message to the symbols. Even though an adult would not be able to read the writing, the child can read what is written although it may not be the same each time the child reads it. S/he will be able to read back the writing because of prior knowledge that print carries a meaning.

41. Which prewriting strategy involves making a list of all the ideas connected with a topic? (Skill 4.2; Average rigor)

A.   Brainstorming
B.   Visual mapping
C.   Observing
D.   Visualizing

Answer A: Brainstorming

Brainstorming is a prewriting strategy that involves making a list of all ideas connected with a topic. It is best used when students allow their minds to work freely, with the student only analyzing the ideas once brainstorming is complete.

42. **A second grader is writing his first book review. He is identifying the purpose of his book report, deciding his main point, and determining the supporting details he will used to make his point. What stage of the writing process is the student at? (Skill 4.3; Rigorous)**

    A.   Discovery stage
    B.   Organization stage
    C.   First draft stage
    D.   Analysis stage

Answer A: Discovery stage

The writing process can be divided into three stages. The discovery stage involves collecting ideas, materials, and supporting details.   The next stage is organization where the purpose, thesis, and supporting points are determined. This is following by the writing stage, and then the editing stage.

43. **The students in Tina's classroom are working together in pairs. Each student is reading another student's paper and asking who, what, when, where, why, and who questions. What is this activity helping the students to do? (Skill 4.4; Rigorous)**

    A.   Draft their writing
    B.   Paraphrase their writing
    C.   Revise their writing
    D.   Outline their writing

Answer C: Revise their writing

Students need to be trained to become effective at proofreading, revising and editing strategies. One way to do this is to have the students read their partners' papers and ask at least three who, what, when, why, how questions. The students answer the questions and use them as a place to begin discussing the piece.

44. **Ms. Michaels is teaching her students about revising. What would Ms. Michaels be best to tell her students about revising? (Skill 4.4; Average rigor)**

   A. Revising is an important part of the writing process and all writing should be revised.
   B. You will only have to revise until you become a good enough writer to get it perfect the first time.
   C. Revising can be skipped sometimes if you think it might ruin your writing.
   D. You will only need to revise work you complete that is to be handed in for assessment.

Answer A: Revising is an important part of the writing process and all writing should be revised.

Revision is probably the most important step for the writer in the writing process. Here, students examine their work and make changes in wording, details and ideas. Students should be encouraged to develop, change, and enhance their writing as they go, as well as once they've completed a draft. Students should also be reminded that all writing must be revised to improve it.

45. **Which sentence has correct subject-verb agreement? (Skill 4.5; Rigorous)**

   A. A workers and his bosses were having a long meeting.
   B. A workers and his bosses was having a long meeting.
   C. A worker and his boss was having a long meeting.
   D. A worker and his boss were having a long meeting.

Answer D: A worker and his boss were having a long meeting.

Subject-verb agreement is correct when a verb agrees in number with its subject. If two singular subjects are connected by **and**, the verb must be plural.

46. **An adolescent has not yet mastered spelling. What would be the best way for a teacher to address this? (Skill 4.5; Rigorous)**

    A.   Provide the student with extra instruction on spelling rules
    B.   Ensure that the student fully understands all the exceptions to rules
    C.   Encourage the student to master the use of a dictionary and thesaurus
    D.   Focus on teaching spelling and grammar in isolation

Answer C: Encourage the student to master the use of a dictionary and thesaurus

The multiplicity and complexity of spelling rules based on phonics, letter doubling, and exceptions to rules - not mastered by adulthood - should be replaced by a good dictionary. As spelling mastery is also difficult for adolescents, our recommendation is the same. Learning the use of a dictionary and thesaurus will be a more rewarding use of time.

47. **A classroom activity involves students writing letters to a mayor to ask for more bike paths to be built. What type of discourse are the students engaged in? (Skill 4.6; Easy)**

    A.   Exposition
    B.   Persuasion
    C.   Narration
    D.   Description

Answer B: Persuasion

Persuasion is a piece of writing, a poem, a play, a speech whose purpose is to change the minds of the audience members or to get them to do something. A letter to a mayor asking for a bike path to be built is being writing to convince the mayor to do something.

48. **Which of the following approaches to student writing assignments is most likely to lead to students becoming disinterested? (Skill 4.6; Average rigor)**

    A.   Designing assignments where students write for a variety of audiences.
    B.   Designing assignments where the teacher is the audience.
    C.   Designing assignments where students write to friends and family.
    D.   Designing assignments where students write to real people such as mayors, the principle, or companies.

Answer A: Designing assignments where students write for a variety of audiences.

In the past, teachers have assigned reports, paragraphs and essays that focused on the teacher as the audience with the purpose of explaining information. However, for students to be meaningfully engaged in their writing, they must write for a variety of reasons. Writing for different audiences and aims allows students to be more involved in their writing. If they write for the same audience and purpose, they will continue to see writing as just another assignment

49. **A teacher is using the sentence "Beautiful Beth is the best girl in the Bradley Bay area" in a writing lesson. What are the students learning about? (Skill 4.7; Easy)**

    A.   Assonance
    B.   Alliteration
    C.   Onomatopoeia
    D.   Metaphor

Answer B: Alliteration

Alliteration occurs when the initial sounds of a word, beginning either with a consonant or a vowel, are repeated in close succession. The sentence "Beautiful Beth is the best girl in the Bradley Bay area" contains alliteration because of the repeated "b" sound.

50. A student writes in a book report that a book they read has a writing style like no other book they have ever read before. When the student revises their report, they write that the book has a unique writing style. What improvement has been made? (Skill 4.8; Rigorous)

   A. The tone is less formal.
   B. The sentence structure is more complex.
   C. Figurative language is removed.
   D. The vocabulary is precise.

Answer D: The vocabulary is precise.

While students may not know all the best words that could summarize their thoughts, whenever one very precise word can take the place of a variety of words, students should use that one precise word. The student improves the report because the precise word "unique" is used in place of the imprecise words "like no other book."

Subarea III. Core Knowledge in the Content Areas

51. What math principle is reinforced by matching numerals with number words? (Skill 5.1; Rigorous)

   A. Sequencing
   B. Greater than and less than
   C. Number representations
   D. Rote counting

Answer C: Number representations

The students are practicing recognition that a numeral (such as 5) has a corresponding number word (five) that represents the same math concept. They are not putting numbers in order (sequencing), and they are not comparing two numbers for value (greater than or less than). In this activity, students are also not counting in order just for the sake of counting (rote counting).

52. How is the following read? (Skill 5.1; Easy)

   3 < 5

   A.   Three is less than five
   B.   Five is greater than three
   C.   Three is greater than five
   D.   Five is less than three

Answer A: Three is less than five

Reading left to right: *three is less than five.*

53. **Which words in a test problem would indicate that an addition operation is needed? (Skill 5.1; Average rigor)**

   A.   Each
   B.   How many
   C.   In each group
   D.   How many more than

Answer B: How many

Addition operations are indicated by the following words: total, sum, in all, join, how many. Subtraction operations are indicated by the following words: difference, how many more than, how many less than, left. Multiplication operations are indicated by the following words: in all, each, of. Division operations are indicated by the following words: in each group, per, divide.

54. **Kindergarten students are participating in a calendar time activity. One student adds a straw to the "ones can" to represent that day of school. What math principle is being reinforced? (Skill 5.4; Rigorous)**

   A.   Properties of a base ten number system
   B.   Sorting
   C.   Counting by twos
   D.   Even and odd numbers

Answer A: Properties of a base ten number system

As the students group craft sticks into groups of tens to represent the days of school, they are learning the properties of our base ten number system.

55. First grade students are arranging four small squares of identical size to form a larger square. Each small square represents what part of the larger square? (Skill 5.5; Average rigor)

    A. One half
    B. One whole
    C. One fourth
    D. One fifth

Answer C: One fourth

Four of the small squares make up the area of the large square. Each small square is one fourth of the larger square.

56. Third grade students are looking at a circle graph. Most of the graph is yellow. A small wedge of the graph is blue. Each colored section also has a number followed by a symbol. What are the students most likely learning about? (Skill 5.5; Rigorous)

    A. Addition
    B. Venn diagrams
    C. Percent
    D. Pictographs

Answer C: Percent

The symbol after the numbers of the sections indicates that students are learning about percents instead of an exact number.

57. A teacher is introducing the concept of multiplication to her third grade students. What is another way she might write 4 x 5? (Skill 5.6; Average rigor)

    A. 4 + 5
    B. 5 + 4
    C. 4 + 4 + 4 + 4 + 4
    D. 5 + 5 + 5 + 5 + 5

Answer C: 4 + 4 + 4 + 4 + 4

The multiplication concept can translate to an addition problem. 4 x 5 is the same as the number 4 added 5 times.

58. **What is the answer to this problem? (Skill 5.7; Easy)**

    25 ÷ 5 =

    A.   5
    B.   30
    C.   125
    D.   20

Answer A: 5

Twenty-five can be divided into five equal groups of five.

59. **Which other equation is a part of this fact family? (Skill 5.7; Rigorous)**

    2 + 6 = 8
    8 – 2 = 6
    6 + 2 = 8

    A.   6 – 2 = 4
    B.   8 + 6 = 14
    C.   8 – 6 = 2
    D.   8 + 2 = 10

Answer C: 8 - 6 = 2

A fact family uses the same three numbers to form two addition and two subtraction problems or two multiplication and two division problems.

60. **What is the main purpose of having kindergarten students count by twos? (Skill 5.8; Rigorous)**

    A.   To hear a rhythm
    B.   To recognize patterns in numbers
    C.   To practice addition
    D.   To become familiar with equations

Answer B: To recognize patterns in numbers

Recognizing patterns in numbers is an early skill for multiplication. It will also help children recognize patterns in word families such as *bit, hit, fit.*

61. **A teacher plans an activity that involves students calculating how many chair legs are in the classroom, given that there are 30 chairs and each chair has 4 legs. This activity is introducing the ideas of: (Skill 5.8; Average rigor)**

    A. Probability
    B. Statistics
    C. Geometry
    D. Algebra

Answer D: Algebra

This activity involves recognizing patterns. It could also involve problem-solving by developing an expression that represents the problem. Activities such as this do not introduce the terms of algebra, but they introduce some of the ideas of algebra.

62. **Square is to cube as triangle is to: (Skill 5.9; Rigorous)**

    A. Sphere
    B. Rectangle
    C. Cone
    D. Tetrahedron

Answer D: Tetrahedron

A square is a two-dimensional polygon, and a cube is a three-dimensional solid made up of squares. A triangle is a two-dimensional polygon, and a tetrahedron is a three-dimensional solid made up of triangles.

63. **Kindergarten students are doing a butterfly art project. They fold paper in half. On one half, they paint a design. Then they fold the paper closed and reopen. The resulting picture is a butterfly with matching sides. What math principle does this demonstrate? (Skill 5.10; Rigorous)**

   A.   Slide
   B.   Rotate
   C.   Symmetry
   D.   Transformation

Answer C: Symmetry

By folding the painted paper in half, the design is mirrored on the other side, creating symmetry and reflection. The butterfly design is symmetrical about the center.

64. **Students completing an activity with tangrams are learning what math principle? (Skill 5.10; Average rigor)**

   A.   Basic geometric concepts
   B.   Repeating patterns
   C.   Counting
   D.   Identity property

Answer A: Basic geometric concepts

The students are learning basic geometric concepts (number of sides and types of angles). The tangram picture may or may not be a repeating design. Counting and the identity property (a number plus zero always equals the original number) are not involved.

65. **When a student completes the following number sentence, which math concept is being learned? (Skill 5.11; Rigorous)**

$$15 - \textbf{+} = 6$$

A. Addition/subtraction and basic algebraic concepts
B. Counting and addition/subtraction
C. Counting and basic algebraic concepts
D. Counting and pattern recognition

Answer A: Addition/subtraction and basic algebraic concepts

Students may use basic addition or subtraction by rearranging the numbers. They are also demonstrating the algebraic concept of finding the value of a missing number.

66. **Students are working with a set of rulers and various small objects from the classroom. Which concept are these students exploring? (Skill 5.12; Average rigor)**

A. Volume
B. Weight
C. Length
D. Temperature

Answer C: Length

The use of a ruler indicates that the activity is based on exploring length.

67. **The term "cubic feet" indicates which kind of measurement? (Skill 5.12; Average rigor)**

A. Volume
B. Mass
C. Length
D. Distance

Answer A: Volume

The word *cubic* indicates that this is a term describing volume.

68. **Which of the following types of graphs would be best to use to record the eye color of the students in the class? (Skill 5.13; Average rigor)**

    A.   Bar graph or circle graph
    B.   Pictograph or bar graph
    C.   Line graph or pictograph
    D.   Line graph or bar graph

Answer B: Pictograph or bar graph

A pictograph or a line graph could be used. In this activity, a line graph would not be used because it shows change over time. Although a circle graph could be used to show a percentage of students with brown eyes, blue eyes, etc. that representation would be too advanced for early childhood students.

69. **Which type of graph uses symbols to represent quantities? (Skill 5.13; Average rigor)**

    A.   Bar graph
    B.   Line graph
    C.   Pictograph
    D.   Circle graph

Answer C: Pictograph

A pictograph shows comparison of quantities using symbols. Each symbol represents a number of items.

70. **Jason has five baseball cards. His friend Marcus gives him six more baseball cards. How many baseball cards does Jason have in all? (Skill 5.14; Easy)**

    A.   5
    B.   11
    C.   30
    D.   1

Answer B: 11

The words *in all* indicate that this is an addition problem: 5 + 6 = 11. The correct answer is 11.

71. **Mr. Lacey is using problem solving to help students develop their math skills. He gives the class a box of pencils. He says that the pencils have to be divided so that each student has the same number of pencils. What step should come first in problem solving? (Skill 5.14; Rigorous)**

    A. Find a strategy to solve the problem
    B. Identify the problem
    C. Count the number of pencils
    D. Make basic calculations

Answer B: Identify the problem

The first step in problem solving is always to identify the problem.

72. **Which of the following should NOT be associated with the early history of Massachusetts? (Skill 6.1; Average rigor)**

    A. Plymouth Colony
    B. Jamestown
    C. Witchcraft
    D. Pilgrims

Answer B: Jamestown

Of all of the original thirteen states of America, Massachusetts is the one most commonly associated with the early history of the nation. Plymouth Rock, the Pilgrims and Puritans, Salem and its witchcraft, the Boston Tea Party, Paul Revere, Lexington and Concord are all names and events that leap to mind when once things of the colonial period. Jamestown was the first settlement in the Virginia colony.

73. **Which of the following ancient civilizations is considered the cradle of democracy? (Skill 6.2; Rigorous)**

    A. Israel
    B. Mesopotamia
    C. Greece
    D. Macedonia

Answer C: Greece

The Greek capital of Athens was known for its practice of pure democracy, which involved direct, personal, and active participation in government by qualified citizens.

74. **Which ancient people practiced what is believed to be the earliest form of monotheism? (Skill 6.2; Rigorous)**

   A.   Chaldeans
   B.   Persians
   C.   Mycenaeans
   D.   Israelites

Answer D: Israelites

The primary contribution of the Israelites was their religion, perhaps the earliest form of monotheism. This religion regulated every aspect of the life of the people with an encompassing legal code, preserved in Scripture, which regulated all aspects of human interaction, both within the community and with outsiders.

75. **Which of the following contributed the most to the growth of densely populated cities? (Skill 6.3; Average rigor)**

   A.   Scientific Revolution
   B.   Agricultural Revolution
   C.   Industrial Revolution
   D.   Information Revolution

Answer C: Industrial Revolution

The Industrial Revolution, which began in Great Britain and spread elsewhere, was the development of power-driven machinery (fueled by coal and steam) leading to the accelerated growth of industry with large factories replacing homes and small workshops as work centers. The lives of people changed drastically, and a largely agricultural society changed to an industrial one.

76. **What does geography include the study of? (Skill 6.4; Easy)**

   A.   Location
   B.   Distribution of living things
   C.   Distribution of the earth's features
   D.   All of the above

Answer D: All of the above

Geography involves studying location and how living things and earth's features are distributed throughout the earth. It includes where animals, people, and plants live and the effects of their relationship with earth's physical features.

77. Which of the following is NOT one of the basic themes of geography? (Skill 6.4; Rigorous)

    A.   Spatial organization
    B.   Polarity
    C.   Location
    D.   Movement

Answer B: Polarity

Geography can be divided into six themes. They are location, special organization, place, human-environment interaction, movement, and regions.

78. Economics is the study of how a society allocates its scarce resources to satisfy: (Skill 6.5; Average rigor)

    A.   Unlimited and competing wants
    B.   Limited and competing wants
    C.   Unlimited and cooperative wants
    D.   Limited and cooperative wants

Answer A: Unlimited and competing wants

Economics is the study of how a society allocates its scarce resources to satisfy what are basically unlimited and competing wants. A fundamental fact of economics is that resources are scarce and that wants are infinite.

79. The two elements of a market economy are: (Skill 6.5; Rigorous)

    A.   Inflation and deflation
    B.   Supply and demand
    C.   Cost and price
    D.   Wants and needs

Answer B: Supply and demand

A market economy is based on supply and demand. Demand is based on consumer preferences and satisfaction and refers to the quantities of a good or service that buyers are willing and able to buy at different prices during a given period of time. Supply is based on costs of production and refers to the quantities that sellers are willing and able to sell at different prices during a given period of time.

80. **Which of the following is NOT one of the branches of government established by the U.S. Constitution? (Skill 6.6; Average rigor)**

    A.   Executive
    B.   Legislative
    C.   Federal
    D.   Judicial

Answer C: Federal

The U.S. Constitution divides the government into three branches. The legislative or law-making branch of the government is called the Congress. The Executive branch of the government, headed by the President, leads the country, recommends new laws, and can veto bills passed by the Legislative branch. The Judicial branch of government is headed by the Supreme Court and has the power to rule that a law passed by the legislature, or an act of the Executive branch is illegal and unconstitutional.

81. **Which of the following powers are reserved to the states by the U.S. Constitution? (Skill 6.6; Rigorous)**

    A.   Regulate intrastate trade
    B.   Raise and support the armed forces
    C.   Govern territories
    D.   Establish courts

Answer A: Regulate intrastate trade

The U.S. Constitution reserves the following powers to the states:
1. To regulate intrastate trade.
2. To establish local governments.
3. To protect general welfare.
4. To protect life and property.
5. To ratify amendments.
6. To conduct elections.
7. To make state and local laws.

82. **Who has the power to veto a bill that has passed the House of Representatives and the Senate? (Skill 6.7; Rigorous)**

    A.   The President
    B.   The Vice President
    C.   The Speaker of the House
    D.   Any member of Congress

Answer A: The President

Once a bill receives final approval by a conference committee, it is signed by the Speaker of the House and the Vice President, who is also the President of the Senate, and sent to the President for consideration. The President may either sign the bill or veto it. If he vetoes the bill, his veto may be overruled if two-thirds of both the Senate and the House vote to do so. Once the President signs it the bill becomes a law.

83. **What is the basic unit of local government and its governing body in Massachusetts? (Skill 6.8; Average rigor)**

    A.   City; city council
    B.   County; county board
    C.   Town; town meeting
    D.   Commonwealth of Massachusetts; Congress of Massachusetts

Answer C: Town; town meeting

The Commonwealth of Massachusetts is governed under a constitution which dates from 1780. The unit of local government is the township, or the town. This form of government originated in Massachusetts. Selectmen, elected at the town meetings, are at the head of affairs in towns.

84. **Which of the following is NOT one of the first ten amendments to the U.S. Constitution, also known as the Bill of Rights? (Skill 6.8; Rigorous)**

    A.   Right to trial by jury, right to legal council
    B.   Right against unreasonable search and seizures
    C.   Right to immediate trial
    D.   Right to jury trial for civil actions

Answer C: Right to immediate trial

The right to trial by jury and the right to jury trial for civil actions are included in the Bill of Rights. However, the right to immediate trial is not a right in the Bill of Rights.

85. **The rights of U.S. citizens also imply certain responsibilities to be exercised. What are the most important responsibilities of citizens? (Skill 6.9; Rigorous)**

    A. Jury duty, voting, freedom of religion, right to due process
    B. Voting, respecting the rights of others, right to due process
    C. Obeying rules and laws, paying taxes, justice, due process
    D. Voting, obeying rules and laws, paying taxes, respecting the rights of others, jury duty

Answer D: Voting, obeying rules and laws, paying taxes, respecting the rights of others, jury duty

The responsibilities of U.S. citizens include respecting others' rights, obeying laws and rules, paying taxes, jury duty, and voting.

86. **Scientific inquiry begins with: (Skill 7.1; Easy)**

    A. A hypothesis
    B. An observation
    C. A conclusion
    D. An experiment

Answer B: An observation

Observations, however general they may seem, lead scientists to create a viable question and an educated guess (hypothesis) about what to expect. The hypothesis can be tested by an experiment, and a conclusion drawn based on the experiment.

87. **Which of the following is true about the human genome project? (Skill 7.2; Average rigor)**

   A.   Its purpose was to map and sequence the human genome.
   B.   It was a United States private project.
   C.   It began in 1950.
   D.   It led to the development of cloning technology.

Answer A: Its purpose was to map and sequence the human genome.

The purpose of the human genome was to map and sequence the human genome. The project was launched in 1986 and an outline of the genome was finished in 2000 through international collaboration.

88. **Science and technology are best described as: (Skill 7.3; Average rigor)**

   A.   Different names for the same thing
   B.   Competing against each other
   C.   Closely related and intertwined
   D.   Independent of each other

Answer C: Closely related and intertwined

Science and technology, while distinct concepts, are closely related. Science attempts to investigate and explain the natural world, while technology attempts to solve human adaptation problems. Technology often results from the application of scientific discoveries, and advances in technology can increase the impact of scientific discoveries.

89. **Which term correctly describes skeletal muscle? (Skill 7.4; Rigorous)**

   A.   Voluntary
   B.   Involuntary
   C.   Active
   D.   Inactive

Answer A: Voluntary

There are three types of muscle tissue. Skeletal muscle is voluntary. These muscles are attached to bones and are responsible for their movement. Cardiac muscle is found in the heart. Smooth muscle is involuntary. It is found in organs and enable functions such as digestion and respiration.

90. Who is known as the father of genetics? (Skill 7.4; Average rigor)

    A.   Charles Darwin
    B.   Carl von Linnaeus
    C.   Gregor Mendel
    D.   Louis Pasteur

Answer C: Gregor Mendel

Gregor Mendel is recognized as the father of genetics. His work in the late 1800s is the basis of our knowledge of genetics. Although unaware of the presence of DNA or genes, Mendel realized there were factors (now known as genes) that were transferred from parents to their offspring.

91. Phase of matter is identified by: (Skill 7.5; Rigorous)

    A.   Shape and mass
    B.   Shape and volume
    C.   Volume and mass
    D.   Shape, mass, and volume

Answer B: Shape and volume

The phase of matter (solid, liquid, or gas) is identified by its shape and volume. A solid has a definite shape and volume. A liquid has a definite volume, but no shape. A gas has no shape or volume.

92. On the moon, an object's _____ will differ from its calculated amount on Earth because of the Moon's lack of gravity. (Skill 7.5; Easy)

    A.   Weight
    B.   Mass
    C.   Volume
    D.   Density

Answer A: Weight

Weight is the measure of the Earth's pull of gravity on an object. The weight of an object would be different on the moon because the gravitational pull would differ.

93. **Which of the following units is a measure of temperature?   (Skill 7.5; Average rigor)**

    A.   Watts
    B.   Joules
    C.   Kelvin
    D.   Ounces

Answer C: Kelvin

There are three units that measure temperature: Kelvin, Celsius, and Fahrenheit. Watts is a measure of power, joules are a measure of energy, and ounce is a unit of mass.

94. **Which of the following causes the Earth to have seasons? (Skill 7.5; Rigorous)**

    A.   The Earth's magnetic field
    B.   The Earth's tilt on its axis
    C.   The Earth's moon
    D.   The Earth's tectonic plates

Answer B: The Earth's tilt on its axis

Seasonal change on Earth is caused by the orbit and axial tilt of the planet in relation to the Sun's Ecliptic: the rotational path of the Sun. These factors combine to vary the degree of insolation (distribution of solar energy) at a particular location and thereby change the seasons.

95. **Which of the following is a vector quantity that refers to the rate at which an object changes its position? (Skill 7.5; Rigorous)**

    A. Speed
    B. Momentum
    C. Velocity
    D. Motion

Answer C: Velocity

Speed is a scalar quantity that refers to how fast an object is moving. Velocity is a vector quantity that refers to the rate at which an object changes its position.

96. **What groups or patterns of stars do astronomers use as reference points in the sky? (Skill 7.5; Average rigor)**

    A. Galaxies
    B. Nebula
    C. Constellations
    D. All of the above

Answer C: Constellations

Astronomers use groups or patterns of stars called constellations as reference points to locate other stars in the sky. Familiar constellations include Ursa Major (also known as the big bear) and Ursa Minor (known as the little bear). Within the Ursa Major, the smaller constellation, The Big Dipper is found. Within the Ursa Minor, the smaller constellation, The Little Dipper is found.

97. **Plate Tectonic Theory proposes that the Earth's surface is composed of: (Skill 7.5; Rigorous)**

    A.   Lithospheric plates
    B.   Atmospheric plates
    C.   Hydrospheric plates
    D.   Biospheric plates

Answer A: Lithospheric plates

Plate Tectonics is the study of the movement of the lithospheric plates and the consequences of that movement. According to the theory, the Earth constantly recycles its materials through a process of upwelling from the center and subducting in the lithosphere, which subsequently causes the movement of Earth's tectonic plates.

98. **What should an experiment have a minimum number of to produce accurate and easily correlated results? (Skill 7.7; Easy)**

    A.   Controls
    B.   Variables
    C.   Samples
    D.   Participants

Answer B: Variables

A variable is a factor or condition that can be changed in an experiment. A good experiment will try to manipulate as few variables as possible, so that the results of the experiment can be identified as occurring because of the change in the variable.

99. **Which hypothesis is valid? (Skill 7.7; Rigorous)**

   A.   An unknown factor causes tomato plants to produce no fruit
        sometimes.
   B.   A tomato plant will produce tasty fruit if it is watered.
   C.   A tomato plant will grow faster in full sunlight than partial sunlight.
   D.   A tomato plant given this fertilizer will produce better fruit than all
        others.

Answer C: A tomato plant will grow faster in full sunlight than partial sunlight.

A valid hypothesis must be able to be proven either right or wrong. "An unknown factor causes tomato plants to produce no fruit sometimes" cannot be proven definitely right or wrong since it is too vague. "A tomato plant will produce tasty fruit if it is watered" cannot be proven either right or wrong because the measurement "tasty" is subjective. "A tomato plant given this fertilizer will produce better fruit than all others" cannot be tested because it cannot be proven that the fruit is better than all others. "A tomato plant will grow faster in full sunlight than partial sunlight" is valid because it can be proven right or wrong.

100. **What is the last step in the scientific method? (Skill 7.7; Average
     rigor)**

   A.   Pose a question
   B.   Draw a conclusion
   C.   Conduct a test
   D.   Record data

Answer B: Draw a conclusion

The steps in the scientific method, in order, are: pose a question, form a hypothesis, conduct a test, observe and record data, and draw a conclusion.

Post Test

Subarea I. Knowledge of Child Development

1. Which of the following is NOT one of Gardner's Multiple Intelligences? (Skill 1.1; Average rigor)

   A. Intrapersonal

   B. Musical

   C. Technological

   D. Logical/mathematical

2. In Bronfenbrenner's Ecological Systems Theory, what type of system is the family or classroom? (Skill 1.1; Average rigor)

   A. Microsystem

   B. Mesosystem

   C. Exosystem

   D. Macrosystem

3. According to Piaget's theory of human development, which stage would a child be in if they understood abstract terms such as honesty and justice? (Skill 1.1; Rigorous)

   A. Concrete operations

   B. Pre-operational

   C. Formal operations

   D. Sensory-motor

4. Which level of Bloom's taxonomy involves having students define, recall, and memorize? (Skill 1.1; Easy)

   A. Application

   B. Analysis

   C. Synthesis

   D. Knowledge

5. What is a good strategy for teaching ethnically diverse students? (Skill 1.2; Rigorous)

   A. Don't focus on the students' culture

   B. Expect them to assimilate easily into your classroom

   C. Imitate their speech patterns

   D. Use instructional strategies of various formats

6. A teacher has a class with several students from low income families in it. What would it be most important for a teacher to consider when planning homework assignments to ensure that all students have equal opportunity for academic success? (Skill 1.2; Rigorous)

A. Access to technology

B. Ethnicity

C. Language difficulties

D. Gender

7. Mr. De Vries observes that a student appears socially awkward, has difficulty expressing himself in words, and is sometimes aggressive. What is most likely to be limiting the student's development? (Skill 1.3; Rigorous)

A. Emotional abuse

B. The recent divorce of the student's parents

C. Lack of verbal interaction

D. Poor nutrition

8. Which of the following best explains why emotional upset and emotional abuse can reduce a child's classroom performance? (Skill 1.3; Rigorous)

A. They reduce the energy that students put towards schoolwork.

B. They lead to a reduction in cognitive ability.

C. They contribute to learning disorders such as dyslexia.

D. They result in the development of behavioral problems.

9. Playing team sports at young ages should be done for the following purpose: (Skill 1.4; Rigorous)

A. To develop the child's motor skills

B. To prepare children for competition in high school

C. To develop the child's interests

D. Both A and C

10. The stages of play development from infancy stages to early childhood includes a move from: (Skill 1.4; Rigorous)

    A.   Cooperative to solitary

    B.   Solitary to cooperative

    C.   Competitive to collaborative

    D.   Collaborative to competitive

11. Which of the following is a true statement? (Skill 1.2; Average rigor)

    A.   Physical development does not influence social development.

    B.   Social development does not influence physical development.

    C.   Cognitive development does not influence social development.

    D.   All domains of development are integrated and influence other domains.

12. One common factor for students with all types of disabilities is that they are also likely to demonstrate difficulty with: (Skill 2.1; Average rigor)

    A.   Social skills

    B.   Cognitive skills

    C.   Problem-solving skills

    D.   Decision-making skills

13. A teacher observes that a student appears sad, shows little interest in people or activities, and is having eating problems. What disorder do these observations suggest? (Skill 2.1; Easy)

    A.   Claustrophobia

    B.   Autism

    C.   Dyslexia

    D.   Depression

14. Which of the following are reasons that young people begin using drugs and alcohol? (Skill 2.1; Easy)

    A.   Curiosity

    B.   To escape from problems

    C.   Due to peer pressure

    D.   All of the above

15. If child abuse is suspected, what action should a teacher take? (Skill 2.2; Average rigor)

   A. Wait to see if the child talks about it again

   B. Talk to your supervisor about your concerns

   C. Call the child's parent

   D. Take no action unless there is proof

16. While children develop at different rates, which of the following can cause learning difficulties? (Skill 2.2; Average rigor)

   A. Lack of sleep

   B. Poor nutrition

   C. Prenatal exposure to nicotine

   D. All of the above

17. When considering whether child abuse could be occurring, what types of abuse should teachers be aware of? (Skill 2.2; Average rigor)

   A. Physical abuse

   B. Mental abuse

   C. Emotional abuse

   D. All of the above

18. Children from age 2 through 5 develop patterns of language from the words and sentences: (Skill 2.3; Rigorous)

   A. They hear on a daily basis

   B. They encounter in learning situations

   C. They read in grade-level books

   D. They learn from other students

19. At what age would a child be expected to have developed speech patterns with 100% intelligibility? (Skill 2.3; Average rigor)

   A. 2

   B. 3

   C. 4

   D. 5

20. A student does not respond to any signs of affection and responds to other children by repeating back what they have said. What condition is the student most likely to have? (Skill 2.4; Average rigor)

   A. Mental retardation

   B. Autism

   C. Giftedness

   D. Hyperactivity

21. Which of the following conditions is more common for girls than boys? (Skill 2.4; Average rigor)

   A. Attention deficit disorder

   B. Aggression

   C. Phobias

   D. Autism

22. The three areas of differentiated instruction are content, process, and: (Skill 2.5; Easy)

   A. Application

   B. Product

   C. Assessment

   D. Structure

23. A teacher attempting to create a differentiated classroom should focus on incorporating activities that: (Skill 2.5; Rigorous)

   A. Favor academically advanced students

   B. Challenge special education students to achieve more

   C. Are suitable for whichever group of students is the majority

   D. Meet the needs of all the students in the class

24. To determine if a child has a disability that may qualify the child for services under IDEA, which of the following pieces of information should the school collect? (Skill 2.6; Average rigor)

   A. The present levels of academic achievement

   B. Vision and hearing screening information

   C. A complete psychological evaluation

   D. All of the above

25. IDEA sets policies that provide for inclusion of students with disabilities. What does inclusion mean? (Skill 2.6; Rigorous)

   A. Inclusion is the name of the curriculum that must be followed in special education classes.

   B. Inclusion is the right of students with disabilities to be placed in the regular classroom.

   C. Inclusion refers to the quality of instruction that is important for student's academic success.

   D. Inclusion means that students with disabilities should always be placed in special classes.

26. Under the IDEA, Congress provides safeguards for students against schools' actions, including the right to sue in court, and encourages states to develop hearing and mediation systems to resolve disputes. This is known as: (Skill 2.6; Rigorous)

   A. Due process

   B. Mediation

   C. Safe Schools Initiative

   D. Parent involvement

27. A student who is deaf has an Individual Family Service Plan (IFSP) in place. This legal document is a way of providing: (Skill 2.7; Average rigor)

   A. Early intervention

   B. Help for the family and the child

   C. Services to deal with the child's disability

   D. All of the above

28. Which of the following should NOT be a purpose of a parent teacher conference? (Skill 2.8; Average rigor)

   A. To involve the parent in their child's education

   B. To establish a friendship with the child's parents

   C. To resolve a concern about the child's performance

   D. To inform parents of positive behaviors by the child

29. The financial support that can be made available by community resources is best described as: (Skill 2.9; Rigorous)

   A. The only financial support available

   B. Only available to students performing well

   C. A valuable additional source of funding

   D. Limited and rarely worth considering

30. A teacher notices that a student is sullen, and has several bruises on his head, arms, and legs. When asked, the student responds that he hit his arm getting out of bed that morning. The teacher should: (Skill 2.10; Average rigor)

   A. Attempt to get more information from the student

   B. Report the suspected abuse

   C. Inform the parents

   D. Wait and see if other signs of abuse become evident

Subarea II. Knowledge of Children's Literature and the Writing Process

31. The works of Paul Bunyan, John Henry, and Pecos Bill are all exaggerated accounts of individuals with superhuman strength. What type of literature are these works? (Skill 3.1; Easy)

   A. Fables

   B. Fairytales

   C. Tall tales

   D. Myths

32. Alphabet books are classified as: (Skill 3.1; Average rigor)

   A. Concept books

   B. Easy-to-read books

   C. Board books

   D. Pictures books

33. Which of the following is NOT a major genre of young children's literature? (Skill 3.2; Easy)

   A. Science fiction

   B. Action and adventure

   C. Current events

   D. Biography

34. During a lesson, a teacher writes the following statement on the board: "His unhappiness was a prison, holding him inside." What type of literary device is the lesson most likely focusing on? (Skill 3.3; Rigorous)

    A. Symbolism

    B. Metaphor

    C. Analogy

    D. Repetition

35. What type of literature are characters, settings, and themes, interpretations, opinions, theories, and research usually found in? (Skill 3.4; Average rigor)

    A. Non-fiction

    B. Fairy tale

    C. Fiction

    D. Folktales

36. Which of the following is an important criterion for evaluating children's literature? (Skill 3.5; Easy)

    A. Character development

    B. Appropriate reading level

    C. Cultural diversity

    D. All of the above

37. Authors portray ideas in very subtle ways through their use of language. What is the perspective through which the story is told called? (Skill 3.6; Average rigor)

    A. Style

    B. Theme

    C. Tone

    D. Point of view

38. Which of the following is NOT a developmental stage of writing? (Skill 4.1; Easy)

    A. Early writing

    B. Role play writing

    C. Pre-conventional writing

    D. Experimental writing

39. Which of the following is NOT a prewriting strategy? (Skill 4.2; Rigorous)

    A. Analyzing sentences for variety

    B. Keeping an idea book

    C. Writing in a daily journal

    D. Writing down whatever comes to mind

40. Writing is a process that can be clearly defined by its various stages. Which of the following is the correct order of the writing stages? (Skill 4.3; Rigorous)

    A. Organization, discovery, writing, editing

    B. Organization, discovery, editing, writing

    C. Discovery, organization, editing, writing

    D. Discovery, organization, writing, editing

41. In the process of writing, the introduction should be written at what stage of the paper? (Skill 4.3; Rigorous)

    A. Before the thesis development

    B. After the entire paper is written

    C. During the brainstorming session

    D. Before writing the body

42. Which of the following is probably the most important step for the writer in the writing process? (Skill 4.4; Average rigor)

    A. Revision

    B. Discovery

    C. Conclusion

    D. Organization

43. Which of the following is an example of a transitional phrase? (Skill 4.4; Easy)

    A. And

    B. In contrast

    C. What

    D. There was

44. Written work of students in Massachusetts should be edited according to the conventions of: (Skill 4.5; Easy)

    A. British English

    B. American English

    C. English Slang

    D. All of the above

45. **What is the function of expository writing? (Skill 4.6; Average rigor)**

   A. To give information

   B. To change the minds of the readers

   C. To describe an experience

   D. To narrate a story

46. **As a part of prewriting, students should identify their audience. Which of the following questions will help students to identify their audience? (Skill 4.6; Average rigor)**

   A. Why is the audience reading my writing?

   B. What does my audience already know about my topic?

   C. Both A and B

   D. None of the above

47. **Which type of text presents information to readers in a quick and efficient manner? (Skill 4.7; Average rigor)**

   A. Essays

   B. Memoirs

   C. Journals

   D. Newspaper articles

48. **Plot is the series of events in a story. Which of the following is the typical sequence of a plot? (Skill 4.7; Rigorous)**

   A. Rising action, exposition, climax, denouement, falling action

   B. Exposition, rising action, climax, falling action, denouement

   C. Denouement, rising action, climax, falling action, exposition

   D. Rising action, exposition, denouement, climax, falling action

49. Mr. Taylor reads the following line of the poem to the students: "The soft sunlight shimmered on the smooth surface." What are the students probably learning about? (Skill 4.7; Easy)

   A. Assonance

   B. Slant rhyme

   C. Alliteration

   D. Onomatopoeia

50. What should the basics of writing to a particular audience include? (Skill 4.8; Easy)

   A. Precise Vocabulary

   B. Figurative language

   C. Illustrations

   D. All of the above

Subarea III. Core Knowledge in the Content Areas

51. Each kindergarten child has a card with the word one, two, three, four, or five on it. As the teacher says a number, the children with the print word for that number stand. What math principle is being practiced? (Skill 5.1; Rigorous)

   A. Rote counting

   B. Number representations

   C. Number sequencing

   D. Addition or subtraction

52. How is the following read? (Skill 5.1; Easy)

   7 > 2

   A. Two is less than seven

   B. Seven is greater than two

   C. Two is greater than seven

   D. Seven is less than two

53. A teacher writes the following problem on the board: "Dan has two white baseball caps and four blue baseball caps. How many more blue baseball caps does Dan have?" Which words indicate that it is a subtraction problem? (Skills 5.1; Rigorous)

   A.   Does Dan have

   B.   Four blue baseball caps

   C.   Two white baseball caps

   D.   How many more

54. Which math principle indicates that a student should "carry" the one in the following addition problem? (Skill 5.4; Rigorous)

   54
   +29
   83

   A.   Counting by tens

   B.   Properties of a base ten number system

   C.   Problem checking

   D.   Adding numbers that are too big

55. At snack time, three friends break a cracker into three equal parts. What portion of the original cracker does each part represent? (Skill 5.5; Easy)

   A.   One fourth

   B.   One half

   C.   One whole

   D.   One third

56. Third grade students are studying percents. When looking at a circle graph divided into three sections, they see that one section is worth 80% and one section is worth 5%. What will the remaining section be worth? (Skill 5.5; Rigorous)

   A.   100%

   B.   85%

   C.   75%

   D.   15%

57. A class has 30 magnets for 6 tables of students. Students are asked to determine how many magnets each table of students should get so that each table of students has the same number of magnets. What math principle would students apply to solve this problem? (Skill 5.6; Rigorous)

   A. Division

   B. Multiplication

   C. Percent

   D. Subtraction

58. What is the answer to this problem? (Skill 5.6; Easy)

   7 x 9 =

   A. 36

   B. 16

   C. 63

   D. 2

59. Which other equation is part of this fact family? (Skill 5.7; Average rigor)

   9 + 3 = 12
   12 – 3 = 9
   3 + 9 = 12
   3 + 9 = 12

   A. 9 – 3 = 6

   B. 3 + 12 = 15

   C. 12 – 9 = 3

   D. 12 + 9 = 21

60. What number comes next in this pattern? (Skill 5.8; Average rigor)

   3, 8, 13, 18, _____

   A. 21

   B. 26

   C. 23

   D. 5

61. Recognizing if the word *fill* belongs in the word family of *bill, hill,* and *mill* or the word family of *king, sing,* and *wing* is an example of using what math principle? (Skill 5.8; Rigorous)

   A. Pattern recognition

   B. Letter counting

   C. Counting by threes

   D. Identity property

62. Students are making three-dimensional figures by folding a net made up of four equilateral triangles. What three-dimensional figure are the students making? (Skill 5.9; Rigorous)

A. Cube

B. Tetrahedron

C. Octahedron

D. Cone

63. Which of the following letters does NOT have a line of symmetry? (Skill 5.10; Rigorous)

A. O

B. D

C. M

D. J

64. Which would be a way for early childhood students to learn about basic geometric concepts? (Skill 5.10; Rigorous)

A. Using a ruler

B. Rote counting

C. Working with tangrams

D. Create an A-B color pattern

65. In which problem would students need an understanding of basic algebraic concepts? (Skill 5.11; Average rigor)

A. 5 + 6 + 5 =

B. 3 + 3 + 3 + 3 + 3 =

C. 10 x 0 =

D. 3 + 6 = 9

66. Students using a measuring cylinder are exploring what concept? (Skill 5.12; Average rigor)

A. Volume

B. Weight

C. Length

D. Temperature

67. The term *millimeters* indicates which kind of measurement? (Skill 5.12; Easy)

A. Volume

B. Weight

C. Length

D. Temperature

68. What type of graph would be best to use to show changes in the height of a plant over the course of a month? (Skill 5.13; Average rigor)

A. Circle graph

B. Bar graph

C. Line graph

D. Pictograph

69. A teacher completes a survey of student eye color. The teacher then creates a graph so students can compare how many students have each eye color. What type of graph should be used? (Skill 5.13; Rigorous)

A. Bar graph

B. Pictograph

C. Circle graph

D. Line graph

70. Annie has three dolls. Sally has eight dolls. How many fewer dolls does Annie have? (Skill 5.14; Easy)

A. 3

B. 5

C. 8

D. 11

71. Which step should come last in problem solving? (Skill 5.14; Rigorous)

A. Write the answer with a label word

B. Identify the problem

C. Check the answer

D. Make basic calculations

72. In which year did the pilgrims arrive on the *Mayflower*? (Skill 6.1; Rigorous)

A. 1602

B. 1614

C. 1620

D. 1625

73. Which ancient civilization contributed the most to literature by writing epic and lyric poetry? (Skill 6.2; Rigorous)

A.   Greeks

B.   Persians

C.   Romans

D.   Israelites

74. Which ancient people contributed the religion that is now known as Jewish? (Skill 6.2; Average rigor)

A.   Chaldeans

B.   Persians

C.   Mycenaeans

D.   Israelites

75. Which of the following occurred first? (Skill 6.3; Average rigor)

A.   Scientific Revolution

B.   Agricultural Revolution

C.   Industrial Revolution

D.   Information Revolution

76. Which term describes an area of lowland formed by soil and sediment deposited at the mouths of rivers? (Skill 6.4; Average rigor)

A.   Plateau

B.   Basin

C.   Mesa

D.   Delta

77. Which of the following divides the continental United States into two main sections? (Skill 6.4; Rigorous)

A.   Grand Canyon

B.   Rocky Mountains

C.   Mississippi River

D.   Great Lakes

78. Which of the following describes how citizens are able to directly participate in their own government by voting for and running for office? (Skill 6.5; Average rigor)

A.   Popular sovereignty

B.   Due process

C.   Rule of law

D.   Democracy

79. What is the study of how a society allocates its scarce resources to satisfy what are basically unlimited and competing wants? (Skill 6.5; Average rigor)

    A. Geography

    B. Economics

    C. Geology

    D. Ecology

80. At what level does the two-party system operate in the United States? (Skill 6.6; Rigorous)

    A. National only

    B. National and state only

    C. Local only

    D. National, state, and local

81. Which of the following powers are reserved to the states by the U.S. Constitution? (Skill 6.6; Rigorous)

    A. To ratify amendments

    B. To declare war

    C. To borrow and coin money

    D. To conduct foreign affairs

82. What is a proposed law called while it is under consideration by Congress? (Skill 6.7; Easy)

    A. Bill

    B. Amendment

    C. Veto

    D. Hopper

83. What does the First Amendment to the U.S. constitution describe? (Skill 6.8; Average rigor)

    A. The right to bear arms

    B. No cruel or unusual punishment

    C. Freedom of religion

    D. Security from the quartering of troops in home

84. At what level is the probate court in Massachusetts? (Skill 6.8; Rigorous)

    A. County

    B. District

    C. State

    D. Municipality

85. The rights of U.S. citizens also imply certain responsibilities to be exercised. Which of the following is NOT a responsibility of U.S. citizens? (Skill 6.9; Rigorous)

    A.   Paying taxes

    B.   Jury duty

    C.   Respecting others' right

    D.   Freedom of religion

86. Each time an experiment is completed, different results are obtained. This indicates that the experiment is not: (Skill 7.1; Rigorous)

    A.   Objective

    B.   Significant

    C.   Reproducible

    D.   Accurate

87. Which of the following can be a source of bias in scientific experiments? (Skill 7.1; Easy)

    A.   Investigators

    B.   Samples

    C.   Instruments

    D.   All of the above

88. Who is known as the father of microscopy? (Skill 7.2; Average rigor)

    A.   Anton van Leeuwenhoek

    B.   Carl von Linnaeus

    C.   Gregor Mendel

    D.   Louis Pasteur

89. Which of the following is NOT one of the three types of cells? (Skill 7.4; Rigorous)

    A.   Eukaryote

    B.   Archaea

    C.   Protist

    D.   Prokaryotes

90. In the human immune system, what is manufactured in response to a foreign invader as a defense mechanism? (Skill 7.4; Average rigor)

    A.   Antigen

    B.   Antibody

    C.   Platelet

    D.   Enzyme

91. **What does a primary consumer most commonly refer to? (Skill 7.4; Average rigor)**

    A. Herbivore

    B. Autotroph

    C. Carnivore

    D. Decomposer

92. **What is a change that produces new material known as? (Skill 7.5; Average rigor)**

    A. Physical change

    B. Chemical change

    C. Phase change

    D. Reversible change

93. **Airplanes generate pressure and remain balanced by: (Skill 7.5; rigorous)**

    A. Fast air movement over wings and slow movement under wings

    B. Slow air movement over wings and fast movement under wings

    C. Air movement that is equal above and below wings

    D. Air movement that only occurs over the wings

94. **Which of the following is the source of sound waves? (Skill 7.5; Rigorous)**

    A. Vibration

    B. Heat

    C. Magnetism

    D. Inertia

95. **The breakdown of rock due to acid rain is an example of: (Skill 7.5; Rigorous)**

    A. Physical weathering

    B. Frost wedging

    C. Chemical weathering

    D. Deposition

96. **What percentage of Earth is covered by water? (Skill 7.5; Average rigor)**

    A. 30%

    B. 50%

    C. 70%

    D. 90%

97. What is a large, rotating, low-pressure system accompanied by heavy precipitation and strong winds known as? (Skill 7.5; Average rigor)

   A.   A hurricane

   B.   A tornado

   C.   A thunderstorm

   D.   A tsunami

98. Which of the following is defined as the identification and application of knowledge to solve a problem? (Skill 7.6; Average rigor)

   A.   Scientific method

   B.   Technological design

   C.   Applied science

   D.   Reverse engineering

99. Which term best describes Newton's universal gravitation? (Skill 7.7; Rigorous)

   A.   Theory

   B.   Hypothesis

   C.   Inference

   D.   Law

100. What would be a good choice when graphing the percent of time that a student spends on various afterschool activities? (Skill 7.7; Average rigor)

   A.   Line graph

   B.   Pie chart

   C.   Histogram

   D.   Scatter plot

Post Test Answer Key

1.	C	35.	A	69.	A
2.	A	36.	D	70.	B
3.	C	37.	D	71.	C
4.	D	38.	C	72.	C
5.	D	39.	A	73.	A
6.	A	40.	D	74.	D
7.	C	41.	B	75.	A
8.	A	42.	A	76.	D
9.	D	43.	B	77.	B
10.	B	44.	B	78.	A
11.	D	45.	A	79.	B
12.	A	46.	C	80.	D
13.	D	47.	D	81.	A
14.	D	48.	B	82.	A
15.	B	49.	C	83.	C
16.	D	50.	D	84.	A
17.	D	51.	B	85.	D
18.	A	52.	B	86.	C
19.	D	53.	D	87.	D
20.	B	54.	B	88.	A
21.	C	55.	D	89.	C
22.	B	56.	D	90.	B
23.	D	57.	A	91.	A
24.	D	58.	C	92.	B
25.	B	59.	C	93.	A
26.	A	60.	C	94.	A
27.	D	61.	A	95.	C
28.	B	62.	B	96.	C
29.	C	63.	D	97.	A
30.	B	64.	C	98.	B
31.	C	65.	D	99.	D
32.	A	66.	A	100.	B
33.	C	67.	C		
34.	B	68.	C		

Post Test Rigor Table

	Easy %20	Average rigor %40	Rigorous %40
Question #	4, 13, 14, 22, 31, 33, 36, 38, 43, 44, 45, 49, 50, 52, 55, 58, 67, 70, 82, 87	1, 2, 7, 11, 12, 15, 16, 17, 19, 20, 21, 24, 27, 28, 30, 32, 35, 37, 42, 46, 47, 59, 60, 65, 66, 68, 74, 75, 76, 78, 79, 83, 88, 90, 91, 92, 96, 97, 98, 100	3, 5, 6, 8, 9, 10, 18, 23, 25, 26, 29, 34, 39, 40, 41, 48, 51, 53, 54, 56, 57, 61, 62, 63, 64, 69, 71, 72, 73, 77, 80, 81, 84, 85, 86, 89, 93, 94, 95, 99

Post Test Answer Key Rationale

Subarea I. Knowledge of Child Development

1. **Which of the following is NOT one of Gardner's Multiple Intelligences? (Skill 1.1; Average rigor)**

    A. Intrapersonal
    B. Musical
    C. Technological
    D. Logical/mathematical

Answer C: Technological

The Multiple Intelligence Theory, developed by Howard Gardner, suggests that students learn in (at least) seven different ways. These include visually/spatially, musically, verbally, logically/mathematically, interpersonally, intrapersonally, and bodily/kinesthetically.

2. **In Bronfenbrenner's Ecological Systems Theory, what type of system is the family or classroom? (Skill 1.1; Average rigor)**

    A. Microsystem
    B. Mesosystem
    C. Exosystem
    D. Macrosystem

Answer A: Microsystem

In his Ecological Systems Theory, Urie Bronfenbrenner outlined four types of nested systems. The first is the microsystem, which includes the family or classroom. The mesosystem refers to the interaction of two Microsystems. The exosystem refers to the influence of external influences on development. The macrosystem is the whole socio-cultural context.

3. **According to Piaget's theory of human development, which stage would a child be in if they understood abstract terms such as honesty and justice? (Skill 1.1; Rigorous)**

    A. Concrete operations
    B. Pre-operational
    C. Formal operations
    D. Sensory-motor

Answer C: Formal operations

Jean Piaget's theory describes how human minds develop through four stages. The first stage is the sensory-motor stage. This occurs up to age 2 and involves understanding the world via the senses. The second stage is the pre-operational stage. It occurs from ages 2 to 7 and involves understanding symbols. The concrete operations stage occurs from ages 7 to 11 and is where children begin to develop reason. The final stage is the formal operations stage. It involves the development of logical and abstract thinking.

4. **Which level of Bloom's taxonomy involves having students define, recall, and memorize? (Skill 1.1; Easy)**

    A. Application
    B. Analysis
    C. Synthesis
    D. Knowledge

Answer D: Knowledge

Bloom's taxonomy classifies critical thinking and learning skills/objectives into six tiered levels. The six levels are: knowledge, understanding/comprehension, application, analysis, synthesis, and evaluation. Tasks at the knowledge stage are the most basic, and include having students define, label, recall, memorize, and list.

5. **What is a good strategy for teaching ethnically diverse students? (Skill 1.2; Rigorous)**

    A.   Don't focus on the students' culture
    B.   Expect them to assimilate easily into your classroom
    C.   Imitate their speech patterns
    D.   Use instructional strategies of various formats

Answer D: Use instructional strategies of various formats

When teaching students from multicultural backgrounds, instructional strategies may be inappropriate and unsuccessful when presented in a single format which relies on the student's understanding and acceptance of the values and common attributes of a specific culture which is not his or her own. A good approach for teaching ethnically diverse students is to use instructional strategies of various formats.

6. **A teacher has a class with several students from low income families in it. What would it be most important for a teacher to consider when planning homework assignments to ensure that all students have equal opportunity for academic success? (Skill 1.2; Rigorous)**

    A.   Access to technology
    B.   Ethnicity
    C.   Language difficulties
    D.   Gender

Answer A: Access to technology

Families with higher incomes are able to provide increased opportunities for students. Students from lower income families will need to depend on the resources available from the school system and the community. To ensure that all students have equal opportunity for academic success, teachers should plan assessments so that not having access to technology does not disadvantage students from low income families.

7. **Mr. De Vries observes that a student appears socially awkward, has difficulty expressing himself in words, and is sometimes aggressive. What is most likely to be limiting the student's development? (Skill 1.3; Rigorous)**

    A. Emotional abuse
    B. The recent divorce of the student's parents
    C. Lack of verbal interaction
    D. Poor nutrition

Answer C: Lack of verbal interaction

When a child has had little verbal interaction, the symptoms can be rather similar to the symptoms of abuse or neglect. The child might have a "deer in the headlights" look and maintain a very socially awkward set of behaviors. In general, such a child will have a drastically reduced ability to express him or herself in words, and often, aggression can be a better tool for the child to get his or her thoughts across.

8. **Which of the following best explains why emotional upset and emotional abuse can reduce a child's classroom performance? (Skill 1.3; Rigorous)**

    A. They reduce the energy that students put towards schoolwork.
    B. They lead to a reduction in cognitive ability.
    C. They contribute to learning disorders such as dyslexia.
    D. They result in the development of behavioral problems.

Answer A: They reduce the energy that students put towards schoolwork.

Although cognitive ability is not lost due to abuse, neglect, emotional upset, or lack of verbal interaction, the child will most likely not be able to provide as much intellectual energy as the child would if none of these things were present. This explains why classroom performance is often negatively impacted.

9. **Playing team sports at young ages should be done for the following purpose: (Skill 1.4; Rigorous)**

    A. To develop the child's motor skills
    B. To prepare children for competition in high school
    C. To develop the child's interests
    D. Both A and C

Answer D: Both A and C

Sports, for both boys and girls, can be very valuable. Parents and teachers, though, need to remember that sports at young ages should only be for the purpose of development of interests and motor skills—not competition. Many children will learn that they do not enjoy sports, and parents and teachers should be respectful of these decisions.

10. **The stages of play development from infancy stages to early childhood includes a move from: (Skill 1.4; Rigorous)**

    A. Cooperative to solitary
    B. Solitary to cooperative
    C. Competitive to collaborative
    D. Collaborative to competitive

Answer B: Solitary to cooperative

The stages of play development move from mainly solitary in the infancy stages to cooperative in early childhood. However, even in early childhood, children should be able to play on their own and entertain themselves from time to time.

11. **Which of the following is a true statement? (Skill 1.2; Average rigor)**

    A. Physical development does not influence social development.
    B. Social development does not influence physical development.
    C. Cognitive development does not influence social development.
    D. All domains of development are integrated and influence other domains.

Answer D: All domains of development are integrated and influence other domains.

Child development does not occur in a vacuum. Each element of development impacts other elements of development. For example, as children develop physically, they develop the dexterity to demonstrate cognitive development, such as writing something on a piece of paper.

12. One common factor for students with all types of disabilities is that they are also likely to demonstrate difficulty with: (Skill 2.1; Average rigor)

    A. Social skills
    B. Cognitive skills
    C. Problem-solving skills
    D. Decision-making skills

Answer A: Social skills

Students with disabilities (in all areas) may demonstrate difficulty in social skills. For a student with a hearing impairment, social skills may be difficult because of not hearing social language. However, the emotionally disturbed student may have difficulty because of a special type of psychological disturbance. An autistic student, as a third example, would be unaware of the social cues given with voice, facial expression, and body language. Each of these students would need social skill instruction but in a different way.

13. A teacher observes that a student appears sad, shows little interest in people or activities, and is having eating problems. What disorder do these observations suggest? (Skill 2.1; Easy)

    A. Claustrophobia
    B. Autism
    C. Dyslexia
    D. Depression

Answer D: Depression

One of the most serious neurotic disorders is depression. Signs of depression include: seeming sad and depressed; crying; showing little or no interest in people or activities; having eating and sleeping problems; and sometimes talking about wanting to be dead. Teachers need to listen to what the child is saying and should take these verbal expressions very seriously.

14. **Which of the following are reasons that young people begin using drugs and alcohol? (Skill 2.1; Easy)**

    A. Curiosity
    B. To escape from problems
    C. Due to peer pressure
    D. All of the above

Answer D: All of the above

Young people start using drugs and alcohol for one of four reasons: out of curiosity; to party; from peer pressure; and to avoid dealing with problems. Teachers should be aware that students are beginning to use drugs and alcohol at young ages. For example, there have been cases of ten year old alcoholics.

15. **If child abuse is suspected, what action should a teacher take? (Skill 2.2; Average rigor)**

    A. Wait to see if the child talks about it again
    B. Talk to your supervisor about your concerns
    C. Call the child's parent
    D. Take no action unless there is proof

Answer B: Talk to your supervisor about your concerns

Child abuse can take many forms including physical, mental, and emotional. If any type of abuse is suspected, the best action is to immediately contact a superior at the school if abuse is suspected.

16. **While children develop at different rates, which of the following can cause learning difficulties? (Skill 2.2; Average rigor)**

    A. Lack of sleep
    B. Poor nutrition
    C. Prenatal exposure to nicotine
    D. All of the above

Answer D: All of the above

Learning difficulties can be caused by a number of factors. Lack of sleep, poor nutrition, and prenatal exposure are all possible causes of learning difficulties. The prenatal exposure to drugs, alcohol, or nicotine can cause moderate to severe brain damage or more subtle impairments such as trouble with breathing or attention deficit disorder. Day-to-day issues, such as lack of sufficient sleep or nutrition, can harm children in a more temporal fashion.

17. **When considering whether child abuse could be occurring, what types of abuse should teachers be aware of? (Skill 2.2; Average rigor)**

 A. Physical abuse
 B. Mental abuse
 C. Emotional abuse
 D. All of the above

Answer D: All of the above

While the symptoms of abuse are usually thought to be physical (and therefore visible), mental and emotional abuse is also possible. Teachers should be aware of all types of abuse, as they can all seriously impact student's wellbeing.

18. **Children from age 2 through 5 develop patterns of language from the words and sentences: (Skill 2.3; Rigorous)**

 A. They hear on a daily basis
 B. They encounter in learning situations
 C. They read in grade-level books
 D. They learn from other students

Answer A: They hear on a daily basis

Children develop patterns of language by learning from the vocal experiences of word and sentence usage that they hear on a daily basis. As children continue through the language development years, the words they hear on a daily basis continue to add to their understanding of language.

19. **At what age would a child be expected to have developed speech patterns with 100% intelligibility? (Skill 2.3; Average rigor)**

 A. 2
 B. 3
 C. 4
 D. 5

Answer D: 5

Speech intelligibility guidelines provide a tracking of a child's oral speech development. Children at 2 years old should have speech patterns that are about 70% intelligible. Children at 3 years old should have an increased 10% speech pattern that is about 80% intelligible. Children at 4 years old should have a 20% speech pattern that is about 90% intelligible. Children at 5 years old should have a speech pattern that is 100% intelligible.

20. **A student does not respond to any signs of affection and responds to other children by repeating back what they have said. What condition is the student most likely to have? (Skill 2.4; Average rigor)**

    A. Mental retardation
    B. Autism
    C. Giftedness
    D. Hyperactivity

Answer B: Autism

There are six common features of autism. They are:

- Apparent sensory deficit – lack of reaction to or overreaction to a stimulus.

- Severe affect isolation – lack of response to affection, such as smiles and hugs.

- Self-stimulation – repeated or ritualistic actions that make no sense to others.

- Tantrums and self-injurious behavior (SIB) – throwing tantrums, injuring oneself, or aggression.

- Echolalia (also known as "parrot talk") – repetition of sounds or responding to others by repeating what was said to him.

- Severe deficits in behavior and self-care skills – behaving like children much younger than themselves.

21. **Which of the following conditions is more common for girls than boys? (Skill 2.4; Average rigor)**

    A. Attention deficit disorder
    B. Aggression
    C. Phobias
    D. Autism

Answer C: Phobias

Many more boys than girls are identified as having emotional and behavioral problems, especially hyperactivity and attention deficit disorder, autism, childhood psychosis, and problems with undercontrol such as aggression and socialized aggression. Girls have more problems with overcontrol, such as withdrawal and phobias.

22. **The three areas of differentiated instruction are content, process, and: (Skill 2.5; Easy)**

    A. Application
    B. Product
    C. Assessment
    D. Structure

Answer B: Product

Differentiated instruction includes the areas of content, process, and product. Content focuses on what is going to be taught. Process focuses on how the content is going to be taught. Product focuses on the expectations and requirements placed on students, where the product refers to the product expected of students.

23. **A teacher attempting to create a differentiated classroom should focus on incorporating activities that: (Skill 2.5; Rigorous)**

    A. Favor academically advanced students
    B. Challenge special education students to achieve more
    C. Are suitable for whichever group of students is the majority
    D. Meet the needs of all the students in the class

Answer D: Meet the needs of all the students in the class

A differentiated classroom is one that meets the needs of special education students, the regular mainstream students, and those that are academically advanced. The purpose of the differentiated classroom is to provide appropriate activities for students at all levels.

24. **To determine if a child has a disability that may qualify the child for services under IDEA, which of the following pieces of information should the school collect? (Skill 2.6; Average rigor)**

   A.   The present levels of academic achievement
   B.   Vision and hearing screening information
   C.   A complete psychological evaluation
   D.   All of the above

Answer D: All of the above

To begin the process of determining if a child has a disability, the teacher will take information about the child's present levels of academic achievement to the appropriate school committee for discussion and consideration. The committee will recommend the next step to be taken. Often subsequent steps may include a complete psychological evaluation along with certain physical examinations such as vision and hearing screening and a complete medical examination by a doctor.

25. **IDEA sets policies that provide for inclusion of students with disabilities. What does inclusion mean? (Skill 2.6; Rigorous)**

   A.   Inclusion is the name of the curriculum that must be followed in special education classes.
   B.   Inclusion is the right of students with disabilities to be placed in the regular classroom.
   C.   Inclusion refers to the quality of instruction that is important for student's academic success.
   D.   Inclusion means that students with disabilities should always be placed in special classes.

Answer B: Inclusion is the right of students with disabilities to be placed in the regular classroom.

Inclusion, mainstreaming and least restrictive environment are interrelated policies under the IDEA, with varying degrees of statutory imperatives. Inclusion is defined as the right of students with disabilities to be placed in the regular classroom. Least restrictive environment is the mandate that children be educated to the maximum extent appropriate with their non-disabled peers. Mainstreaming is a policy where disabled students can be placed in the regular classroom, as long as such placement does not interfere with the student's educational plan.

26. **Under the IDEA, Congress provides safeguards for students against schools' actions, including the right to sue in court, and encourages states to develop hearing and mediation systems to resolve disputes. This is known as: (Skill 2.6; Rigorous)**

   A. Due process
   B. Mediation
   C. Safe Schools Initiative
   D. Parent involvement

Answer A: Due process

Under the IDEA, Congress provides safeguards for students against schools' actions, including the right to sue in court, and encourages states to develop hearing and mediation systems to resolve disputes. No student or their parents/guardians can be denied due process because of disability.

27. **A student who is deaf has an Individual Family Service Plan (IFSP) in place. This legal document is a way of providing: (Skill 2.7; Average rigor)**

   A. Early intervention
   B. Help for the family and the child
   C. Services to deal with the child's disability
   D. All of the above

Answer D: All of the above

An IFSP is an Individual Family Service Plan and is a legal document. This plan is put in place for young children who have disabilities, such as deafness or other special needs. The focus of the plan is to help the family and the child by providing services, such as family based programs and the services of professionals to deal with the child's disability. The IFSP is a way of providing early intervention under IDEA (Individuals with Disabilities Education Act). It is not only designed to enhance the child's education but it is also designed to help the family facilitate the child's development.

28. **Which of the following should NOT be a purpose of a parent teacher conference? (Skill 2.8; Average rigor)**

    A.   To involve the parent in their child's education
    B.   To establish a friendship with the child's parents
    C.   To resolve a concern about the child's performance
    D.   To inform parents of positive behaviors by the child

Answer B: To establish a friendship with the child's parents.

The purpose of a parent teacher conference is to involve parents in their child's education, address concerns about the child's performance and share positive aspects of the student's learning with the parents. It would be unprofessional to allow the conference to degenerate into a social visit to establish friendships.

29. **The financial support that can be made available by community resources is best described as: (Skill 2.9; Rigorous)**

    A.   The only financial support available
    B.   Only available to students performing well
    C.   A valuable additional source of funding
    D.   Limited and rarely worth considering

Answer C: A valuable additional source of funding

Community resources can supplement the minimized and marginal educational resources of school communities. With state and federal educational funding becoming increasingly subject to legislative budget cuts, school communities welcome the financial support that community resources can provide in terms of discounted prices on high end supplies, along with providing free notebooks, backpacks and student supplies for low income students who may have difficulty obtaining the basic supplies for school.

30. **A teacher notices that a student is sullen, and has several bruises on his head, arms, and legs. When asked, the student responds that he hit his arm getting out of bed that morning. The teacher should: (Skill 2.10; Average rigor)**

    A.   Attempt to get more information from the student
    B.   Report the suspected abuse
    C.   Inform the parents
    D.   Wait and see if other signs of abuse become evident

Answer B: Report the suspected abuse

The most important concern is for the safety and wellbeing of the student. Teachers should not promise students that they won't tell because they are required by law to report suspected abuse. Failure or delay in reporting suspected abuse may be a cause for further abuse to the student. In some cases, a teacher's decision to overlook suspected abuse may result in revoking the teacher's license. Teachers are not required to investigate abuse for themselves or verify their suspicions.

Subarea II. Knowledge of Children's Literature and the Writing Process

31. **The works of Paul Bunyan, John Henry, and Pecos Bill are all exaggerated accounts of individuals with superhuman strength. What type of literature are these works? (Skill 3.1; Easy)**

    A.   Fables
    B.   Fairytales
    C.   Tall tales
    D.   Myths

Answer C: Tall tales

Tall tales are purposely exaggerated accounts of individuals with superhuman strength. The works of Paul Bunyan, John Henry, and Pecos Bill are all examples of tall tales. Fables are usually stories about animals with human features that often teach a lesson. Fairytales usually focus on good versus evil, reward and punishment. Myths are stories about events from the earliest times.

32. **Alphabet books are classified as: (Skill 3.1; Average rigor)**

    A. Concept books
    B. Easy-to-read books
    C. Board books
    D. Pictures books

Answer A: Concept books

Concept books are books that combine language and pictures to show concrete examples of concepts. One category of concept books is alphabet books, which are popular with children from preschool through to grade 2.

33. **Which of the following is NOT a major genre of young children's literature? (Skill 3.2; Easy)**

    A. Science fiction
    B. Action and adventure
    C. Current events
    D. Biography

Answer C: Current events

The major themes of young children's literature can be classified into seven major genres. They are: science fiction; fantasy; horror and ghost stories; action and adventure; historical fiction; biography; and educational books.

34. **During a lesson, a teacher writes the following statement on the board: "His unhappiness was a prison, holding him inside." What type of literary device is the lesson most likely focusing on? (Skill 3.3; Rigorous)**

    A. Symbolism
    B. Metaphor
    C. Analogy
    D. Repetition

Answer B: Metaphor

An analogy is where one thing is compared to another using the word "like" or "as." The statement "His happiness was like a prison, holding him inside" is an analogy. The statement "His unhappiness was a prison, holding him inside" is a metaphor.

35. **What type of literature are characters, settings, and themes, interpretations, opinions, theories, and research usually found in? (Skill 3.4; Average rigor)**

    A. Non-fiction
    B. Fairy tale
    C. Fiction
    D. Folktales

Answer A: Non-fiction

In fiction, students can generally expect to see plot, characters, setting, and themes. In nonfiction, students may see a plot, characters, settings, and themes, but they will also experience interpretations, opinions, theories, research, and other elements.

36. **Which of the following is an important criterion for evaluating children's literature? (Skill 3.5; Easy)**

    A. Character development
    B. Appropriate reading level
    C. Cultural diversity
    D. All of the above

Answer D: All of the above

In selecting appropriate literature for children, teachers must consider several factors. Primary among these factors is the composition of the class (including diversity) and the preferences of the children. Children love to identify with the characters in books; therefore it is important to select books with characters that provide positive role models for children. Books should be chosen at an appropriate reading level and should be challenging enough to promote vocabulary growth.

37. Authors portray ideas in very subtle ways through their use of language. What is the perspective through which the story is told called? (Skill 3.6; Average rigor)

      A. Style
      B. Theme
      C. Tone
      D. Point of view

Answer D: Point of view

Point of view is the perspective through which the story is told. While most of us think of point of view in terms of first or third person (or even the points of view of various characters in stories), point of view also helps explain a lot of language and presentation of ideas in non-fiction and fiction texts.

38. Which of the following is NOT a developmental stage of writing? (Skill 4.1; Easy)

      A. Early writing
      B. Role play writing
      C. Pre-conventional writing
      D. Experimental writing

Answer C: Pre-conventional writing

Children develop writing skills through a series of steps. These steps are: role play writing, experimental writing, early writing, and then conventional writing. During role playing writing, the child writes in scribbles and assigns a message to the symbols. With experimental writing, the child usually writes with letters according to the way they sound. In early writing stages, young children start to use a small range of familiar text forms and sight words in their writing. Conventional writing is the final stage.

39. **Which of the following is NOT a prewriting strategy? (Skill 4.2; Rigorous)**

    A. Analyzing sentences for variety
    B. Keeping an idea book
    C. Writing in a daily journal
    D. Writing down whatever comes to mind

Answer A: Analyzing sentences for variety

Prewriting strategies assist students in a variety of ways. Common prewriting strategies include keeping an idea book for jotting down ideas, writing in a daily journal, and writing down whatever comes to mind, which is also called "free writing." Analyzing sentences for variety is a revising strategy.

40. **Writing is a process that can be clearly defined by its various stages. Which of the following is the correct order of the writing stages? (Skill 4.3; Rigorous)**

    A. Organization, discovery, writing, editing
    B. Organization, discovery, editing, writing
    C. Discovery, organization, editing, writing
    D. Discovery, organization, writing, editing

Answer D: Discovery, organization, writing, editing

The first stage of the writing process is the discovery stage, which is when ideas, materials, and supporting details are deliberately collected. The next stage is organization where the purpose, thesis, and supporting points are determined. This is followed by the writing stage. Finally, once the paper is written, the editing stage is necessary.

41. **In the process of writing, the introduction should be written at what stage of the paper? (Skill 4.3; Rigorous)**

    A. Before the thesis development
    B. After the entire paper is written
    C. During the brainstorming session
    D. Before writing the body

Answer B: After the entire paper is written

It is important to remember that in the writing process, the introduction should be written last. This is necessary because, until the body of the paper has been determined, it's difficult to make strategic decisions regarding the introduction.

42. **Which of the following is probably the most important step for the writer in the writing process? (Skill 4.4; Average rigor)**

   A. Revision
   B. Discovery
   C. Conclusion
   D. Organization

Answer A: Revision

Revision is probably the most important step for the writer in the writing process. Here, students examine their work and make changes in wording, details, and ideas. So many times, students write a draft and then feel they're done. Students must be encouraged to develop, change, and enhance their writing as they go, as well as once they've completed a draft.

43. **Which of the following is an example of a transitional phrase? (Skill 4.4; Easy)**

   A. And
   B. In contrast
   C. What
   D. There was

Answer B: In contrast

As writers transition from one paragraph to another or from one sentence to another they will usually provide transitional phrases that give sign-posts to readers about what is coming next. Words like "however," "furthermore," "although," and "likewise" are examples of transition words.

44. **Written work of students in Massachusetts should be edited according to the conventions of: (Skill 4.5; Easy)**

   A. British English
   B. American English
   C. English Slang
   D. All of the above

Answer B: American English

Rules should be applied according to the American style of English. For example, spelling "theater" instead of theatre and placing terminal marks of punctuation almost exclusively within other marks of punctuation.

45. **What is the function of expository writing? (Skill 4.6; Average rigor)**

   A.   To give information
   B.   To change the minds of the readers
   C.   To describe an experience
   D.   To narrate a story

Answer A: To give information

Expository writing is not interested in changing anyone's mind or getting anyone to take a certain action. It exists to give information. Some examples are: driving directions to a particular place or the directions for putting together a toy that arrives unassembled.

46. **As a part of prewriting, students should identify their audience. Which of the following questions will help students to identify their audience? (Skill 4.6; Average rigor)**

   A.   Why is the audience reading my writing?
   B.   What does my audience already know about my topic?
   C.   Both A and B
   D.   None of the above

Answer C: Both A and B

As part of prewriting, students should identify the audience. Make sure students consider the following when analyzing the needs of their audience: why the audience is reading the writing; what the audience already knows about the topic; what the audience needs or wants to know; what will interest the reader; and what type of language will suit the reader.

47. **Which type of text presents information to readers in a quick and efficient manner? (Skill 4.7; Average rigor)**

   A.   Essays
   B.   Memoirs
   C.   Journals
   D.   Newspaper articles

Answer D: Newspaper articles

Nonfiction comes in a variety of styles and can include opinion and perspective. Newspaper articles are short texts which rely completely on factual information and are presented in a very straightforward, sometimes choppy manner. The purpose of these texts simply is to present information to readers in a quick and efficient manner.

48. **Plot is the series of events in a story. Which of the following is the typical sequence of a plot? (Skill 4.7; Rigorous)**

   A. Rising action, exposition, climax, denouement, falling action
   B. Exposition, rising action, climax, falling action, denouement
   C. Denouement, rising action, climax, falling action, exposition
   D. Rising action, exposition, denouement, climax, falling action

Answer B: Exposition, rising action, climax, falling action, denouement

Exposition is where characters and their situations are introduced. Rising action is the point at which conflict starts to occur. Climax is the highest point of conflict, often a turning point. Falling action is the result of the climax. Denouement is the final resolution of the plot.

49. **Mr. Taylor reads the following line of the poem to the students: "The soft sunlight shimmered on the smooth surface." What are the students probably learning about? (Skill 4.7; Easy)**

   A. Assonance
   B. Slant rhyme
   C. Alliteration
   D. Onomatopoeia

Answer C: Alliteration

Alliteration occurs when the initial sounds of a word, beginning either with a consonant or a vowel are repeated in close succession. The function of alliteration might be to accentuate the beauty of language in a given context, or to unite words or concepts through a kind of repetition.

50. **What should the basics of writing to a particular audience include? (Skill 4.8; Easy)**

   A. Precise Vocabulary
   B. Figurative language
   C. Illustrations
   D. All of the above

Answer D: All of the above

Teachers should allow students to write to a variety of audiences. The basic of writing to a particular audience would include a focus on using precise vocabulary, using figurative language, and using illustrations.

Subarea III. Core Knowledge in the Content Areas

51. **Each kindergarten child has a card with the word one, two, three, four, or five on it. As the teacher says a number, the children with the print word for that number stand. What math principle is being practiced? (Skill 5.1; Rigorous)**

    A.   Rote counting
    B.   Number representations
    C.   Number sequencing
    D.   Addition or subtraction

Answer B: Number representations

In this activity, students are practicing different ways to represent numbers (verbal word, printed word). They are not rote counting (counting without meaning). They are not arranging numbers in order (sequencing), and they are not adding or subtracting two numbers.

52. **How is the following read? (Skill 5.1; Easy)**

    $7 > 2$

    A.   Two is less than seven
    B.   Seven is greater than two
    C.   Two is greater than seven
    D.   Seven is less than two

Answer B: Seven is greater than two

Reading left to right: *seven is greater than two.*

53. A teacher writes the following problem on the board: "Dan has two white baseball caps and four blue baseball caps. How many more blue baseball caps does Dan have?" Which words indicate that it is a subtraction problem? (Skills 5.1; Rigorous)

A. Does Dan have
B. Four blue baseball caps
C. Two white baseball caps
D. How many more

Answer D: How many more

The other answers indicate numbers in the problem (*two, four*) or that it is a question (*does Dan have*). The words "how many more" shows that the problem is an addition problem.

54. Which math principle indicates that a student should "carry" the one in the following addition problem? (Skill 5.4; Rigorous)

$$\begin{array}{r} 54 \\ +29 \\ \hline 83 \end{array}$$

A. Counting by tens
B. Properties of a base ten number system
C. Problem checking
D. Adding numbers that are too big

Answer B: Properties of a base ten number system

In a base ten number system, groups of ten ones are regrouped and carried into the tens column. In the addition problem shown, four ones plus nine ones is equal to 13 ones. The ten ones are regrouped and carried into the tens column.

55. **At snack time, three friends break a cracker into three equal parts. What portion of the original cracker does each part represent? (Skill 5.5; Easy)**

   A.   One fourth
   B.   One half
   C.   One whole
   D.   One third

Answer D: One third

If the cracker is broken into three equal parts, each part represents one third of the whole.

56. **Third grade students are studying percents. When looking at a circle graph divided into three sections, they see that one section is worth 80% and one section is worth 5%. What will the remaining section be worth? (Skill 5.5; Rigorous)**

   A.   100%
   B.   85%
   C.   75%
   D.   15%

Answer D: 15%

Percentages use the base ten number system. Percentages of a total amount will always add up to 100%. Since the two sections add to 85%, the third section must be 15%.

57. **A class has 30 magnets for 6 tables of students. Students are asked to determine how many magnets each table of students should get so that each table of students has the same number of magnets. What math principle would students apply to solve this problem? (Skill 5.6; Rigorous)**

   A.   Division
   B.   Multiplication
   C.   Percent
   D.   Subtraction

Answer A: Division

The magnets need to be divided equally between 6 tables of students. The division principle is applied to solve this problem ($60 \div 6 = 5$). Each table gets five magnets.

58. **What is the answer to this problem? (Skill 5.6; Easy)**

$7 \times 9 =$

A.   36
B.   16
C.   63
D.   2

Answer C: 63

The answer to this multiplication problem is 63. It can also be computed by adding seven nine times. $7 + 7 + 7 + 7 + 7 + 7 + 7 + 7 + 7 = 63$

59. **Which other equation is part of this fact family? (Skill 5.7; Average rigor)**

$9 + 3 = 12$
$12 - 3 = 9$
$3 + 9 = 12$
$3 + 9 = 12$

A. $9 - 3 = 6$
B. $3 + 12 = 15$
C. $12 - 9 = 3$
D. $12 + 9 = 21$

Answer C: $12 - 9 = 3$

A fact family uses the same set of three numbers to form two addition problems and two subtraction problems, or two multiplication problems and two division problems.

60. **What number comes next in this pattern? (Skill 5.8; Average rigor)**

3, 8, 13, 18, _____

A.   21
B.   26
C.   23
D.   5

Answer C: 23

This pattern is made by adding five to the preceding number. The next number is found by adding 5 to 18, which gives the answer 23.

61. Recognizing if the word *fill* belongs in the word family of *bill, hill,* and *mill* or the word family of *king, sing,* and *wing* is an example of using what math principle? (Skill 5.8; Rigorous)

   A. Pattern recognition
   B. Letter counting
   C. Counting by threes
   D. Identity property

Answer A: Pattern recognition

To understand which is the correct word family for *fill*, the student must recognize the pattern *i-l-l* as opposed to the pattern *i-n-g.*

62. Students are making three-dimensional figures by folding a net made up of four equilateral triangles. What three-dimensional figure are the students making? (Skill 5.9; Rigorous)

   A. Cube
   B. Tetrahedron
   C. Octahedron
   D. Cone

Answer B: Tetrahedron

A net is a two-dimensional figure that can be cut out and folded up to make a three-dimensional solid. A tetrahedron is made by folding a net made up of four equilateral triangles.

63. Which of the following letters does NOT have a line of symmetry? (Skill 5.10; Rigorous)

   A. O
   B. D
   C. M
   D. J

Answer D: J

For an object to show symmetry, it must be able to be divided into identical halves. The letter O has an unlimited number of lines of symmetry. The letter D has a horizontal line of symmetry. The letter M has a vertical line of symmetry. The letter J does not have a line of symmetry.

64. **Which would be a way for early childhood students to learn about basic geometric concepts? (Skill 5.10; Rigorous)**

    A.   Using a ruler
    B.   Rote counting
    C.   Working with tangrams
    D.   Create an A-B color pattern

Answer C: Working with tangrams

Tangrams, or puzzle pieces, are excellent manipulatives for children to use to explore geometric shapes and relationships. They allow students to transform shapes through flips and rotations as well as to take them apart and put them together in different formations.

65. **In which problem would students need an understanding of basic algebraic concepts? (Skill 5.11; Average rigor)**

    A. $5 + 6 + 5 =$
    B. $3 + 3 + 3 + 3 + 3 =$
    C. $10 \times 0 =$
    D. $3 + \square = 9$

Answer D: $3 + \square = 9$

By rearranging the numbers in this equation to calculate for the missing value, students are demonstrating basic algebraic concepts. The other choices are simple computation problems.

66. **Students using a measuring cylinder are exploring what concept? (Skill 5.12; Average rigor)**

    A.   Volume
    B.   Weight
    C.   Length
    D.   Temperature

Answer A: Volume

The amount of liquid in a cylinder would be a measure of volume. A balance or scale would be used to measure weight. A ruler or meter stick would be used to measure length. A thermometer would be used to measure temperature.

67. **The term *millimeters* indicates which kind of measurement? (Skill 5.12; Easy)**

   A. Volume
   B. Weight
   C. Length
   D. Temperature

Answer C: Length

The term *millimeters* is a reference to length in the metric system.

68. **What type of graph would be best to use to show changes in the height of a plant over the course of a month? (Skill 5.13; Average rigor)**

   A. Circle graph
   B. Bar graph
   C. Line graph
   D. Pictograph

Answer C: Line graph

A line graph shows trends over time. A line graph would show how the plant's height changed over time.

69. **A teacher completes a survey of student eye color. The teacher then creates a graph so students can compare how many students have each eye color. What type of graph should be used? (Skill 5.13; Rigorous)**

   A. Bar graph
   B. Pictograph
   C. Circle graph
   D. Line graph

Answer A: Bar graph

Bar graphs are used to compare various quantities. In this case, the bar graph would show the number of students with each eye color. By looking at the graph, students would be able to compare how many students have each eye color.

70. Annie has three dolls. Sally has eight dolls. How many fewer dolls does Annie have? (Skill 5.14; Easy)

    A.   3
    B.   5
    C.   8
    D.   11

Answer B: 5

The words "how many fewer" indicates that this is a subtraction problem: $8 - 3 = 5$. Annie has five fewer dolls than Sally.

71. Which step should come last in problem solving? (Skill 5.14; Rigorous)

    A.   Write the answer with a label word
    B.   Identify the problem
    C.   Check the answer
    D.   Make basic calculations

Answer C: Check the answer

Typically, there are four steps to problem solving. The first step is to understand the problem. The second step is to devise a plan. This is followed by carrying out the plan. The final step of problem solving is to look back. This involves checking the answer to make sure it is correct.

72. In which year did the pilgrims arrive on the *Mayflower*? (Skill 6.1; Rigorous)

    A.   1602
    B.   1614
    C.   1620
    D.   1625

Answer C: 1620

The real history of Massachusetts began in 1620 with the arrival of 102 pilgrims who arrived in search of a place that allowed them to worship as they chose. The *Mayflower* brought them to Plymouth, where they struggled against the elements to survive with little food. Almost half of the pilgrims died during their first winter in Massachusetts. The spring and summer allowed a bountiful harvest, and the first Thanksgiving Day was a great celebration.

73. **Which ancient civilization contributed the most to literature by writing epic and lyric poetry? (Skill 6.2; Rigorous)**

    A.   Greeks
    B.   Persians
    C.   Romans
    D.   Israelites

Answer A: Greeks

The Greeks are credited with influencing drama, epic and lyric poetry, fables, myths centered on the many gods and goddesses, science, astronomy, medicine, mathematics, philosophy, art, architecture, and recording historical events.

74. **Which ancient people contributed the religion that is now known as Jewish? (Skill 6.2; Average rigor)**

    A.   Chaldeans
    B.   Persians
    C.   Mycenaeans
    D.   Israelites

Answer D: Israelites

The primary contribution of the Israelites was their religion, perhaps the earliest form of monotheism. This religion regulated every aspect of the life of the people with an encompassing legal code, preserved in Scripture, which regulated all aspects of human interaction, both within the community and with outsiders. Until the 1940s, the Israelite (Jewish) people have lived scattered throughout the world. The formation of the nation of Israel gave them a "land" and a political existence.

75. **Which of the following occurred first? (Skill 6.3; Average rigor)**

    A.   Scientific Revolution
    B.   Agricultural Revolution
    C.   Industrial Revolution
    D.   Information Revolution

Answer A: Scientific Revolution

The Scientific Revolution was characterized by a shift in scientific approach and ideas, and occurred near the end of the sixteenth century. The Agricultural Revolution occurred next, then the Industrial Revolution, and the Information Revolution the most recently.

76. **Which term describes an area of lowland formed by soil and sediment deposited at the mouths of rivers? (Skill 6.4; Average rigor)**

   A. Plateau
   B. Basin
   C. Mesa
   D. Delta

Answer D: Delta

Deltas are areas of lowlands formed by soil and sediment deposited at the mouths of rivers. The soil is generally very fertile and most fertile river deltas are important crop-growing areas.

77. **Which of the following divides the continental United States into two main sections? (Skill 6.4; Rigorous)**

   A. Grand Canyon
   B. Rocky Mountains
   C. Mississippi River
   D. Great Lakes

Answer B: Rocky Mountains

The continental United States is bordered by the Pacific Ocean on the west and the Atlantic Ocean on the east. The country is divided into two main sections by the Rocky Mountains, which extend from New Mexico in the south through the Canadian border on the north.

78. **Which of the following describes how citizens are able to directly participate in their own government by voting for and running for office? (Skill 6.5; Average rigor)**

   A. Popular sovereignty
   B. Due process
   C. Rule of law
   D. Democracy

Answer A: Popular sovereignty

Popular sovereignty grants citizens the ability to directly participate in their own government by voting and running for public office. This ideal is based on a belief of equality that holds that all citizens have an equal right to engage in their own governance, and is established in the United States Constitution.

79. **What is the study of how a society allocates its scarce resources to satisfy what are basically unlimited and competing wants? (Skill 6.5; Average rigor)**

    A.   Geography
    B.   Economics
    C.   Geology
    D.   Ecology

Answer B: Economics

Economics is the study of how a society allocates its scarce resources to satisfy what are basically unlimited and competing wants. A fundamental fact of economics is that resources are scarce and that wants are infinite. The fact that scarce resources have to satisfy unlimited wants means that choices have to be made.

80. **At what level does the two-party system operate in the United States? (Skill 6.6; Rigorous)**

    A.   National only
    B.   National and state only
    C.   Local only
    D.   National, state, and local

Answer D: National, state, and local

The American political system is a two-party system, consisting of the Democratic and Republican parties. The two-party system in America operates at the national, state, and local levels.

81. **Which of the following powers are reserved to the states by the U.S. Constitution? (Skill 6.6; Rigorous)**

    A. To ratify amendments
    B. To declare war
    C. To borrow and coin money
    D. To conduct foreign affairs

Answer A: To ratify amendments

The U.S. Constitution reserves the following powers to the states:
1. To regulate intrastate trade.
2. To establish local governments.
3. To protect general welfare.
4. To protect life and property.
5. To ratify amendments.
6. To conduct elections.
7. To make state and local laws.

82. **What is a proposed law called while it is under consideration by Congress? (Skill 6.7; Easy)**

    A. Bill
    B. Amendment
    C. Veto
    D. Hopper

Answer A: Bill

The first step in the passing of a law is for the proposed law to be introduced in one of the houses of Congress. A proposed law is called a bill while it is under consideration by Congress. A bill becomes a law once it is signed by the President.

83. **What does the First Amendment to the U.S. constitution describe? (Skill 6.8; Average rigor)**

   A. The right to bear arms
   B. No cruel or unusual punishment
   C. Freedom of religion
   D. Security from the quartering of troops in home

Answer C: Freedom of religion

The first ten amendments to the U.S. Constitution are also known as the Bill of Rights. They are summarized as follows:

1. Freedom of Religion.
2. Right To Bear Arms.
3. Security from the quartering of troops in homes.
4. Right against unreasonable search and seizures.
5. Right against self-incrimination.
6. Right to trial by jury, right to legal council.
7. Right to jury trial for civil actions.
8. No cruel or unusual punishment allowed.
9. These rights shall not deny other rights the people enjoy.
10. Powers not mentioned in the Constitution shall be retained by the states or the people.

84. **At what level is the probate court in Massachusetts? (Skill 6.8; Rigorous)**

   A. County
   B. District
   C. State
   D. Municipality

Answer A: County

The judiciary of Massachusetts is made up of a supreme judicial court, a superior court, district and municipal courts and land courts. Each county has its own probate court.

85. The rights of U.S. citizens also imply certain responsibilities to be exercised. Which of the following is NOT a responsibility of U.S. citizens? (Skill 6.9; Rigorous)

   A.   Paying taxes
   B.   Jury duty
   C.   Respecting others' right
   D.   Freedom of religion

Answer D: Freedom of religion

The responsibilities of U.S. citizens include respecting others' rights, obeying laws and rules, paying taxes, jury duty, and voting. Freedom of religion is a right of U.S. citizens, not a responsibility.

86. Each time an experiment is completed, different results are obtained. This indicates that the experiment is not: (Skill 7.1; Rigorous)

   A.   Objective
   B.   Significant
   C.   Reproducible
   D.   Accurate

Answer C: Reproducible

The question stage of scientific inquiry involves repetition. By repeating the experiment you can discover whether or not you have reproducibility. If results are reproducible, the hypothesis is valid. If the results are not reproducible, one has more questions to ask.

87. Which of the following can be a source of bias in scientific experiments? (Skill 7.1; Easy)

   A.   Investigators
   B.   Samples
   C.   Instruments
   D.   All of the above

Answer D: All of the above

Although bias related to the investigator, the sample, the method, or the instrument may not be completely avoidable in every case, it is important to know the possible sources of bias and how bias could affect the evidence. Moreover, scientists need to be attentive to possible bias in their own work as well as that of other scientists.

88. **Who is known as the father of microscopy? (Skill 7.2; Average rigor)**

   A.   Anton van Leeuwenhoek
   B.   Carl von Linnaeus
   C.   Gregor Mendel
   D.   Louis Pasteur

Answer A: Anton van Leeuwenhoek

Anton van Leeuwenhoek is known as the father of microscopy. In the 1650s, Leeuwenhoek began making tiny lenses that yielded magnifications up to 300 times. He was the first to see and describe bacteria, yeast plants, and the microscopic life found in water.

89. **Which of the following is NOT one of the three types of cells? (Skill 7.4; Rigorous)**

   A.   Eukaryote
   B.   Archaea
   C.   Protist
   D.   Prokaryotes

Answer C: Protist

The cell is the basic unit of all living things. There are three types of cells. They are prokaryotes, eukaryotes, and archaea. A protist is an organism, not a cell type.

90. **In the human immune system, what is manufactured in response to a foreign invader as a defense mechanism? (Skill 7.4; Average rigor)**

   A.   Antigen
   B.   Antibody
   C.   Platelet
   D.   Enzyme

Answer B: Antibody

An antigen is any foreign particle that elicits an immune response. An antibody is manufactured by the body and recognizes and latches onto antigens, hopefully destroying them. They also have recognition of foreign material versus the self. Memory of the invaders provides immunity upon further exposure.

91. **What does a primary consumer most commonly refer to? (Skill 7.4; Average rigor)**

    A.   Herbivore
    B.   Autotroph
    C.   Carnivore
    D.   Decomposer

Answer A: Herbivore

Autotrophs are the primary producers of the ecosystem. Producers mainly consist of plants. Primary consumers are the next trophic level. The primary consumers are the herbivores that eat plants or algae. Secondary consumers are the carnivores that eat the primary consumers. Tertiary consumers eat the secondary consumer. These trophic levels may go higher depending on the ecosystem.

92. **What is a change that produces new material known as? (Skill 7.5; Average rigor)**

    A.   Physical change
    B.   Chemical change
    C.   Phase change
    D.   Reversible change

Answer B: Chemical change

Matter constantly changes. A physical change is a change that does not produce a new substance. The freezing and melting of water is an example of physical change. A chemical change (or chemical reaction) is any change of a substance into one or more other substances.

93. **Airplanes generate pressure and remain balanced by: (Skill 7.5; rigorous)**

    A.   Fast air movement over wings and slow movement under wings
    B.   Slow air movement over wings and fast movement under wings
    C.   Air movement that is equal above and below wings
    D.   Air movement that only occurs over the wings

Answer A: Fast air movement over wings and slow movement under wings

Airplanes or fixed-wing aircraft are heavier than aircraft that utilize the laws of physics to achieve flight. As the aircraft is propelled forward by thrust from the engines, air moves faster over the top of the wings and slower under the bottom. The slower airflow beneath the wing generates more pressure, while the faster airflow above generates less. This difference in pressure results in upward lift.

94. **Which of the following is the source of sound waves? (Skill 7.5; Rigorous)**

   A.   Vibration
   B.   Heat
   C.   Magnetism
   D.   Inertia

Answer A: Vibration

Sound waves are produced by a vibrating body. The vibrating object moves forward and compresses the air in front of it, then reverses direction so that pressure on the air is lessened and expansion of the air molecules occurs. The vibrating air molecules move back and forth parallel to the direction of motion of the wave as they pass the energy from adjacent air molecules closer to the source to air molecules farther away from the source.

95. **The breakdown of rock due to acid rain is an example of: (Skill 7.5; Rigorous)**

   A.   Physical weathering
   B.   Frost wedging
   C.   Chemical weathering
   D.   Deposition

Answer C: Chemical weathering

The breaking down of rocks at or near to the Earth's surface is known as weathering. Chemical weathering is the breaking down of rocks through changes in their chemical composition. The breakdown of rock due to acid rain is an example of chemical weathering.

96. **What percentage of Earth is covered by water? (Skill 7.5; Average rigor)**

   A.   30%
   B.   50%
   C.   70%
   D.   90%

Answer C: 70%

Earth is considered a water planet because 70% of its surface is covered by water. This property of Earth differs from all other planets in the Solar System.

97. **What is a large, rotating, low-pressure system accompanied by heavy precipitation and strong winds known as?** (Skill 7.5; Average rigor)

     A.   A hurricane
     B.   A tornado
     C.   A thunderstorm
     D.   A tsunami

Answer A: A hurricane

Hurricanes are storms that develop when warm, moist air carried by trade winds rotates around a low-pressure "eye". These form a large, rotating, low-pressure system and are accompanied by heavy precipitation and strong winds. They are also known as tropical cyclones or typhoons.

98. **Which of the following is defined as the identification and application of knowledge to solve a problem?** (Skill 7.6; Average rigor)

     A.   Scientific method
     B.   Technological design
     C.   Applied science
     D.   Reverse engineering

Answer B: Technological design

Technological design is the identification of a problem and the application of scientific knowledge to solve the problem.

99. **Which term best describes Newton's universal gravitation? (Skill 7.7; Rigorous)**

   A. Theory
   B. Hypothesis
   C. Inference
   D. Law

Answer D: Law

A hypothesis is an unproved theory or educated guess followed by research to best explain a phenomenon. A theory is the formation of principles or relationships which have been verified and accepted. It is a proven hypothesis. A law is an explanation of events that occur with uniformity under the same conditions, such as laws of nature or laws of gravitation.

100. **What would be a good choice when graphing the percent of time that a student spends on various afterschool activities? (Skill 7.7; Average rigor)**

   A. Line graph
   B. Pie chart
   C. Histogram
   D. Scatter plot

Answer B: Pie chart

The type of graphic representation used to display observations depends on the data that is collected. A pie chart is useful when organizing data as part of a whole. A good use for a pie chart would be displaying the percent of time students spend on various after school activities.

WEBSITES FOR TEACHERS

The following sites provide additional resources and information:

AllPsych Online
http://allpsych.com/psychology101/moral_development.html

Biology Corner
http://www.biologycorner.com/

BBC History
http://www.bbc.co.uk/history/

Busy Teacher's Website K-12/Biology
http://www.ceismc.gatech.edu/busyt/bio_cell_bio.shtml

Discovery Education
http://school.discoveryeducation.com/schrockguide/

EducationAtlas.com
http://www.educationatlas.com/elementary-education-teaching-resources.html

Education Place
http://eduplace.com/

Educator's Reference Desk
http://www.eduref.org/

Education World
http://www.education-world.com/

Elementary Teachers' Resource Site
http://www.ket.org/Education/IN/elem.html#music

ERIC
http://www.eric.ed.gov/

Illuminations
http://illuminations.nctm.org/

Library of Congress
http://www.loc.gov/index.html

Massachusetts Department of Education
http://www.doe.mass.edu/educators/

Massachusetts Studies Project
http://www.msp.umb.edu/theme.html

Math Achieves
http://archives.math.utk.edu/k12.html

Merlot
http://www.merlot.org/merlot/index.htm

National Center for Improving Student Learning and Achievement in Mathematics and Science
http://www.wcer.wisc.edu/ncisla/teachers/index.html

National Council of Teachers of Mathematics
http://www.nctm.org/

National Education Association
http://www.nea.org/parents/nearesources-parents.html

National Research Center on the Gifted and Talented
http://www.gifted.uconn.edu/nrcgt.html

Public Broadcasting System
http://www.pbs.org/

Scholastic.com
http://www2.scholastic.com/browse/teach.jsp

School Psychology Resources Online
http://www.schoolpsychology.net/

Smithsonian Education
http://www.smithsonianeducation.org/educators/lesson_plans/history_culture.html

Teachers.net
http://www.teachers.net/

The Geological Society of America
http://www.geosociety.org/educate/resources.htm

MASSACHUSETTS TEST FOR EDUCATOR LICENTURE - MTEL - 2007

PO#   Store/School:

Address 1:

Address 2 (Ship to other):

City, State Zip

Credit card number_____-_____-_____-_____   expiration_____

EMAIL _____

PHONE _____   **FAX** _____

ISBN	TITLE	Qty	Retail	Total
978-1-58197-875-9	MTEL Communication and Literacy Skills 01			
978-1-58197-876-6	MTEL General Curriculum (formerly Elementary) 03			
978-1-58197-878-0	MTEL History 06 (Social Science)			
978-1-58197-879-7	MTEL English 07			
978-1-58197-880-3	MTEL Mathematics 09			
978-1-58197-881-0	MTEL General Science 10			
978-1-58197-684-7	MTEL Physics 11			
978-1-58197-883-4	MTEL Chemistry 12			
978-1-58197-884-1	MTEL Biology 13			
978-1-58197-676-2	MTEL Early Childhood Education 02			
978-1-58197-683-0	MTEL Earth Science 14			
978-1-58197-893-3	MTEL Visual Art Sample Test 17			
978-1-58197-8988	MTEL Political Science/ Political Philosophy 48			
978-1-58197-886-5	MTEL Physical Education 22			
978-1-58197-887-2	MTEL French Sample Test 26			
978-1-58197-888-9	MTEL Spanish 28			
978-1-58197-889-6	MTEL Middle School Mathematics 47			
978-1-58197-890-2	MTEL Middle School Humanities 50			
978-1-58197-891-9	MTEL Middle School Mathematics-Science 51			
978-1-58197-892-6	MTEL Foundations of Reading 90 (requirement all El. Ed)			
			SUBTOTAL	
			Ship	$8.25
			TOTAL	

Printed in the United States
144825LV00001B/76/P